BASIC EQUALITY

Basic Equality

PAUL SAGAR

PRINCETON UNIVERSITY PRESS

PRINCETON & OXFORD

Published by Princeton University Press
41 William Street, Princeton, New Jersey 08540
99 Banbury Road, Oxford OX2 6JX

press.princeton.edu

All Rights Reserved

Library of Congress Cataloging-in-Publication Data

Names: Sagar, Paul, author.
Title: Basic equality / Paul Sagar.
Description: Princeton: Princeton University Press, 2024 |
    Includes bibliographical references and index.
Identifiers: LCCN 2023021711 (print) | LCCN 2023021712 (ebook) |
    ISBN 9780691255347 (hardback) | ISBN 9780691257792 (ebook)
Subjects: LCSH: Equality. | Equality—Philosophy. | Equality—
    Political aspects.
Classification: LCC HM821.S134 2024 (print) | LCC HM821 (ebook)
LC record available at https://lccn.loc.gov/2023021711
LC ebook record available at https://lccn.loc.gov/2023021712

British Library Cataloging-in-Publication Data is available

Editorial: Ben Tate and Josh Drake
Production Editorial: Theresa Liu
Jacket/Cover Design: Katie Osborne
Production: Danielle Amatucci
Publicity: William Pagdatoon
Copyeditor: Hank Southgate

This book has been composed in Classic Arno

Printed in the United States of America

10 9 8 7 6 5 4 3 2 1

CONTENTS

IN LATE MAY 2020, I was rock climbing in England's Peak District with my then partner, Jess. Due to a mixture of complacency and poor judgement whilst leading the second pitch of the climb, I took a fall of about six meters onto a protruding ledge. My left foot was immediately dislocated by the force of the impact, coming to be positioned outside of, rather than beneath, my leg. The fall also broke my talus bone, and left the bottom of my tibia sticking out of my skin. Luckily, there was no major blood-loss, so I was not in immediate mortal danger. I was, however, in a great deal of shock, and rapidly increasing pain. Unfortunately, Jess and I were now stuck about twenty meters off the ground. An abseil retreat was possible but hardly desirable under the conditions. Ignoring my shock-induced insistences that we descend immediately, Jess did the eminently sensible thing and called Mountain Rescue. Thus began a two-hour wait as the rescue team first located and then safely reached us. I wish I could tell you that I behaved with stoic self-detachment throughout. I did not. Eventually, a terrified paramedic was lowered down, greeting me with a syringe of morphine, a bottle of nitrous oxide, and (believe it or not) a box of paracetamol.[1] Those duly administered, the task of getting me off the cliff, and into hospital, began.

When Jess placed that call to Mountain Rescue, a team of over twenty people mobilised immediately, without question, to come and help. By the time they finally got me down (about three hours after the accident occurred), an ambulance crew and field doctors were waiting. I was promptly driven well over an hour, at high speed, to the specialist ankle unit at Sheffield Northern General Hospital. There a team of doctors and nurses took over my care. Given the severity of the damage, a specialist surgeon who had not been scheduled to work that day was contacted, and he came immediately to assess the situation. Judging that surgery was required that night if I was to have a chance of full recovery, I was taken to the operating theatre. When I awoke the next day, my foot was back where it was supposed to be, albeit in a cast that I would wear for the next three months. A long road to recovery stretched ahead, but the worst had been averted.

At no point in this series of events—from when we first called Mountain Rescue, to being stretchered to the waiting ambulance by a team of volunteers, to arriving at the hospital, to the contacting of the surgeon who dropped everything for me—did anyone ask to know anything about me other than that I needed help. Nobody asked about my race, my gender, my sexuality. Nobody asked whether I was a productive member of society, a layabout, or (closer to the truth) something in between. Nobody asked how clever I was, or how creative, or how kind or good or generous or otherwise deserving. They instead focused singularly on this one principle: a human being is hurt and in need, and we must help. And the most inspiring—indeed, amazing—thing about this is that they did not do this as some kind of one-off, or just for me. In that time and that place, they would have done it for *anybody*.[2]

The following book is, at least in part, inspired by what I saw put into action on that late spring day. It is an attempt to understand this extraordinary idea: that there is something that matters about human beings *just because* they are human beings—and that in light of this fact, the rest of us have a special kind of ethical relationship to them, and to all of them *equally*. It is not difficult to imagine another kind of world. A world in which the support I received from the emergency services might have been conditional on some particular characteristic I did or did not possess: membership of a certain race, or caste, or gender; or my being deemed to have a sufficient level of intelligence, or social usefulness, or moral worthiness. Failing in one or more of these regards I might have been abandoned, or told to wait until more worthy or higher-status individuals had been attended to first, even if their need was less severe than mine. Most human societies have been like that. Many *still are* like that. Furthermore, it is undoubtedly of great importance that I was lucky enough to experience my accident in a wealthy developed country, and where I was classed as part of the relevant citizen in-group to whom scarce resources are extended. As I write these words, human beings in need drown in the English Channel, as my own government takes a posture of excluding refugees from the demands of rescue on the basis that they lack the relevant citizenship status, whilst cynically hoping to disincentivize others who might be tempted to follow them.[3] It is undoubtedly the case that my being rescued that day wasn't *solely* due to my status as a human; I also needed to be lucky in various other regards. Nonetheless, when the chips were indeed down for me that day, all that mattered, given the otherwise fortunate features of my situation, was that I was a human in need. Any other human in need, in that time and that place, would have been viewed exactly the way I was. That is an amazing thing—more amazing, perhaps, than we always appreciate and remember. This book tries to deepen our appreciation of, and help us to remember, what is at stake when human beings treat each other as all equally important *just because* they are human beings.

The writing of this book began during the long period of convalescence that followed my accident. But I had been thinking about the ideas that went into it for quite some time before I found myself with nothing better to do for an entire summer than finally put words on the page. The long genesis of the argument is hence deeply indebted to a great number of conversations with other people, spanning a period of more than a decade. Some of them read drafts of (what became) the argument, in various stages of development. To them, I am especially grateful. In particular, Robin Douglass and Ed Hall gave me continuous feedback on chapter drafts as they were being produced, initiating some vital course-corrections, as well as multiple improvements both large and small. Nikhil Krishnan has been an invaluable interlocutor on this topic (and countless more) for many years, and he provided crucial improvements to the arguments that follow, particularly on the thornier metaethical issues. Hallvard Lillehammer read the entire manuscript in draft and pointed to the need for numerous subtle yet important corrections—I have tried to do justice to his advice (but likely failed on many counts). Bernardo Zacka also read the entire manuscript, and likewise gave me much to think about, and I have benefited enormously from his conversation (more infrequent in recent years than I would like!) for some time now. Anne Phillips also read the entire thing, and although we continue to disagree, it is a disagreement born of proximity, and I am grateful for her generosity in offering comment on a draft dumped on her out of the blue. David Livingstone Smith, Matthieu Queloz, and Matt Sleat all read the penultimate version of what follows, and important final changes were made in light of their comments. I must also thank the following for their conversation and critique (not always directly on the question of basic equality, but in ways that nonetheless helped me work out my thoughts): Richard Bourke, Chris Brooke, Clare Chambers, John Dunn, John Filling, Nick Gooding, Kinch Hoekstra, the late Istvan Hont, Rob Jubb, Nik Kirby, Diana Popescu, Andrea Sangiovanni, Sophie Smith, David Livingstone Smith, Amia Srinivasan, Adam Tebble, and Sam Zeitlin. My thanks also to Ben Tate and Josh Drake at Princeton University Press, whose editorial support in this project has been invaluable.

Lastly, I must once more thank Jess Williams: not only for looking after me that day in the Peak District (and for many days afterwards), but for all the love she showed me before and since. Our paths may since have parted, but the many days when they ran parallel will forever live fond in my memory.

BASIC EQUALITY

1

The Basic Problem

CONTEMPORARY ANGLO-ANALYTIC POLITICAL theory now takes place on what Ronald Dworkin dubbed an "egalitarian plateau."[1] Whilst thinkers of the past might have started from presumptions of fundamental difference and inequality between (say) the genders, or people of different races, this is no longer the case. In political theory, we are all now presumed to be, in some fundamental sense, *basic equals*. Of course, what follows from this putative fact of basic equality remains enormously controversial: liberals, libertarians, conservatives, socialists, republicans, and others continue to disagree vigorously with each other, despite all being on the plateau. Likewise, specific questions as to who gets what, how much, and why, remain sites of protracted disagreement.[2] But the starting point—that all people are in some sense deserving of prima facie equal consideration—has become an axiom of our moral and political thinking.

But *why*? Why are we basic equals? The trouble is that as soon as one asks for an explanation of this foundational premise, it begins to look very shaky. After all, on any conceivable metric, human beings are notably *unequal*, and often to striking degrees. Such inequality ranges from the apparently trivial—differences in physical attributes such as height, weight, eyesight, hearing, capacity to grow hair, athletic ability, etc.—to things that moral and political philosophers (as well as ordinary people in ordinary life) typically take to be much less trivial: our intellectual capacities; the ability to make and adhere to rational resolutions; emotional sensitivity; our capability of relating to others in appropriate ways—and so on. Whatever you pick, when you examine the human population at large, what you will discover is not equality, but *in*equality. This is true even just within the subset of "normal" adult humans, and becomes dramatically more so when we include those such as the profoundly mentally disabled, or very young children, or those suffering senile dementia, and so forth, recognition of whom greatly expands the range of inequalities that human beings exhibit. Furthermore, there is also the question of what exactly it is we are basic equals regarding. Philosophers in this area tend to talk of equal *worth*, but often without trying to specify what exactly that means. Other contenders include equal status, and also equal authority (i.e., as regards political participation and the legitimacy of how power is exercised by some over others).[3] So why, given all these apparent difficulties and unclarities, are we nonetheless basic equals?

Over the past two decades, in large part thanks to the prompting of Jeremy Waldron, philosophers and political theorists have begun to focus on what, if anything, can explain and justify basic equality.[4] So far, however, the results have not been good. Despite some valiant attempts (which I survey in the next chapter), the situation remains highly unsatisfactory. Richard Arneson puts the point well when he says that, as things stand, basic equality is neither acceptable nor rejectable.[5] It is not *rejectable* because we appear to be, as a matter of fact, profoundly committed to the claim that we are all one another's basic equals (no matter how much we disagree about what rightly follows from that). This is one of our deepest normative assumptions, and one we are not prepared to let go of lightly. But as things stand, there appear to be no good arguments for believing in basic equality. Hence—at least as philosophers and theorists concerned with establishing a normative claim and its grounds—basic equality does not appear to be *acceptable*, either.

The aim of this book is to try and show why basic equality *is* acceptable. To do so, however, it will also contend that we need to approach the question rather differently to how it has mostly been handled so far. In particular, it maintains that we cannot hope to solve the issue by doing philosophy alone: by just thinking very hard, from our armchairs, of putative justifications against which we test our intuitions, and that we try to defend from counterexamples thought up by our cleverest opponents. Certainly, we are going to need some (in fact, a great deal of) philosophy to make progress. The tools of analytic distinction, rational probing of claims and their plausibility, and our reflective willingness and ability to endorse (or indeed, reject) what we find—all of which are the hallmarks of good philosophy—will be indispensable. But our philosophy will need to be what Bernard Williams described as *impure*: it must take on board and learn from other areas of human intellectual endeavour.[6] In particular, we are going to need to look to insights available from research in psychology, what we know of our history, and how we go about practicing basic equality in our collective lives. Furthermore, when it comes to basic equality, we are also going to need to consider what we think philosophy itself is capable of achieving— what it is *for*—if we are to use it in the right kinds of ways.

What I mean by all of this will become clearer later, as the argument is built up over the chapters that follow. For now, I simply warn the reader that various reorientations and choices will be required in due course. We can, however, begin to make progress by specifying, somewhat more precisely, what it is we are looking for when it comes to basic equality.

Waldron has put the matter helpfully when he says that basic equality signals a refusal to draw the kinds of distinctions within the human set that we are typically comfortable drawing within the set of nonhuman animals, as well as between humans on the one hand and nonhuman animals on the other.[7] Consider: amongst the nonhuman animals we do not assign equal value to all creatures. Domestic dogs and cats are typically accorded much higher status (at least in the West) than farmyard animals like cows and sheep, which in turn sit above creatures like pigeons, feral rats, and below them again, insects and arachnids, with bacteria probably at the very bottom.[8] What the thesis of basic equality denies is that any such gradations or distinctions of the sort that we are comfortable drawing between different kinds of animals might be made *within the human set.*[9]

It was, of course, not always like this—and indeed in many places in the world today, it is still not like this. Throughout most of human history, most people have been entirely comfortable with gradations and distinctions *within* the human set, in light of which significant differences of worth, and in turn of moral and political status, were widely believed to obtain. Gender remains an obvious and far-reaching example. For most of history, and in most societies, women have been variously subjugated by men, widely presumed to be "lesser" in some fundamental sense (with a great many political and social evils following from that). But race and ethnicity have clearly also been taken, and by no means in the recent history of the West alone, as signalling a demarcation of fundamental status within the human set, of the sort we are still comfortable and familiar drawing between animals, and that most of us want to draw between animals and humans, but now refuse to draw between humans alone. We deny that any such differentiations as posited by the patriarchal or racist societies of old do in fact exist, and we affirm that within the human set we are all equal. But on what grounds?

Furthermore, this is not a story of the crude unthinking masses postulating false differences of worth but which philosophers, via careful reflection, have consistently rejected via an affirmation of fundamental equality. On the contrary, many philosophers have taken it as evident that human beings are *not* basic equals. Plato and Aristotle, clearly enough, did not hold there to be basic equality within the human set. In *The Republic* we learn that hierarchical political rule is to reflect the fundamental differences in intellectual and spiritual capacities of the citizenry, whilst *Politics* teaches not only the inherently lesser status of women and "natural slaves," but of barbarian and savage races as compared to educated male Greeks. Nor is this just a feature of ancient philosophy. Even

Enlightenment thinkers, who in their theoretical writings sometimes affirm something like basic equality in terms of inclusion
and worth within political affairs, did not consistently extend such
considerations throughout the human set. Thus Rousseau, for all
his emphasis on the necessary equality of citizens in any legitimate
political regime, was entirely comfortable excluding women from
such considerations. Kant—often appealed to as the paragon of a
philosopher who postulated the equal worth of all humans insofar
as they were all possessed of the capacity for rational agency and
thus obedience to the moral law, generating for them a special kind
of dignity—was also capable of a level of racism that calls into serious doubt his holding any thoroughgoing commitment to basic
equality within the entire human set.[10] Even Hobbes, sometimes
appealed to as an early proponent of basic equality due to his infamous pronouncement that in the state of nature all humans are
equally vulnerable to violent death, turns out to have held a more
complex position: that equality must be publicly affirmed as part
of a pragmatic collective survival strategy, that is, as a way of securing peace precisely because humans are markedly *un*equal on all
relevant metrics (including the ability to kill and to fend off would-
be killers), and if not somehow contained, this inequality was
likely to be a casus belli. Thus whilst Hobbes does not affirm basic
*in*equality in the way some other notable philosophers have, it isn't
straightforwardly the case that he offers arguments for their basic
equality, either.[11]

Indeed, in the history of Western political thought, the figure
who seems to have done the most sustained thinking about the
substance and grounding of basic equality is one whose writings
many contemporary theorists now consider to be a dead end. As
Waldron has shown, the body of work left to us by John Locke
represents perhaps the most serious attempt to grapple with basic
equality that we possess (although, as Waldron also notes, even
Locke was unable to free himself from the pervasive sexism of his
age[12]). Yet Locke worked from an explicitly theistic perspective:
that we are basic equals because we are "all the Workmanship of

one Omnipotent, and infinitely wise Maker; All the servants of one Sovereign Master, sent into the World by his order and about his business."[13] This means that Locke's thinking, for most contemporary political theorists, is deeply unsatisfactory, insofar as what most of us now want is a *secular* account of basic equality. Waldron has long been sceptical that a purely secular account can indeed be had, and in his more recent work he has proposed an explicitly Christian-inspired approach to the problem.[14] But that won't do for those of us who find that there are no good reasons to believe in any form of higher power, or supernatural maker, and hold out for an entirely nontheistic account of why we are, indeed, basic equals. Yet as we will see in the next chapter, all of the current secular attempts at a solution are unconvincing.

Further Complexities

Thus far I have been discussing basic equality as though it is merely a philosophical puzzle: how to account for this common intuition that we apparently all now have about us all being somehow on a level when it comes to our fundamental moral status. This, indeed, is how most of the literature on basic equality is currently framed. But it will not do. First, because the problem has crucial *historical* dimensions, to which we must also attend. Second, because the idea that we are all basic equals is in practice more *contested*, and is also far more *recent*, than one would guess from reading only the scholarly publications of academic political theorists and moral philosophers as produced in the last half century or so. Yet these facts matter.

We must be careful not to overestimate the extent to which those outside of the polite society that informs current academic discourse do endorse the basic equality claim.[15] Certainly, it is now the case that explicitly racist or eugenicist work predicated on the inferiority of some kinds of people, and especially fascist or Nazi political thought positing (for example) biological hierarchies of race and inequality within the human set, are now beyond the pale of civilised discourse, and in turn such views are not found in any reputable centre of learning. But that doesn't mean that such views don't continue to exist. At the extreme end of the spectrum there remain (for example) hardened racists and White supremacists, who use online forums, websites, and also public meetings and rallies, to disseminate an explicit denial of basic equality. For them, the "White race" ought to be accorded special status within the set of human animals, one that also involves exercising power over all the other races. Writing in the early 2020s, following the resurgence in openly ethnonationalist politics in America in particular, these people seem to be both more numerous, and less of a fringe political force, than at any previous time in the past half century. Basic equality is not yet universally accepted, even in the democratic West, and sadly it looks like it never really has been. Less extreme, but in some ways just as troubling, there are the more garden-variety forms of bigotry that one is apt to encounter if one leaves the confines of polite (and especially, academic) discourse. Think of the racist uncle one is forced to endure at Christmas dinner, with his views about Muslims, Blacks, and the "fact" that all major historical civilisational progress is due to the inherent superiority of European culture. Or the pub boor who foists his opinions about Asian communities on you unbidden at the bar. The truth is that beyond the confines of civilised discourse, there remain a disturbing number of people who are *not* fully signed up to basic equality.

Yet it is also significant that civilised discourse, for now at least, *has won*. It is a remarkable truth of recent history that basic equality has become a position which it is typically impermissible to publicly reject, at least outside of the purposefully artificial explorations of the philosophy seminar. In the democratic West at least, politicians of all stripes, if they wish to be taken seriously and to continue a career in politics, now at least pay lip service to the principle of basic equality. Take for example the following statement made by Boris Johnson, six years before he became UK prime minister:

No one can ignore the harshness of that competition, or the inequality that it inevitably accentuates; and I am afraid that violent economic centrifuge is operating on human beings who are already very far from equal in raw ability, if not spiritual worth.[16]

Johnson, a politician of the right, was trying to justify the vast inequalities in life chances that result from allowing extensive market competition to obtain. Notable, however, is that although Johnson is eminently comfortable with vast inequalities of *outcome* for individuals in a society, as allegedly stemming from their inequalities of talent (their "raw ability"), he nonetheless affirms a commitment to an underlying basic equality (their "spiritual worth"). Yet it was not always so. Prior to the Second World War, eugenicist ideas—i.e., that some people were of less worth than others, and that their traits should be bred out of the general population accordingly—flourished across the political spectrum, being by no means the preserve of the right. Members of the left-wing Fabian Society in Britain were for a time staunch supporters of eugenicist policies, and many self-identified liberals subscribed to eugenicist ideas that explicitly posited the lesser worth of some kinds of people compared to others (John Maynard Keynes, for example, was the first treasurer of the Cambridge Eugenics Education Society).[17] By contrast, whilst today there certainly are racists, eugenicists, and just garden-variety bigots, they are either fringe political elements, or are required to hide their denial of basic equality when appearing in public. Whilst racist politics, and the depressing efficacy of appealing to racially charged divisions to obtain electoral success, have certainly not disappeared, what is remarkable today is that such activity is predominantly conducted through "dog-whistle" tactics, more or less under the guise of equal consideration for all, even if this is merely a cynical ploy.[18] No serious politician with a shot at power anymore comes out and just affirms as a fact that (for example) Whites are superior to Blacks, or that men are superior to women, and that therefore such-and-such a policy must follow in turn. Even Donald Trump's race baiting of Mexicans prior to the 2016 presidential election focused on criminality and illegal immigration, stopping short of explicitly declaring Mexicans to be of less inherent worth than Americans (or rather, Republican-voting White Americans) *simply because* they were Mexican. In France, Marine Le Pen's ability to seriously challenge for the presidency has required her to first abandon the explicitly racist and Islamophobic pronouncements that her father, Jean-Marie Le Pen, and his Front National party previously employed. Some politicians might continue to *think* things that deny basic equality, on lines of race, or gender, or sexuality, or some other metric of discrimination, and may attempt to signal to the like-minded amongst the electorate that they think these things. But it is understood that *saying* them is no longer acceptable.

This is a remarkable historical development. After all, throughout the vast majority of human history, the vast majority of people *have not* held basic equality to be true, and the vast majority of human societies *have not* been organised around even a minimal commitment to it, nor a concomitant understanding that all decent people agree on this premise (even if they disagree, sometimes fiercely, about what follows from it). This is evidently so in the history of the Western powers, mired as those are in the blood of colonial conquest and indigenous genocide, with wealth plundered high and wide from other civilisations, not least through the horrors of the Atlantic slave trade and an accompanying ideology of the inherent superiority of Whites over Blacks.[19] But it is by no means unique to the West. The long-lasting and extensive Arab slave trade drew its legitimation in part from the denial of equal basic status to non-Muslims. For centuries, Japanese culture was predicated on the inherent ethnic superiority of the Japanese people, which served as legitimation for horrors periodically perpetrated on neighbouring Chinese and Korean populations, and later on captured Western soldiers in POW camps. The caste system in India is as explicit a denial of basic equality as could be imagined, and its legacy remains a feature of modern Indian society. China's infamous one-child policy led to significant population imbalances between men and women due to the levels of infanticide and illegal abortion that tracked preexisting prejudices about the superiority of males over females. And for all of John Locke's attempts to derive an account of basic equality from Christian ideas, it is not hard to find in the Bible, particularly the Old Testament, ammunition for a view that God favours some kinds of human over others (not just the Nation of Israel, but heterosexual men in particular). Likewise, it ought to be remembered that racial segregationists in the American South were typically also staunch Christians. The Ku Klux Klan, after all, chose burning crosses as their preferred motif.

And once again, even just within the West (where basic equality has now become a widespread political axiom) what we have is not a simple history of vulgar prejudice being combatted by noble philosophers, but on the contrary, ready examples of intelligent and sincere philosophical partisans of the view that humans are *not* fundamentally equal. Take, as a case in point, the somewhat ghastly figure of Reverend Hastings Rashdall, whom Waldron has previously drawn our attention to. In the second edition of his *The Theory of Good and Evil: A Treatise on Moral Philosophy*, published in 1924, Rashdall could write words such as these:

> I will now mention a case in which probably no one will hesitate. It is becoming tolerably obvious at the present day that all improvement in the social condition of the higher races of mankind postulates the exclusion of competition with the lower races. That means that, sooner or later, the lower Well-being—it may be ultimately the very existence of—countless Chinamen or negroes must be sacrificed that a higher life may be possible for a much smaller number of white men. It is impossible to defend the morality of such a policy upon the principle of equal consideration taken by itself and in the most obvious sense of the word.[20]

What is remarkable about this statement is not just the—to us, now—deeply shocking claim that "countless Chinamen and negroes" must be sacrificed to allow the "higher" White races to flourish, but Rashdall's presumption that "no one will hesitate" in agreeing with his claim. In 1924, somebody could publish an explicitly racist denial of basic equality and *expect it to be uncontroversial.*

I take it that these facts—of wider history, of contemporary widespread acceptance of basic equality, of what is now politically beyond the pale when once it was entirely mainstream—are not likely to be incidental to any satisfactory account. What we are confronted with is not just a philosophical puzzle; it is also a historical one. How is it that only relatively recently in the history of Western societies, something which had previously been denied—or at the very least ignored, or gone unrecognised—and which all other human civilisations also seem to have denied throughout *their* histories, has nonetheless now come to be widely accepted as the only permissible outlook?

Most existing enquiries in this area proceed as though the historical issues can be treated in isolation from the philosophical question of why we are basic equals. This appears to be because most who have considered the matter seem to take it that there must be a fact of basic equality that stands *independent* of whatever particular historical contingencies happen to have obtained up until now. There are thus supposedly two separate questions: why we *are* basic equals, and why *people have come to believe* that we are basic equals. The philosopher's job (they take it) is to work out the answer to the first in terms of an independent *justification* for why commitment to basic equality is warranted, whilst the historian or social scientist can deal with the second in terms of offering a causal *explanation* of how and why ordinary people might have come to hold such a belief. There is thus a neat division of labour appropriate in this area. By contrast, I reject this perspective and this putative division of labour. I do so for the following reasons.

First, I take it that the persistent failure of philosophers to establish any fact of the matter about basic equality that is simply "there," waiting to be discovered through the power of reason and reflection alone, is strongly indicative that such an endeavour is a hiding to nothing. By this point, too many highly intelligent thinkers have tried and failed. This is a clue that the strategy isn't working, and won't be made to work by some clever philosopher coming along with a yet cleverer theory. If basic equality could be sorted out by standard philosophical methods of pure argument and analysis, I suspect that it already would have been. Now it might be replied that working out answers to such questions is very difficult, and we just need more time: after all, it took human beings millennia to discover the Pythagorean theorems about triangles, although once they had been established, they could then be taught to intelligent ten-year-olds. Might basic equality not be like that? I doubt it, however, because I doubt very much that understanding basic equality requires grasping some fact or truth of the matter that is simply there, independent of us and of the history which led us to become committed to it—which brings me to my second point.

Namely, I doubt very much that it is simply a coincidence that academic philosophers and political theorists, on the one hand, and the general mass of ordinary peoples within Western societies, on the other, just so happened, at around the same time, in the same societies, to simultaneously converge on a widespread belief in basic equality. On the contrary, I suspect that this convergence is indicative of the very nature of the commitment we are trying to make sense of. In turn, I find it even less likely that ordinary people converged on some rough version of this idea (which is also an ideal) *because* the philosophers were doing so.[21] Any attribution of decisive causal efficacy on behalf of academic thinkers here would be the height of delusion. (And indeed, it definitely cannot be true: as Waldron has pointed out, until he started raising the question in a persistent manner about twenty years ago, few had interrogated the reasons for us all being on Dworkin's plateau, and those who had done so confessed themselves deeply puzzled.) Although many philosophers proceed as though this matter is simply irrelevant—that they are interested in discovering the truth of the matter, and whether or not ordinary people happen to believe in that truth is beside the point—I take it that the shift onto the egalitarian plateau in the West, in roughly the period since the Second World War, by academic philosophers and theorists at the same time as much of the general population, is a sign that all are moving in response to changes that have taken place in wider society. In this case, I suspect, the changes in philosophy are largely causally downstream of changes in social reality. And so, if we want to understand what our commitment to basic equality now consists in, we had better take seriously its history. In this area, doing "pure" philosophy will not give us what we need.

It might be replied that what I have just said is all well and good, but it doesn't really affect the heart of the matter, for what philosophers ultimately seek to know is not how particular beliefs came about, but whether our normative commitment to basic equality can be *justified*—and isn't that simply a separate question from explaining whether and how various people did (or did not) come to believe in it at a particular point in time? My position here, however, is that these questions are in fact not separable: that in order to be able to say whether or not commitment to basic equality is normatively justified *requires* taking account of the explanation of how the commitment arose and became widespread.[22] Hence (I want to argue) it is hopeless in this case to try and do normative philosophy in isolation from the history of the phenomenon under examination. Seeing why this is so will, however, take a little time, and indeed constitutes the first step in the positive account put forward in this book. I thus beg the reader's patience; a fuller answer on these points is coming, beginning in chapter 3.

For reasons similar to those just noted (and which are again expanded on below), I treat it as a serious mark against any attempt to account for basic equality if what we are given is a hyper-intellectualist theory that is only accessible to those with extensive technical philosophical training, and which nobody could ever have thought of, let alone understood, unless they were already a professional philosopher with the benefit of many years of advanced study. Whatever basic equality consists in, it has to be something that *ordinary people* can have gotten a grasp on, and indeed something that moved not just ordinary people, but all of those professional political theorists who found themselves on Dworkin's egalitarian plateau by the early 1980s, despite most of them having nothing to say about *why* they believed all acceptable political theory had indeed to start from *there*. Given that for much of Western intellectual history basic *in*equality has been the default position, the speed and extent to which basic equality became the dominant outlook is something that itself needs to be acknowledged, but which cannot be explained through recourse to any theory so complex that only a handful of elite academic thinkers can even understand what it says.[23]

This is not to say that ordinary people, the vast majority of whom go about their daily lives without any advanced philosophical (or indeed any other intellectual) training, will themselves all need to be able to understand a particular philosophical account in order for that account to be correct. If that were the bar to be cleared, then no philosophy would ever clear it, and it would certainly be to demand far too much. But the point I am making is different: it is that any explanation offered needs to be plausible *as an explanation* (which is not the same as saying that the explanation itself must be universally intelligible). The explanation for why people in the West now widely subscribe to a belief in basic equality cannot be that they are consciously committed to complex philosophical theorems which they have never encountered, and probably couldn't understand even if they did encounter them, lacking as they do the necessary years of advanced intellectual training required to do so. But it does not follow from this that a successful philosophical account of basic equality must *itself* be intelligible to those same people whose beliefs and attitudes it is trying to explain. It may turn out to be intelligible only to those who have the benefit of the advanced training, even if it posits as part of its explanation only materials that are plausibly available to those whose beliefs and values it is trying to explain. And that is fine, because the two things may be entirely distinct. (To draw a rough analogy with science: the biologist explaining how breathing gets oxygen into red blood cells had better come up with a robust scientific account that explains why and how all healthy humans do indeed get oxygen into their red blood cells. But it clearly doesn't follow that all healthy humans—especially those lacking biological training—should be able to follow in full the technicalities of the account the biologist puts forwards *in order* for the account to be considered correct.)

What we are looking for, then, is a way to explain not just a philosophical puzzle—in virtue of what are we basic equals?—but what is also a dramatic historical development: how is it that in Western societies, in a period of less than a century, we went from basic equality being one view in competition with others, to being the only game in town? Both of these elements, I argue, are going to be important if we want to gain a proper understanding of the phenomenon in question. History matters, I will here be maintaining, because basic equality is a value that has arisen—and only makes sense—in a specific historical context. But philosophy matters, because what we are trying to explain and reflectively endorse is indeed a normative commitment, and in order to understand what that commitment consists in, we need normative analysis and critique—and that requires doing philosophy. My point, however, is that we need both *together*. I am not a historian, so I will not attempt to offer a detailed history of the dramatic rise of basic equality in Western societies in this book. But I will try to show, and make good on, the reasons why our philosophical analysis had better pay attention to the relevant history at key points.

Do We Even Need an Answer?

Before proceeding further, however, we might ask whether we even need an answer at all. Does it *matter* if we can't account for basic equality, and should the current lack of any satisfactory account bother us? After all, I've already referred to basic equality as, precisely, an *axiom*—and the point about axioms is that they do not need to be (indeed, standardly cannot be) proven. Can we not just say that basic equality is *simply what we believe*—a sort of normative ground zero—and leave it at that?[24]

There is something important in this line of response (and I return to it later in the book). For indeed there are times and places when it is eminently appropriate. Most obviously, if one is confronted by (say) a neo-Nazi who is affirming the subhuman status of Jews, then a straightforward affirmation of the principle of basic equality may well be the correct response, whereas getting drawn into a "debate" about what makes us all basic equals is likely to be a serious strategic error, where it would be foolish to think that one is entering into a genuine exchange of ideas undertaken in good faith.

There is also the entirely correct point that whilst it may be very hard to come up with an account of why we are all basic equals, it is not as though the opponent of basic equality holds better cards—or at least, not under the guises that basic *in*equality usually gets affirmed. After all, whilst it is certainly the case that human beings appear markedly unequal on any conceivable metric whatsoever, it is also evident that those inequalities do not track the usual candidates that are claimed for making divisions within the human set. The variation between the races and genders (and so on) are as dramatic as the variations within them. It is simply not the case that (for example) *all* Whites are superior as regards to X than *all* Blacks, or that *all* women are inferior to *all* men when it comes to Y. Quite the contrary, and far from it. On any conceivable metric, some individual member of some grouping within the human set will be in possession of more (or less) of whatever it is we might choose to consider, than some individual member of some other group. Whilst we are all unequal in varying ways, and to varying degrees, that inequality is randomly distributed amongst and between different groups of human beings and does not track other identifiable characteristics in any reliable or predictable form. Can we not therefore simply leave the matter there, and go on affirming basic equality as an axiom in light of the fact that there are no good arguments for basic *in*equality?

Again, this may sometimes be an entirely appropriate response, in particular when we are occupied with the business of trying to regulate and improve the social world and where pausing to ask foundational philosophical questions is liable to be unhelpful. But this will not do from the perspective of reflective enquiry.[25] After all, and as indicated above, it seems that we have a commitment to basic equality that is a great deal more substantive than it simply being the thing we have plumbed for in the absence of any good argument for the opposite. Our belief in the basic-ness of basic equality both feels and functions like a lot more than just an arbitrary decision, or brute preference. Even more importantly, insofar as we are engaged in reflective enquiry, we want to know *why* we believe and value certain things, and in turn, whether those things are *correct*, and whether we ought in the light of critical reflection to go on endorsing them or not. The question of why we are basic equals has now been raised, and it cannot be un-asked. Critical reflection on its status has begun, and such critical reflection, as Max Weber put it, is not a taxicab one can hail at will. We are going to have to see where it takes us.[26]

Furthermore, there is an important point here about what we want to say in the light of *challenges* to the idea of basic equality. As mentioned above, rejection of basic equality, even within the recent West, never entirely went away, and worryingly it appears as though it may be once more on the rise. Globally speaking, given the fact that for most of human history it is basic *in*equality that has been the default, we ought to think carefully about what we want to say in defence of what appears to be a foundational aspect of our present normative outlook. After all, there is no good reason to think that our outlook is guaranteed to survive simply because it now exists. (One thing that history teaches us is that moral outlooks can and do change—and sometimes die.) Thus, whereas in mathematics it may be perfectly acceptable to say "that's just an axiom: it grounds the proof but it cannot itself be proven," basic equality is not like that. As reflective agents, we need *reasons* to adhere to some normative principles rather than others, at least if we are to continue to endorse them once reflection has begun, and in opposition to those who deny what we hold to be an important normative commitment.

However, we should also not demand or expect too much of our reasons and our reflection. When offering a defence of basic equality, it is not necessary that we set the bar so high that the only acceptable account is one that could convince a thoroughgoing moral sceptic, or a full-blooded opponent of basic equality, to change their mind.[27] There are some people who are just never going to be convinced by what we say, either because they reject our values so thoroughly that there is nothing for us, using our values, to get a grip on, or because they deny the validity of any values at all (consider the perhaps fanciful spectre of the nihilist who rejects *all* claims of normativity, whatsoever). What we should look for here is something less, but nonetheless entirely adequate: what we can say, to each other, about why we believe in the value of basic equality, and why we are right to uphold this in the face of opposition that we may encounter (which is not necessarily the same thing as *convincing* those opponents that we may encounter), and hence why we should continue to strive for a world in which no fundamental divisions within the human set are viewed as legitimate. What we need here is not an argument so powerful that it can compel anybody and everybody—even the committed racist, or the thoroughgoing moral sceptic—to accept the truth of basic equality. What we need is an account that we, who *are* already within a particular worldview that includes basic equality, find compelling in the right kind of ways, and which provides us with reasons for continuing to endorse it following serious reflection.

Now that the question of why we should believe in basic equality has been raised, we need to say something substantive in reply. We cannot—either as philosophers seeking the best account, nor as moral agents navigating a contested ethical and political landscape—simply assert it as an axiom that requires no further comment (even if, for practical political purposes, or at other levels of theoretical reflection, we do indeed, and quite correctly, sometimes treat it that way). The strategy adopted in what follows, in light of all this, is an attempted reorientation of how to think about both the problem and its solution. As will be seen in the next chapter, the existing approaches to the question of basic equality treat things as though there is some independent fact of the matter about why we *are* basic equals, and hence view basic egalitarianism—the disposition to treat each other *as* equals—as both explanatorily and conceptually downstream of that putatively independent fact. The problem (as we shall see) is that there just appear to be no good reasons for establishing any such putatively independent, and prior (we might say, grounding) fact of basic equality. Basic egalitarianism thus looks imperilled: a commitment without a foundation. But what if we approach the matter, so to speak, the other way around? That is the strategy adopted in what follows. Let us ask instead: what is this disposition to treat each other as basic equals, that is, to adopt a commitment to basic *egalitarianism*? Where did this disposition come from, and how does it work? Once we have a clear answer to the problem posed in this manner, I suggest, we will then be in a position to understand what is going on when we think of each other *as* basic equals. Hence whereas the standard approaches treat the egalitarian disposition as a principle made concrete, I treat the principle as the disposition made abstract. Where others defend the egalitarian disposition by arguing for the basic equality principle, I argue for accepting the basic equality principle by presenting what has come to be known as a vindicatory genealogy of the disposition. In proceeding this way, we can in turn entirely avoid the need to offer some sort of foundation for the commitment to basic equality (which is a significant advantage, given that no such foundation appears to exist). Crucially, however, we can do this without giving up on the normative importance that the commitment to basic equality now genuinely has for us. Getting to the point where this all makes sense will, however, take some time, requiring various stages of reorientation. We begin, therefore, by first considering the most promising attempts to account for the basis of basic equality that have thus far been suggested, but none of which are adequate to the task.

2

Answers That Don't Work

IN THIS CHAPTER, I consider the main attempts to account for basic equality that have so far been suggested. My coverage is neither comprehensive nor definitive; I aim merely to survey the more prominent strategies and the more serious obstacles that they face. This is because my core aim is to argue that we need to adopt an entirely different kind of approach to those tried so far, and the reasons for this will be easier to see after first examining the current state of the field. Readers who wish more detail on any of the arguments surveyed here can follow the references provided. Those already familiar with the literature on basic equality might skip this chapter, proceeding directly to the next.

An Underlying Feature?

An obvious way to try and account for basic equality is to locate some *underlying feature* that all humans might be found to possess, and in virtue of which they can all be said to be basic equals. Yet this seems doomed to fail. In the first place, it appears impossible to locate any feature that is not only shared by all humans, but shared by them *equally*, or in virtue of which they should be taken to *be equals*. Take any metric—physical, rational, emotional, etc.—and what you will discover when examining the human set is vast inequality, not equality. Furthermore, what feature could be so important that upon discovery of its possession we would wish to grant that basic equality follows from it? Presumably such a feature would have to be *nontrivial*: if we discovered that all humans equally possessed the same number of nostril hairs, for example, nobody would want to say that we are basic equals because of *that*. But even if the feature were something that seems more normatively weighty, that alone would not necessarily be enough. Let us imagine (as is not true) that all humans were equally possessed of the same level of rationality, which most would consider a nontrivial feature. But imagine that they also continued to be vastly unequal in (say) the extent to which they relate to others emotionally, and thus treat people respectfully and with care; or in their capacity for artistic appreciation; or their sensitivity to the naturally sublime; or their physical prowess— and so on and so forth. Why should these latter sorts of inequalities, especially if taken together, not outweigh the former equality? If we found something that we did all possess equally, it would have to be not only nontrivial, but *normatively decisive*, such that it could trump the vast range of *in*equalities we also know to obtain along-side it. Yet what feature could that possibly be? Furthermore, there is a question of *supervenience*: we need to explain how possession of some feature X generates a supervening strong claim not just of worth (or rank, or status, or authority—which further complicates the picture; what *is* the value being generated?) in its possessor, but *equal* worth amongst *all* possessors. How do we get from the fact of some feature, to the value of basic equality, simply in virtue of the former being found to obtain?

For these sorts of reasons, it seems that basic equality is not going to be straightforwardly grounded in the possession of any simple underlying feature (or features). Indeed, if any such feature existed, we would surely already know about it. No underlying feature is possessed by all humans such that it is nontrivial, possessed equally, and can account for why the strong, normatively weighty, claim of basic equality should follow merely from its possession.

The Capacity for Rational Agency?

Perhaps it is a mistake to look for a generic *feature*, and we should instead focus on the *possession of a capacity*, which whilst it may be exercised to different degrees, is nonetheless shared by all humans. A popular candidate here is the capacity for rational agency, that is, of living a life that is (amongst other things) informed by a self-directed will, in which one makes choices according to desires that one is able to reflectively weigh and evaluate, whose consequences are understood as fanning out over time to shape one's life. Even though we exercise the capacity to be rationally self-directed to markedly different degrees, we do indeed all possess such a capacity, at least as regards all normal adult humans (the profoundly disabled, young infants, the senile, and the like being special cases that we might hope to account for later). In turn, it might be said that because we all possess this capacity—which animals, notably, do not—we thus have the grounds upon which to begin to build an account of basic equality within the human set. In turn, it might be said that insofar as one meets a threshold requirement for a certain level of rational agency, then one is a *person*.[1] And insofar as one is a person, then one is entitled to equal moral consideration merely as such. As Arneson puts it, "The basic equality idea is that all individual beings that possess rational agency capacities at the threshold level that qualifies for personhood are equally persons, and have equal basic moral entitlements."[2]

Unfortunately, the reasoning here is not sound. We cannot, without assuming what needs to be proved, get from the possession of rational capacity, and a putative attribution of personhood in light of that, to a claim about *equality*. As Arneson goes on,

On any remotely plausible view, all of the psychological traits that combine to generate rational agency capacity vary by degree, and any plausible standard that integrates the various traits into a single measure of personhood capacity will also vary by degree. If the fact that I possess greater rational agency capacity than a normal cat or chimp justifies my claim to have a moral status and accompanying moral entitlements greater than they possess, by the same token it would seem that the fact that I possess less rational agency capacity than many other humans would seem to show that I am less morally considerable than they are. The rational agency account does not yield a basis for a basic equality claim but rather for its denial. I have greater affective and cognitive and volitional ability than even a very competent gorilla but much less of such abilities than many of my fellow humans.[3]

The capacity for rational agency strategy turns out to face the same problems as the search for an underlying feature. For again, we can simply ask why possession of rational agency should be so important, and so decisive, such that its mere possession should trump our other normatively salient inequalities, such as the capacity for emotional engagement with others, the capacity for various social and moral virtues, for artistry, creativity, physical ability, and so on and so forth. Philosophers who focus on rationality tend to do so at the exclusion of all else, whilst assuming that normativity is at base regulated by reason (a view which is itself strenuously disputed by those who want a much more prominent role for the emotions). But this is to beg the question: to simply assume that rationality is not only what ultimately defines our status as persons—which is implausible; think of all the things we do that separate us from nonpersons that are not simply based in, or a function of, reason—but that the capacity for rationality is normatively decisive in the face of all else. There are no good grounds, just as it stands, to accept this.

Furthermore, the fact that rational agency cannot account for the basic equality of some members of the human set, except in a derivative way, or by explicitly treating them differently, is in fact a serious problem for it. The partisan of the rational agency view might say that children can be accorded the status of basic equals because they have the *potential* for rational agency, and so we are to treat them as though they already had it (knowing that one day, if all goes well, they in fact will do so). As regards the profoundly mentally disabled, or those who have lost rational agency due to illness or accident, the rational agency account is forced to say that such humans are not, or are no longer, *persons*. Whilst we may still have to accord them important normative status, it is not the status of (fully fledged) persons, and we are therefore presumably to treat wrongs done to them as less serious than the wrongs done to (fully fledged) persons. But this seems wrong as an account of what we want to say when we say that all humans are basic equals. I take it that young children are basic equals with adults *now*, and not because of some promise regarding what they will later become, but because of what they currently are, as things stand today. Similarly, I take it that when we say that all of us are basic equals, we want to *include* the profoundly disabled, or the senile, or the brain-damaged, who cannot exercise rational agency. Part of the appeal of basic equality as a normative commitment is that it puts a *block* on treating some, no matter how profoundly incapacitated, as somehow differentiated from those within the set of equals, and therefore claiming that the wrongs they are liable to suffer are less morally weighty because they are not (really) persons. The whole *point* of basic equality, I take it, is to say that no matter how impaired your rational capacities, you are still a basic equal with the rest of us. This is one of the things that Bernard Williams is driving at when he points out that to state that somebody is equal *simply because* they are human may initially seem trivial, but upon closer inspection, is not trivial at all.[4]

Of course, the rational agency account is in some guises prepared to be radically *revisionary* of our moral intuitions here: "you may have thought that the profoundly disabled or the senile are our moral equals, but actually they are not (though we still have moral obligations towards them, just not the same ones)."[5] Yet basic equality is the claim that they *are* our equals. The rational agency account asks us to restrict the set of humans over which basic equality applies, and that entails a significant weakening in our ethical aspirations. Yet it is unacceptable to agree to any such weakening given that the very position which demands it cannot plausibly account for basic equality even within the set of humans that it *does* want to include as basic equals. We must, therefore, look elsewhere.

A Range Property?

Following John Rawls, it might be thought that basic equality is best thought of not in terms of a single underlying feature or capacity, but as a *range property*.[6] A range property is something which all those who possess it may possess to different degrees, but so long as they are all above a certain threshold of possession, and so can be considered as being within the relevant range, they are all to that extent considered equal. For example, it does not matter whether I am sitting in San Francisco or have just driven over the state line from Oregon: in either case I am equally *in California*. Thus "to possess a range property is to possess some other, scalar property, within a specified range," where the scalar property is then ignored once within the range.[7] Rawls suggests that basic equality might be such a thing, with the criterion we use for the range being "moral personality," by which he means being able to form and revise a conception of the good and possessing a sense of justice. Crucially, "while individuals presumably have varying capacities for a sense of justice, this fact is not a reason for depriving those with a lesser capacity of the full protection of justice. Once a certain minimum is met, a person is entitled to equal liberty on a par with everyone else."[8] We need not necessarily follow Rawls in thinking the range property is moral personality, however, and might construct a different range based on other criteria, should we think those more appropriate to capturing what basic equality pertains to.[9]

Yet despite its initial appeal, the range property strategy faces severe obstacles.[10] In the first place, there is the problem of exclusion: we are committed to saying that anybody who falls even only just below the threshold of inclusion nonetheless falls outside of it completely (and likewise, somebody who only just scrapes through falls *inside* of it completely). But basic equality is a very weighty idea: what threshold could we set, and based on what reasons, such that it could legitimately have the dramatic effect of denying inclusion in the set of human equals to some, but granting it to others who are only very slightly different to them? If the response here is to make the line which one must cross in order to be above the threshold "thick" rather than "thin," in order to try and reduce the number of marginal cases, then a different problem arises: establishing why some who might otherwise have been candidates for inclusion now get excluded, simply as a consequence of our being uncomfortable about marginal cases when the line was thin. There is also the point that given how complex it seems to be to establish the relevant criteria for basic equality, how would we know not only where to draw the threshold (and what it takes to cross it) but why indeed it should be *there*, and not somewhere else, and why it should be that thick or that thin, when the consequences for those not included are very dramatic? Furthermore, it is not as though just any range property that humans happen to share will do. The one we choose has to be nonarbitrary, and highly normatively significant. But what could that be?

Furthermore, there are problems about persistent inequality within the range, even for those who are above the threshold. Why, once some are within the range, do inequalities that we normally take to be normatively weighty suddenly stop counting? Somebody who clears the threshold comfortably will remain in unequal possession of whatever qualities the range is concerned with, as compared to somebody who only scrapes in. Why should those inequalities now stop mattering? Likewise, the inequalities that somebody at the top of the range displays as compared to somebody at the very bottom will be much greater than that between the person at the very bottom, and somebody at the edge of the threshold, yet who didn't quite make the cut. Why should the first two be treated as equals, but the latter two not? In the case of "being in California," this kind of range property is by its essence arbitrary, precisely because it is a function of the arbitrariness of this kind of human geographical arrangement. And that is fine, because nothing of normative importance turns on it merely as such. But basic equality isn't like that. Given the level of normative seriousness that basic equality is taken to possess, we do not want our reasons for inclusion and exclusion to be arbitrary. We want them, precisely, to be *reasons*. But it is unclear what those reasons could be, especially when they carry such weight.

In addition, there is the question not only of what subvening properties the range is supposed to be based on (and anything one chooses looks likely to be highly controversial if it is not to be trivial), but of why we should then *ignore* those subvening properties, and focus only on the range. If what gives the range its significance is precisely what it is based on, why not focus on the basis? Why is it the range, and only the range, that is morally relevant? And of course, any adequate answer here cannot make recourse to the idea that we focus on the range *because* we are basic equals—for that is precisely what the range is supposed to establish.[11]

Finally, it looks certain that any range property we select as constitutive of basic equality is likely to exclude, for example, the profoundly mentally disabled, the senile, young infants, and the like, as by necessity they will lack whatever features the range picks out. Unless, that is, the range is so wide that it picks out only things that are very basic, so that all humans get included by default. But then it would presumably have to grant inclusion to, for example, primates and other higher mammals at the very least (or if the threshold is set especially low, maybe even to plants and bacteria), which will also exhibit the chosen features common to all humans, but thus failing to establish why there is basic equality within the human set, and within the human set *specifically and alone*. Despite the initial promise of a range property approach, upon closer inspection it seems unlikely to succeed, and indeed seems to face the same structural problems that confront the rational agency approach.

Doubling Down on Personhood?

An alternative strategy is to double down on the notion of a person, and claim that once we get clear on what is involved in that, basic equality follows as a necessary consequence. The most famous and influential attempt to do something like this was put forward by Immanuel Kant (whom Rawls is clearly influenced by in his account of "moral personality"). On Kant's picture, what we fundamentally are is *rational agents*, able to not only set ourselves ends, but who are able to choose whether we attempt to conform our wills to the moral law, which binds us all equally as rational agents, and the content of which we can know in virtue of our being such. For Kant, the capacity to set oneself an end is what is distinctive of humans as opposed to animals—and it doesn't matter, ultimately, what the quality of the ends we set ourselves in practice turns out to be; this ability to set ourselves ends is itself what is distinctive of personhood. Yet because every rational agent is able to choose, and because (Kant thinks) every rational agent has the capacity to be properly overawed by the moral law when encountering it, in turn registering this law as something categorical to which one must conform one's will regardless of all else, it follows that each individual is possessed of a pure practical reason that enables them to know, and at least in theory be moved by, the moral law. This in turn means that every person (every end-chooser) is a locus of moral worth, because able to recognise and conform their will to the moral law: "To satisfy the categorical command of morality is within everyone's power at all times."[12] In turn, we owe respect not just to the moral law, but to those capable of recognizing the moral law, and that in part is why we are to treat each individual, in Kant's famous maxim, never only as a mere means, but also as an end in themselves.[13] Insofar as we are all rational agents capable of recognizing the moral law, we all therefore ourselves have individual moral worth. In turn, we are all due moral respect, merely as such.[14]

Despite its enormous influence in subsequent moral philosophy, however, it is not at all clear that the Kantian picture can establish the grounds for basic equality. For a start, if one is to strictly follow Kant, then it has to be remembered that all of what Kant says about morality—about pure practical reason, about moral worth, about the moral law, etc.—is predicated on his radical transcendental metaphysics: that despite our empirical selves being bound by the deterministic constraints of the causally regulated "phenomenal" realm, we nonetheless also exist as pure rational agents in the "noumenal" realm, beyond such constraints, and where we are radically free to choose, and thus to act morally. Kant's picture of moral agency—our ability to choose our ends free from not just our inclinations and passions, but of the causal constraints of the phenomenal world that we empirically inhabit—is dependent upon an enormously ambitious metaphysical account that is, to say the least, controversial. No matter how often neo-Kantian moral philosophers try to do so, one cannot coherently pluck Kant's moral claims out on their own, expecting them to function just fine without their original metaphysical grounding. Truly Kantian pictures of agency come at a prohibitively high cost—or else are merely asserted in the absence of precisely the kind of metaphysical support that Kant himself thought was unequivocally necessary for them to succeed.[15]

Second, it is not even clear that moral personality understood in terms of Kant's idiosyncratic metaphysical picture even establishes basic *equality*. As Waldron points out, given that Kant himself accepts that the capacity to choose and set ends varies wildly, what we are dealing with is a range property.[16] But then it is not clear why the fact that each moral agent is capable of recognizing the moral law, and is therefore a site of individual moral worth, means that others must therefore value each agent *equally*, or why therefore each agent has the status of *equal* worth, and not just (say) some varying level of worth above a threshold. Moral worth can be both *unconditional* and yet also *unequally distributed*. Why should it not matter if some agents are much better than others (as evidently they are) in not only choosing certain ends, but in successfully conforming their wills to the moral law?[17] Even if we agree with Kant that our humanity (our being rational agents who choose ends) is itself the "objective end" of morality, "something the *existence of which in itself* has an absolute moral worth, something which *as an end in itself* could be a ground of determinate laws," how do we get from that to the claim that the moral worth that each of us possesses is possessed by all of us *equally*?[18] As Waldron further points out, the idea of respect—either in a loose sense, or in Kant's more technical understanding—does not automatically generate basic equality.[19] Something more needs to be said. But what?

Finally, there is the point already made above: that exclusive focus on *rationality*, although it has tended to be shared by the kinds of moral and political philosophers whom Kant already appeals to, looks unjustifiably narrow. Is it really the case that we are persons simply and only because we can set rational ends (in accordance with a putative moral law knowable via reason)? This looks wrong. We are persons because of a great many other things besides our rational agency: our capacity for language; our ability to use tools; our living in different cultures; our ability to create art; our proclivity to enjoy (or not enjoy) playing and watching sports; our enormously complex emotional relationships with humans and also some animals, all of which we experience and develop over time. All of these (and many more) are deep and important markers and aspects of personhood. The Kantian asks us to ignore all of these, and the great inequalities that obtain between them, and focus only on rational agency. But why should we do that?

Some have attempted to do away with specifically Kantian metaphysical foundations and put forward accounts of personhood that it is claimed generate a putative commitment to basic equality in turn.[20] The problems with these sorts of accounts, however, tend to be twofold. First, any philosophical, criterion-based theory of personhood is inevitably going to be controversial. As indicated a moment ago, the number of things that personhood ranges across seems too wide and too complex for any one theory to adequately capture without controversy (even more so if privileging one feature above all others, such as rationality). Any account of basic equality that requires us to first embrace a contentious theory of personhood is going to be especially shaky: we do not have any firm or generally accepted views about what it means to be a person, and so positing a controversial theory about personhood looks especially unpromising if what we are after is an account of basic equality.[21] Second, philosophical theories deriving basic equality from a putative concept of personhood tend to be hyperintellectualised accounts requiring high-powered arguments to get established, and therefore are typically arguments that only somebody who has spent years training as a professional philosopher can even begin to understand, let alone decide whether they agree with. Remember, however, what was said in the previous chapter: that we are looking to explain not just a philosophical puzzle, but a major historical development. Basic equality is something which most ordinary people in the contemporary West now subscribe to, as do the vast majority of moral and political philosophers—even though neither group has apparently thought much about *why* they do so, and when pressed on the issue, tend to find a satisfactory explanation elusive. Given this, it seems unlikely that the kinds of answers we seek will be provided by complex philosophical theories that only a handful of specialist academic theoreticians even know about, let alone have read and fully understood.[22]

Opacity Respect?

Maybe the solution is to try and combine the insights of the range property approach with an emphasis on respect for agents. The most impressive attempt to do this has come from Ian Carter and his idea of "opacity respect."[23]

The core idea here is quite simple, although the execution is certainly not. Carter's core idea is to say that above the threshold for inclusion in the range of basic equals, we stop paying attention to the kinds of subvening inequalities that a range property of basic equality is based on, treating everybody within the range as basically equal. We do this for reasons of *respect*. According to Carter, above the threshold, individuals within the basic equality range are treated as *opaque*—we refrain from "looking inside" them, and treat them as though they were all the same in their subvening properties, even if we know this not to be the case. The reason we are to treat people as opaque is because we owe them a duty of respect on two grounds: 1) what Carter calls a naturalised Kantian view of agents being worthy of respect simply because they are agents entitled to a certain kind of "internal" dignity; and 2) because insofar as we are liberals, who are in turn fundamentally committed to respect for agents and upholding their "outward" dignity, and this liberalism grounds a commitment to basic equality in our political relationships. This means that Carter need not deny that there are times when it is appropriate *not* to treat others as opaque, for example in personal relationships with friends and family where paying attention to each other's specific personal differences and inequalities is important and morally correct (and indeed, when respecting their dignity *requires* abandoning opacity respect). Nonetheless, when it comes to respecting each other in a *political* sense (which is for Carter ultimately a deeply moral sense), then opacity respect is what we owe to others as agents as part of our commitment to their dignity, and explains why we ought to treat all agents as basic equals.

Despite—or perhaps indeed because of—its ingenious nature, Carter's opacity respect faces a raft of objections.[24] In the first place, there is the point already made about hyperintellectualist philosophical theories: how could something like *this* be the grounds for not just the idea of basic equality, but also explain the astonishing rise of a real-world commitment to basic equality in the recent history of the Western democracies? Carter seems to be arguing for why we (or at least, why liberals) *ought* to be normatively committed to basic equality, as a function of other, deeper, commitments about agency and respect. But if we lack those more basic commitments—as many clearly do—then it is not clear why we should be moved by Carter's argument. If basic equality obtains only insofar as it is entailed by controversial commitments about autonomy, especially when those are themselves comprehensible only to advanced theoreticians of a particular ideological stripe, then it hardly seems to deliver the basis that might undergird Dworkin's egalitarian plateau. Perhaps Carter himself is simply uninterested in providing such a basis; but as I will try to show in the rest of this book, such lack of interest would be a mistake.

There are also serious problems with Carter's arguments for the respect that we allegedly owe agents merely as such. Carter simply asserts that agents are owed "internal" dignity, claiming that this remains so even if we abandon Kant's two-tier metaphysics. But why? It is not obviously true that the notion of another's agency automatically entails, or even just brings along with it, the notion (let alone the *duty*) of respect for their dignity. The racist or sexist bigot need not deny that Black people or women are *agents*. They may simply deny that *these* agents are owed a certain kind of (equal) respect. Certainly, the racist or sexist has bad reasons for their belief (insofar as they have reasons at all). But what is going wrong here is not a mistake about agency: the problem is with their morally objectionable and ill-founded evaluative attitudes. If one wishes to claim that the logic of agency entails respect for dignity, one needs to present an argument for *why* that is so, and why those who deny it are not just bigots (i.e., that they have the wrong, objectionable sorts of attitudes towards others), but are in some way committing a demonstrable intellectual error as regards the concept of agency and what follows from it. Kant's metaphysics seemed to promise a way of doing this. But it is precisely the high cost of that metaphysic that drives Carter to a putatively naturalised outlook. But once the outlook is indeed naturalised, it is not good enough to simply assert that the logic of agency entails respect for dignity. We are owed some argument about how the empirical features of another necessarily commit us to certain kinds of normative response. Until we have an argument, Carter is proceeding on Kantian faith whilst having renounced the grounds of Kantian argument. But those who do not share that faith will simply be unmoved, and that means Carter's attempt to ground basic equality is inert for anybody who does not already agree with his controversial views of agency and respect for "internal" dignity. In other words, Carter's account is insufficiently ecumenical to shore up commitment to basic equality even for those who otherwise share that commitment—and hence is unable to explain what needs explaining.

This becomes an even more serious issue when we consider Carter's arguments for "outward" dignity, especially his insistence that this is yielded by prior commitment to respect for agency, which is itself the defining feature of a commitment to liberal politics. Carter's proposal here is again too controversial to yield what we are after. On the one hand, it is simply not the case that even if one is a liberal this is more fundamentally because one is committed to respect for agency in Carter's specific sense. For example, somebody who follows Judith Shklar in advocating the "liberalism of fear" is interested primarily in the avoidance of the evils of cruelty, humiliation, suffering, and so forth, not with the abstract notion of agency.[25] Agency certainly comes into this picture, as does dignity, but not as the fundamental grounding normative commitment that Carter presents it as being. And of course, many are not liberals, and yet nonetheless affirm a commitment to basic equality. Republicans, for example, *might* be committed to something like a fundamental respect for agency, but then again they might not be, insofar as they see the primary goal of legitimate political arrangements to be the securing of a particular form of freedom—understood in terms of nondomination—and which may stand independently of Carter's specific claims about agency, or be thought to be prior to it.[26] Similarly, libertarian theorists might wish to affirm the importance of basic equality, whilst seeing their primary commitments as grounded in claims of self-ownership.[27] If we take Dworkin's idea of an egalitarian plateau seriously, then Carter's strategy is too controversial to explain why so many are now on it. And this is even before we recognise that the majority of ordinary people who seem committed to the idea of basic equality have no worked-out theoretic position on the basis of their political views at all, be it one of agency-respect or otherwise. Carter's suggestion does not help us to make sense of an egalitarian *plateau*, because what he is offering is an alleged consequence generated by only one particular (and highly controversial) understanding of one version of liberalism.

Furthermore, it is not clear that even if we accept many of Carter's starting points about a "political conception of justice" and commit ourselves to his controversial understanding of liberalism, that opacity respect can anyway be the sort of independent prior moral duty that he claims it to be. Arneson points out that even in political relationships under Carter's liberal conception of justice, "it is not so that there is any general moral principle that commands refraining from gauging someone's agency capacities or determining how to behave toward the person on the basis of one's beliefs about their characteristics."[28] Plausible fundamental principles of justice might require bringing it about that people lead good lives to an equal, or good enough, or priority-weighted degree (and so on), but doing so effectively—i.e., in line with a meaningful commitment to liberal justice—may require assessments of what people are owed based on determinations of their agency capacities. Respecting agents may, at important times and within political relationships even on a liberal conception of the kind Carter envisages, require precisely *not* treating them as opaque. But if that is the case, then opacity respect will not be the sort of prior moral duty that can ground basic equality in the way Carter requires.

Yet if we abandon Carter's commitment to opacity respect as a prior and fundamental moral duty, and instead see it as something like a prima facie duty we owe to all people within the range of normal agency capacities before we make judgements about how to treat them on individual case-by-case bases (what Arneson labels "minimal opacity respect"), then the question reemerges of *why* we should do this. For what we will have is a range of humans exhibiting differences in subvening scalar properties (on Carter's picture, agential ones), differences which we take to be morally relevant. But for some reason we are now going to act as though they either do not exist, or if they do, are not morally relevant after all. As Arneson puts it, this more minimal understanding of opacity respect "just says, ignore what should not be ignored." And this lands us back where we started: "To rebut this claim, one would have to show that variations in overall agency capacity within the normal range do not in fact generate differences in moral considerability. But that is just the deeply puzzling question that has been baffling us all along."[29] In sum, Carter's opacity respect does not deliver what we require, even if we are liberals on his conception, and let alone if we are not—which most people aren't.

A Locus of Subjectivity?

Perhaps we have been looking in the wrong kinds of places. An alternative is suggested by George Sher, who urges that we pick up on Bernard Williams's reminder that each human being has a life to live, and experiences that life "from the inside."[30] Each of us is, after all, a locus of *subjectivity*, and even if that subjectivity differs in its content, quality, intensity, depth, and so on, all of us (or almost all, excluding perhaps the most extreme cases of mental incapacity) have the experience of what it is like *to have experiences*, and to go through the world accordingly. Once we recognise that all people are possessed of subjectivity, of something that it is like to be them, do we have grounds for considering them basic equals?

Sher notes that all humans possessed of a certain level of subjectivity thereby exhibit certain "generic" features of the phenomenon. Examples include believing the world to be spatially and temporally ordered; conceiving of oneself as temporally embodied within the physical world and as persisting over time; of being aware that various courses of action are open to one, and that the world gives us reasons to choose some of them over others; that within certain limits we have reason to find out what it is better for us to do or not do, and act accordingly. From these generic features, "we can infer that each person necessarily projects himself into the future as the continuing subject of a certain kind of life . . . as a continuing conscious subject whose earlier and later experiences will be related by anticipation and memory, and whose earlier and later actions will be structured around plans that are aimed at implementing his stable though evolving reason-based aims."[31] Sher thinks this is what enables "each person to *live a characteristically human life*."[32] He then points out that we all have certain interests that enable us to go on living, and that are prerequisites for, a characteristically human life. These include remaining alive long enough to realise our goals; having enough food, water, shelter, etcetera, to decently survive; being free to form, revise, and pursue our intentions in line with our perceived strongest reasons, and so on. However, insofar as we are all loci of subjectivity, and insofar as we all equally need these interests fulfilled if we are to be able to go on realizing our subjectivity, Sher claims that by "linking the features that structure the consciousness of each normal human being to the interests of whose equal importance our moral equality consists, we can decisively block the objection [made by Carter] that our subjectivity is too undifferentiated to sustain the claim that we are moral equals."[33]

Unfortunately, however, Sher's argument appears to beg the question. As he goes on to say, although our subjectivity requires certain interests being met, and these are interests that we *all* need to be met in order for us to go on experiencing the world and hence exhibiting subjectivity, the claim that our interests all matter *equally*—the basic equality claim—requires appeal to a different sort of fact: "that each of us occupies a distinct subjectivity."[34] But why should the mere fact that each of us occupies a distinct subjectivity generate the further conclusion that each subjectivity matters *equally*? It can't simply be that we *have* subjectivity that matters—there has to be something more. But what? Sher has not said.

Stan Husi presses the point home by showing that it is not going to be enough to find something—say, subjectivity—that all (normal) humans possess to some degree. We need a further reason for why being above the threshold of possession generates egalitarian conclusions about the status of all who possess that subjectivity, whilst simultaneously excluding others who possess some level of subjectivity, but not to a sufficient degree to be granted basic equality status. Yet as a result the subjectivity approach turns out to be vulnerable to the same kinds of objections that we have already encountered above. After all (and here following Husi), there is surely something that it is like to be a chimpanzee. Call it C-subjectivity. Sher would rightly point out that C-subjectivity lacks the generic features of ordinary human subjectivity, and to that extent we have reasons for not according chimpanzees equal status with humans, insofar as we think there is something particularly valuable about normal human subjectivity. So far so good, assuming that we can non-question-beggingly give an account of that. But then even if we can, why are we simultaneously going to ignore significant differences of subjectivity *within the human set*? Husi offers the example of a psychopath, somebody who is unable to form emotional attachments with others, and treats them as akin to self-propelled vending machines, to be manipulated and taken advantage of for purely selfish ends: "there's no connection, no empathy, no love, no care. Nothing exists in the in world of the psychopath to reach out to, nothing exists to reach back; it is all dark and lonely, nobody's there."[35] It is surely wildly implausible to say that the subjectivity of the psychopath and that of the ordinary person are the same. One is manifestly much more impoverished than the other. So why shouldn't we assign more moral weight to one over the other, accordingly? Yet we do still want to say, I take it, that for all the psychopath's impoverished subjectivity vis-à-vis a normal person, he *is* still a basic equal with others (even if his behaviour means he is likely to be treated very differently by others in practice, as a legitimate consequence of his actions). The problem is that simply saying "but there is something that it is like to be the psychopath, from the inside" does not get us to *equality*. And it is not clear how it could get us there, absent some explanation of why within the human set we are going to ignore differences in the quality, nature, intensity, shape, and so forth, of human subjectivity, which a moment's reflection shows to be considerable, and which we normally take to be highly normatively salient. And that means we are back to where we started.

Furthermore, there are stark differences even within just the set of "normal" adult humans, that is, excluding special cases like psychopaths, and which we need to say something about. Some people experience a wide range of experiences in their subjective lives: emotional, artistic, creative, sporting, cultural, and so on. Others, by contrast, experience very few, and restricted over a much smaller range of things. We normally want to say that such differences in subjectivity matter: that the quality of a life immersed in literature and theater and friendship and hiking in the mountains is *more worthwhile* than one spent addicted to reality TV and drowned in cheap beer whilst sitting alone on the sofa, ranting on social media. That two such contrasting subjectivities are nonetheless both subjectivities does not, by itself, seem to get us to the idea that both are nonetheless to count equally in some important sense. Mere subjectivity is not enough.

Indeed, near-persons (e.g., the mentally impaired who lack subjectivity) or nonpersons (e.g., chimpanzees with C-subjectivity) are presumably to be excluded from basic equality on Sher's understanding precisely because they lack the "generic features" of subjectivity that Sher wants to pick out as "distinctively human." Yet this leads again to the problem encountered above: that actually we often *do* want to include some who lack generic human subjectivity within the set of basic equals—e.g., the profoundly mentally disabled—whilst excluding others, such as chimpanzees, who on some metrics experience *more* subjectivity than some humans. As with the rational capacity accounts, we are being asked to restrict the set of humans who get to count as basic equals, and that should give us pause, because we are not getting what we thought we were being given: an explanation for why within the human set we do *not* draw the kinds of distinctions that we happily draw between humans and animals, and that most of us are comfortable drawing within the wider set of nonhuman animals.

As Husi points out, switching the focus to subjectivity appears no more successful than appealing to rational capacity due to the problems associated with accounting for why differentiation within the normal range is not to count. Arneson's long-standing challenge thus remains, even if one substitutes "subjectivity" for "rational agency capacities":

> Suppose someone asserts that the difference between the rational agency capacities [or, we might add, subjectivity] of the most perceptive saints and the most unreflective and animalistic villains defines a difference in fundamental moral status that is just as important for morality as the difference between the rational agency capacities [or subjectivity] of near-persons and marginal persons. What mistake does this claim embody?[36]

Mere possession of subjectivity cannot establish basic equality, for the now-familiar reason that we manifestly possess subjectivity to different degrees, and we need a reason why those differences are supposed to stop mattering above a threshold, but without locating that threshold in a way that assumes the truth of basic equality— which is what the threshold is itself supposed to establish.

More Promising Directions

Three further accounts are worth considering, which, whilst I do not consider to be successful, deserve mention insofar as they point in more promising directions. These are, first, Andrea Sangiovanni's suggestion that vulnerability to cruelty may serve for the basis of moral equality. Second, Grant J. Rozeboom's claim that basic equality is grounded in a social practice, one orientated to concerns about mutual respect in conditions of "inflamed *amour propre*." Third, John Charvet's argument that we start from a communitarian political-theoretic perspective and understand basic equality as making sense only if drawing upon the materials of our wider existing normative commitments.

Sangiovanni suggests that what we need to focus on is the vulnerability to *cruelty* that individuals are liable to, realizing that insofar as each of us is both susceptible to suffering acts of cruelty, and yet each has an irreducible interest in not being so treated, from this we can establish a common moral equality. Sangiovanni eschews the terminology of "basic equality" insofar as he believes that doing so risks committing one to a foundationalist view—the search for some underlying property or feature—which he convincingly argues is not going to be successful.[37] However, Sangiovanni's attempt to establish the case for "moral equality" is nonetheless functionally the same as what I have been referring to as "basic equality," and I treat it as such here.

Sangiovanni's case is as follows. First, we are all deeply sociable beings, who require interactions with others to live a flourishing and meaningful existence, and who also need to be able to maintain a stable sense of self, which is a precondition of living well. In part, this means being able to conceal aspects of ourselves from the gaze of others when we so require. But even more importantly, it requires not being vulnerable to things that others can do to us that attack not just our physical being, but our capacity to hold a stable sense of self. Sangiovanni identifies a broad range of things that can make individuals vulnerable in this way, classing them under five paradigmatic headings of dehumanizing, infantilizing, objectifying, instrumentalizing, and stigmatizing, all of which he heads under the broad label of cruelty.[38] Insofar as cruelty attacks the deep interest that everyone has in their sense of self, Sangiovanni posits that there is a moral duty incumbent upon all of us not to engage in cruelty. In practice, this means that we must adopt Carter's idea of "opacity respect": treating others as moral equals, insofar as we refuse (ceteris paribus, and when appropriate) to pry beyond the fact that all individuals are vulnerable to cruelty. Instead, we are to take the fact of the wrongness of treating some as inferior (and thus liable to acts of cruelty), and move from that to assert the fact of moral equality. We treat each other with *humanity*, as Sangiovanni puts it, when we treat each other as equals—and indeed, this established practice of so treating each other is itself part of what has brought about, and continues to sustain, the social and normative reality of moral equality.

This account is ingenious, and in its emphasis on attempting to account for moral equality in terms not that some moral sceptic, or basic equality-denying opponent, could be expected to endorse merely as such, but through the values and reasons that we already recognise as structuring our moral lives, is very promising. But unfortunately it does not work in the form presented.[39] Sangiovanni claims that he avoids the "variation" objections levelled at foundationalist accounts (i.e., explaining why manifest variation of worth is irrelevant, if the worth is what is supposed to confer value), but it is unclear why this is so. Sangiovanni recognises that individuals vary in their vulnerability to cruelty, and he claims to embrace this difference. But if there is such variation, why is it that all are nonetheless moral *equals*, simply because all are vulnerable to (different degrees of!) cruelty? The answer is unclear, but it appears to rest in the independent importance of the duty of opacity respect: once this kicks in, it kicks in equally for all. But if so, Sangiovanni is remarkably underspoken about the grounds for this alleged duty, how exactly it is supposed to work, and why we are compelled by it to extend a concomitant judgement of moral equality. Indeed, Sangiovanni credits Carter with having worked out the philosophical foundations of opacity respect—but that won't do for the reasons we have already seen. If Sangiovanni's account presumes the success of Carter's in order for it to work, then it fails for the same reasons as Carter's does. Nonetheless, Sangiovanni's insistence that we pay sustained attention to the social dimensions of basic equality, and concentrate on offering an account that is addressed to those of us who *do already* have a commitment to basic equality—rather than trying to think of something that might convince a thoroughgoing moral sceptic, or some agent who shared none of our normative values whatsoever—seems to me entirely right. Subsequent chapters shall, indeed, proceed accordingly.

Rozeboom by contrast proposes that basic equality is something we have come to affirm as a way of managing to live together in conditions where the desire to be looked at and thought well of by others structures all our social and political relations, but which is potentially socially destabilizing because assigning unequal status to those who have a high opinion of themselves is a deeply provocative act. Taking inspiration from Jean-Jacques Rousseau, and calling this psychological state enflamed *amour propre*, Rozeboom argues that we should think of basic equality as being accorded to each of us as a result of a constructed social practice that we have developed in democratic conditions, in which it is imperative to respect each other as equals insofar as we now participate as such in a wider politically egalitarian environment. "To remove the conditions of inflamed *amour propre*, we need a social practice that grants us all the same basic decision-making authority over our lives and interactions with others—the anti-inflammatory practice of moral equality."[40]

Yet Rozeboom's account, whilst pointing in a promising direction with its emphasis on social practice and how we interact with others in political settings, has at least two major problems. The first is that it relies upon a particular, and highly controversial, theory of moral psychology—Rousseau's notion of enflamed *amour propre*—which there is good reason to be sceptical about in terms of its being a satisfactory account of the complexities of moral and political psychology.[41] Second (and as Rozeboom himself acknowledges), his account makes basic equality *derivative*: we affirm basic equality as a value that enables us to live together in stable political communities through its dampening effects upon *amour propre*. But that makes it look like something we value only, and only insofar, as it turns out to be instrumentally useful. Yet it seems wrong to present the claim of basic equality as derivative, as merely instrumental for securing some other good(s). Basic equality is typically viewed as itself normatively foundational, and independently salient: that certain political ways of going on are required *because* we are basic equals, not the other way around. I take it that most of us would want to say that we remain basic equals even if we were somehow, by some other route, cured of the competitive and destabilizing *amour propre* that Rozeboom makes central to his account. Rozeboom's view makes basic equality too downstream of the social practice of mutual respect. Instead, I take it that we want to say that, at least in part, the social practice of mutual respect is good precisely because it *embodies and makes good on* our prior basic equality. Rozeboom's account seems to put the cart before the horse, though the difficult issues raised here are ones my own account will also have to wrestle with (see chapter 6).

Charvet, not dissimilarly, suggests (against what have been mostly self-consciously liberal accounts) that "the ethical community" is the source of individual ethical worth, and that from recognizing this, we can in turn get to the idea of ethical worth being equal amongst members of a relevant community.[42] According to Charvet, "there is a fundamental moral worth that all human beings possess the capacity for and this is the capacity to participate in ethical communities organized through a system of rights and duties. Each person possesses a threshold-level capacity to recognize, and govern himself by, such a scheme. In this sense they possess equal moral worth."[43] Whilst Charvet's emphasis on wider political and moral practices—rather than some supposed underlying empirical feature of individuals—as the source of the idea and ideal of basic equality is attractive, the account he gives of how this works is not satisfactory. In the first place, and as we have just seen, he falls back on some sort of threshold account for determining inclusion, and it seems inevitable that all the problems associated with threshold accounts noted above will reemerge here. Furthermore, Charvet's own particular brand of communitarianism—as well as the more general demand that we accept communitarian political theory as a prerequisite of coherently affirming basic equality—is too sectarian. Most political theorists, let alone most ordinary people, are not committed political-theoretic communitarians, and demanding that one be a communitarian in order to coherently affirm basic equality is too high a price to pay, not least insofar as commitment to basic equality is typically regarded as *prior* to more substantive political commitments (such as communitarianism).[44] Thus whilst Charvet is right to point to the need to pay attention to wider aspects of our moral and political lives if we are to get a grip on basic equality—i.e., rather than questing after some underlying feature, or capacity, that could act as a prior and independent grounding of our values—we need an account with less weighty and sectarian theoretical baggage, and which offers the correct sequencing of the relevant ideas. After all, what we are trying to explain is an egalitarian *plateau*. By contrast, Charvet suggests that basic equality is something communitarianism has a uniquely coherent claim to, and the implication of this is that if we are genuinely committed to basic equality, we must all in turn adopt a communitarianism of a particularly theoretically demanding sort. Yet we can nonetheless agree with Charvet that making sense of basic equality first requires understanding the wider historical and social context in which such an idea has arisen and makes sense, whilst rejecting the claim that this commits one to a specifically communitarian political theory or ideological stance more generally. On the contrary, one of the hallmarks of basic equality is that the social and historical context it has arisen amidst is one inhabited by people with markedly different and incompatible political commitments (and sometimes, worked-out theories) who nonetheless sincerely converge on the egalitarian plateau—and that convergence needs to be explained and accounted for, rather than ruled out as a demonstration of the alleged incoherence of anyone with a noncommunitarian outlook. Charvet, that is, falls into the same trap of putting the cart of theory before the horse of practice as the accounts he criticizes. In what follows, I try to avoid this pitfall.

Conclusion

Sangiovanni, Rozeboom, and Charvet all point us in more promising directions by urging that we pay attention to the wider, and in particular, the socially embedded, features of our normative commitments. Nonetheless, and as Arneson has put it with admirable bluntness, "In this area of thought, the available alternative positions are all bad. Choose your poison."[45] This chapter has agreed that Arneson is right about how things currently stand. But it is usually best to try and avoid poison. Indeed, if one finds that all one is getting from the apothecary is variations upon the same kinds of poison, it must surely be worth finding out if another chemist, who works with different ingredients and prepares them in a different manner, can do better. In that spirit, the rest of this book tries to do things differently. I begin the process in chapter 3 by asking what kind of philosophical approach we should even be bringing to bear here, and in turn what we should and should not expect philosophy to be able to do for us in this area. The aim is to set up the reorientation promised at the close of chapter 1: of asking what this disposition to treat each other as basic equals—of being committed to basic *egalitarianism*—consists of, and in turn using that as a way of attempting to get clear on the idea of basic equality in turn. Approaching matters in this way will allow us to understand basic equality not as some putatively preexisting and independent fact about us (for which there appear to be no plausible candidates, as this chapter has demonstrated), but rather as something that we have brought into being through our practices and dispositions. To this reorientation we now turn.

3

The Basis of an Alternative

I HAVE SUGGESTED in the two previous chapters that when it comes to basic equality, we need not just a different answer, but a different kind of approach. This is in part because the various answers currently on offer simply are not working. But it is more fundamentally because of a problem that is rarely made explicit, let alone addressed, in this area. This pertains to explaining why so many people—in fact, the vast majority of human beings, throughout most of history, and indeed in many parts of the world today—have *not* subscribed to basic equality. This must be acknowledged and accounted for. But doing so means getting clear on what kind of thing we therefore take basic equality to be. And this points us towards a different kind of answer to those currently available. This chapter brings these issues out. In turn, it provides the rationale and orientation underlying the positive case that the rest of the book goes on to offer.

Who Needs an Error Theory?

When confronted with the fact that most people, throughout most of history, have not subscribed to basic equality, one possible response is to say that we—i.e., those in broadly speaking the West, in relatively recent history, and who adhere to the expectations of polite discourse—are simply right about the fact that we are all basic equals, and those who have denied it in previous history (and for that matter, who continue to deny it in other parts of the world today, or who may come to deny it in the future) have simply been wrong. On this view, basic equality consists of some fact or facts about us that any impartial and rational enquirer armed with the right information and arguments could expect to hit upon. We, now and around here, have hit upon it. In the past, other people failed to do so, and were therefore in error. Too bad for them, hurrah for us.

The problem with this view is that it is staggeringly implausible, for several reasons. The first is that—and as the previous chapter showed—we *don't* appear to have arguments for establishing the fact of basic equality that any impartial and rational enquirer could be expected to converge upon simply as such. Indeed, quite the opposite: once we start to interrogate basic equality, we seem to confound rather than establish its credentials. Insofar as people in this part of the world, at this moment in history, subscribe to a belief in basic equality, they do so *in spite of* a lack of good theoretical grounding. This indicates that commitment to basic equality is not founded in the available theoretical arguments, but comes from elsewhere. Indeed, this must certainly be the case, given that so few people have actually read, let alone understood, the technical philosophical accounts: *that* simply cannot be where most people have gotten their ideas from.

Second, it surely cannot be that the reason (say) Genghis Khan, or Aristotle, or an American slave holder in the 1850s, or a Fabian Eugenicist in the 1920s, all rejected basic equality, is that they were simply mistaken about the available facts and arguments, or were lacking some future development in theoretical knowledge, whereas we have now arrived at a higher stage of learning that enables us to access a truth that was hidden from them. This is where basic equality is different to a scientific discovery, such as the double-helix structure of DNA. In the case of DNA, there is a straightforward story to tell about why people in the past did not know about what it was and how it works: they did not have access to relevant scientific knowledge and relevant theoretical explanations, which required centuries of intellectual advancement to eventually make comprehensible, as happened by the mid-twentieth century. What we readily have available in the case of DNA, therefore, is an *error theory* about why people prior to the twentieth century were mistaken about, for example, the causes of certain diseases or variations of phenotype: we possess facts and scientific explanations that they didn't have access to. But there is just no comparable story to tell in the case of basic equality. If we are simply right about the fact of basic equality, and they are simply wrong, *why* have most people simply been wrong, whereas we are now right? What is the error theory that explains why most humans, for most of history, have been making a mistake, one that we are now free from? What would such an error theory even *look* like?

A more promising way forward here is to embrace the fact that whatever basic equality consists in, and whatever reasons we have for believing in it now, those reasons are not going to be the sort that show that other peoples, in other times and places, were simply wrong, in the way that (for example) people who did not know about the structure of DNA, and how that causes variations in different animal species, were simply wrong. The reason that most human beings in most of history have denied basic equality is not because they were simply mistaken about the facts, or that they lacked sufficiently good arguments, but because they did not share the values and history that we (i.e., in roughly speaking the developed West, in polite society, in relatively recent history) presently hold. Consequently, basic equality did not make sense to them— *could* not make sense to them—in the kinds of ways that it makes sense to many of us, now.[1]

Looked at this way, however, the need for an error theory dissolves, for there simply is no error to explain, at least not in the way that there would be if basic equality was a fact comparable to a scientific truth like the structure of DNA. The reason most people throughout most of human history have not subscribed to the idea of basic equality is not because they have been simply mistaken,

but because they have been *different*: they lived in different kinds
of societies, and held different normative commitments, because
they had different constituting histories, in the context of which an
idea like basic equality did not make sense to them in the ways that
it does to us now. But as a result, in order to understand why basic
equality *does* make sense to us, at least more or less and now and
around here, we need to investigate the preconditions and groundings of the idea in the practices and history that we actually find
ourselves with. The next two chapters undertake precisely this kind
of investigation by focusing first on crucial aspects of human psychology regarding how we conceive of living creatures, and then by
considering relevant features of history and the important role that
fictions often play for us. Taken together, these factors can help us
make sense of what is going on when it comes to basic equality.

Before turning to the substantive case as presented in those
chapters, however, some further issues need to be addressed. First,
we must consider who any account of basic equality is supposed
to be *for*, and hence what we should expect it to be able to achieve.
Second, we must indicate why the approach I advocate here is not
vulnerable to claims of having committed the so-called genetic
fallacy: in particular, that I illegitimately conflate the distinct en-
deavours of *normative justification* (the task of the philosopher)
versus *causal explanation* (that of the historian or social scientist).
Once those matters have been addressed, we turn to the positive
argument that the rest of the book sets out.

Who Are We Talking To?

If we take seriously the idea that basic equality is something that
only makes sense to specific peoples in specific times and places,
then what we can usefully say about it will depend in part on who
we take ourselves to be talking to. This is because the reasons and
considerations that we can expect to be found compelling, or that
will even make sense on a subject like this, are going to depend
on whether we are speaking to somebody who already accepts

(something like) the idea of basic equality, versus somebody who actively denies it, or who lacks the relevant surrounding beliefs and historical preconditions for subscribing to such an idea.

If confronted with somebody who actively denies basic equality—some sceptic who denies the claims of *any* values, or a thoroughgoing bigot who is intransigently committed to the relative superiority of some kinds of humans over others—there may be nothing we can hope to say *to them*, that somehow forces *them* to change their mind. Even assuming we can get them to sit down long enough to hear us out, perhaps they just won't listen, perhaps they are unwilling to be moved by good arguments, perhaps they are too deeply committed to ethical premises that we reject for us to have enough common ground to even begin a meaningful dialogue, let alone hope to get them to see things our way. Similarly, if we imagine ourselves in debate with some historical figure—an Aristotle, or a Genghis Khan—it may be that there is too much unbridgeable distance between us and them for us to say anything that gets a grip on what they would count as reasons for seeing things our way. Insofar as they take it to simply be a fact that (for example) some people are natural slaves, or that women are biologically defective versions of men whose proper role is obedience, or that non-Mongol peoples exist only to be subjugated or slaughtered by the horsemen of the great Khan, then it is not clear there is anything we could say that would make them give up their existing worldviews, and in turn come to adopt our values instead. In all these cases, reasoned argument may simply lack the power to change minds.[2]

But even if that is so, it is a different matter entirely what we— who *do* find ourselves with a commitment to basic equality at this point in our history—might nonetheless want to say *to ourselves and each other* about the reasons that *we* have for subscribing to basic equality. Even if we cannot reasonably expect to convince the sceptic, bigot, or imagined historical figure to see it our way, there may nonetheless be things we can say to ourselves that help us understand why we *do* see it this way—and potentially, in turn, why we think that we are *right* to go on seeing it this way.

But how can I talk about our being *right*, if we do not have arguments that can prove those who disagree to be *wrong*? And did I
not say above that it is wildly implausible to suppose that those
who deny basic equality are simply making a mistake? What is
going on here?

The crux of the matter relates to the point made above: that
whatever basic equality consists in, it is a different kind of thing to
(say) a scientific truth like the fact of DNA. What makes such
things true are not the same in each case. In the latter case, facts
about DNA—for example, that it has a double-helix structure—
exist independently of the beliefs and commitments of any particular observer. The observer could attempt to deny that DNA has
a double-helix structure if they liked, but they would simply be
wrong to do so (and we would know they were wrong, even if they
stubbornly refused to see or admit it). Basic equality is not like
that, however, because basic equality *is* structured by the beliefs
and commitments of particular observers. Specifically, of human
observers now and around here: of people, like us, who possess
particular histories and are operating with particular ideas about
what values are appropriate. Insofar as one lacks that history and
those sorts of commitments, then claims of basic equality *won't* be
true. Hence why we cannot say that others who reject basic equality are *simply* making a mistake, as they would be if they denied
that DNA has a double-helix structure. If they lack the relevant
history and normative commitments, then it *won't* be true, in a
way that makes sense to them, to say that all humans are basic
equals. Another way of putting it is to say that basic equality will
be true for us but not for them—hence we can say that *we* think
we are right (and hence that they are wrong), but also understand
that from their perspective, it will be the other way around. That,
however, is a feature and not a bug when it comes to normative
values. That is just the way it is.

Some readers will find this deeply alarming. I am, after all,
openly admitting that basic equality is *relative*—relative to the values and histories of the people who do or do not believe in it. But

if it is relative, how can I claim that it is *true* that human beings are basic equals? If it is true, surely this must be true for everyone, regardless of their histories and existing commitments? And if it isn't true for everyone, then surely it isn't true for anybody? The mistake here, however, is thinking that truth has to universally take the form that it does in cases of scientific facts, as with the structure of DNA. In such cases—e.g., where the relevant facts and considerations are not dependent on the beliefs of observing agents, because they are given by prior and freestanding facts of organic chemistry—truth is not relative: it is the same for all persons (DNA *just does* have a double-helix structure, whether or not you think so). Not all truths, however, are like that. Truths about morality, for example, get their meaning and content in a different way.

Consider, in this regard, David Hume's famous example of "wilful murder" in *A Treatise of Human Nature*:

> Take any action allow'd to be vicious: Wilful murder, for instance. Examine it in all lights, and see if you can find that matter of fact, or real existence, which you call *vice*. In whichever way you take it, you find only certain passions, motives, volitions and thoughts. There is no other matter of fact in the case. The vice entirely escapes you, as long as you consider the object. You never can find it, till you turn your reflexion into your own breast, and find a sentiment of disapprobation, which arises in you, towards this action. Here is a matter of fact; but 'tis the object of feeling, not of reason. It lies in yourself, not in the object.[3]

Hume is not denying that *it is true* that wilful murder is vicious—on the contrary, he entirely agrees that it is. What Hume is saying is that what *makes* it true that wilful murder is vicious are certain facts about our sentimental responses to such acts (what goes on in "your own breast"). I agree with Hume: normative judgements receive their content and meaning from features that the relevant normative agents themselves bring to bear, in particular to do with their sentimental responses. And that is fine: that just is what morality in large part consists of, when we get down to brass tacks (and basic equality will, to that extent, be no different). It is a mistake, however, to think that because facts of morality are not like scientific facts, that they are therefore *lesser*, somehow not the real deal: that the only truths that are *really* truths are scientific ones, which present themselves equally to all observers, regardless of what the observers happen to otherwise believe or be committed to. But why should we think or accept that? Just because basic equality—like wilful murder—gets its truth conditions from a different source (from the practices, dispositions, commitments, and so forth, of the agents who subscribe to it) than does the fact of DNA having a double-helix structure (which gets them from underlying facts of organic chemistry), that doesn't mean it isn't *really* true that basic equality obtains for agents like us, and that for agents like us it isn't an important normative commitment. It *is* true—but what makes it true are wider facts about our beliefs and commitments as they presently stand.

Of course, the same will not be the case for people(s) who lack our beliefs and commitments. So how can we say that they are wrong? Well, we can say that *given* our beliefs and commitments, we think that they are wrong to deny basic equality—and that if they had our beliefs and commitments, then they would (properly) see things the way that we do. Of course, we may also accept that getting them to that point may prove impossible—though I take it to be a genuinely open question whether or not we might think it worth trying (a lot here will depend on who exactly we are talking to, and in what circumstances). Likewise, we must accept that if *we* didn't have these beliefs and commitments, then *we* wouldn't believe in the truth of basic equality, either. Our commitment to basic equality is contingent on a number of other facts about ourselves: facts about our psychologies and histories that could well have been otherwise than they are (we will come back to this matter in more detail in chapter 6).

To some, this revelation of contingency can induce a kind of ethical vertigo: if our ethical commitments are contingent, doesn't that make them *arbitrary*? And if they are arbitrary, doesn't that mean that they should lose their normative claim on us? But this is a mistake—in fact, the same mistake as noted above: of thinking that the only truths and facts that really count are those that are beyond contingency, because the only permissible model for making sense of anything is one drawn from science. After all, given the underlying facts of physics, and thus of chemistry, and thus of organic chemistry, it is not a contingent fact that DNA exhibits a double helix structure. If it didn't have this structure, then it simply wouldn't be DNA (and we wouldn't be us). In order for our values and commitments to *really* be values and commitments, must they not also look like that? Must they not be necessary, in the way that it is necessary that DNA has a double helix? The answer is again no, and for the same reason as given above: normative phenomena—what constitutes them, and what gives them their meaning and truth—are not the same as scientific phenomena. That doesn't make them lesser; it just makes them different.

As a result, however, we should not expect from normative phenomena the same features we expect of scientific phenomena—in particular, that their truths be noncontingent. What this also means however is that in *practical* terms, nothing needs necessarily to change: realising that our values are contingent has no necessary impact upon our commitment to them, and hence of how we live our lives (even if it feels, initially, as though it must). Whilst one might think—rather like Dostoyevsky—that if values are contingent then everything is permitted, one need not come to that conclusion. Importantly, "need" here may be coextensive with trying hard enough, or indeed just giving it enough time. It is quite possible to come to think of one's value commitments as having different origins to what may previously have been supposed (i.e., if one previously thought of them as having to approximate scientific facts, but now realises that such a picture can't be right), but also to see—unlike Dostoyevsky—that precisely because they are *our* values, then they will go on applying to *us*, just as they did before we became properly aware of where they came from.

Ethical vertigo, like the regular kind, is apt to pass when you realise that you are not in fact falling.[4]

This in turn allows us to avoid a mistake often associated with relativism (both by some of its advocates, as well as its critics): of inferring that because moral truths will be true to us, but not true to those who do not share our constituting histories, contingencies, backgrounds, experiences, and so forth, that therefore when it comes to normativity anything goes, and no moral outlook can be judged better or worse than any other: that all value judgements are on a level because all are true relative to the perspective of the holder. But this is a very bad inference, once again trading on the idea (appropriate in science, but not in ethics) that moral values could only *really* be of worth if absolutely true, noncontingently, from some perspective outside of human experience. But when we see that this is a confusion, based on mistakenly thinking that scientific truth is the only form of truth that exists or may legitimately be admitted, this inference can be stopped in its tracks. Just because our values are relative, nothing follows about their status *as values* from that fact alone. In turn, it remains open to us to judge and rank different kinds of values, and reflect on which of them we wish to go on upholding, and why, especially as compared to alternatives we may already know of, or otherwise encounter or consider. The fact of ethical relativism does not preclude this (as indeed I hope to demonstrate in the chapters that follow). On the contrary, it is a more accurate diagnosis of how such value judgement could even be possible in the first place.

Discovering that our values and commitments—such as our commitment to basic equality—are contingent in a way that scientific facts are not, need in turn have no destabilising (no vertigo-inducing) consequences. Our commitments can still be our commitments, and still have continued value and meaning for us, even once we accept that they could all have been otherwise. And of course, it will be the case that others who have different contingent formations may turn out not to share our values. Many in the past have not done so, and presumably others in the future will not do so either (these are facts of life we had better learn to live with, rather than trying to ignore or imagine away). What we *do* about such disagreement is a complex matter, often likely to be in large measure a political question, about how and whether we can successfully live with others with whom we profoundly disagree. But the mere fact of disagreement itself, which is a result of the underlying contingency of all values, need not mean the status of our values *as values* is in any way impugned. Bernard Williams (whose work my thinking is heavily influenced by in this regard) put the point well:

> Precisely because we are not unencumbered intelligences selecting in principle among all possible outlooks, we can accept that this outlook is ours just because of the history that has made it ours; or, more precisely, has both made us, and made the outlook as something that is ours. We are no less contingently formed than the outlook is, and the formation is significantly the same. We and our outlook are not simply in the same place at the same time. If we really understand this, deeply understand it, we can be free of what is indeed another scientistic illusion, that it is our job as rational agents to search for, or at least move as best we can towards, a system of political and ethical ideas which would be the best from an absolute point of view, a point of view that was free of contingent historical perspective.[5]

Given that now and around here we (or at least, most of us) *do* find ourselves committed to an idea like basic equality, but accepting that reason and argument alone are not going to convince others to see it our way if they don't also share our histories and values to some sufficient degree, then what is the point of doing philosophy at all?

The answer comes back to who we take ourselves to be talking to, and why. Even if we cannot expect to convince all possible comers simply through reason and argument alone (they may simply be too far away, in terms of their normative starting points, to get them to see it our way), it doesn't follow that we therefore have nothing to say to ourselves and each other about why we see things in the particular ways that we do. This, however, will involve at least two things. First, I take it that we will want to *explain* why we see things this way (and hence why others don't). Second, once we have that explanation in place, we will want to look critically at our values and commitments, and ask if, in the light of our best explanations, we now want to go on holding them—or if they ought instead to be revised, or perhaps even rejected entirely, in light of what we have come to know about them. The goal here is to be *critically self-reflective*, in order ultimately to be confident in the values and commitments that we possess, whilst being sufficiently convinced that we possess them for the right kinds of reasons, and in the right kinds of ways.[6] That confidence comes from being truthful about why we believe what we believe—and that truthfulness can be forwarded, at least in part, by certain kinds of philosophical enquiry. But precisely because what we need to explain here is contingent in its formation and origin, any such enquiry must accept that it cannot *just* be philosophy, done from the armchair alone and without instruction from other areas of human intellectual endeavour. On the contrary, it must be—as I said in chapter 1—*impure*. With regards specifically to basic equality, it must take on board insights from (as I will attempt to show in the next two chapters) what we know of human psychology, and of relevant facts of history, as well as the human capacity to employ and become immersed in various kinds of fiction. At any rate, it is crucially important to make clear that relativism and subjectivism on this matter in no way necessitate scepticism about our values and commitments. On the contrary, if things go well, we can hope for more, not less, confidence in our values—as indeed I hope to show by the end of this book.

To some readers, my baseline acceptance of ethical subjectivism—and therefore of a species of relativism—will already be enough to disqualify my account entirely. For them, the only kind of account regarding basic equality that will be acceptable will be one that presents itself as "objective": as somehow valid and binding on all agents regardless of their existing beliefs, commitments, dispositions, psychologies, and so forth. For my part, I believe that this response is a hiding to nothing, primarily because *no* normative features of our lives look like that. But those who disagree are welcome to keep trying if they wish; to quest on after some fact or facts establishing the basis of basic equality that necessarily present as true to all rational enquirers, merely as such, and that are somehow normatively decisive in turn.[7] I suspect that doing so will sooner or later terminate in the sorts of cul-de-sacs surveyed in the last chapter. And even if not, we will still be owed an error theory as to why most humans, throughout most of history, have failed to discern these facts, but which the philosopher has now apparently revealed (and they will also need to explain how the rest of us, now and around here, nonetheless stumbled upon these facts in the absence of, and prior to, the philosopher's revelations). Alternatively, I suggest we take a different path.

The Genetic Fallacy?

Before turning to the substantive account of basic equality built over the next three chapters, it is important to first address an objection: that I am committing the so-called genetic fallacy in complaining that existing accounts of basic equality do not explain why and how people have come to believe in basic equality. The objection goes like this. The route via which ordinary people (including many philosophers and political theorists) have come to arrive at a belief is not what matters most: what matters most is that their belief is true, and hence that they are justified in holding to it, and acting appropriately in the light of it. How the belief was formed is one thing; its status as a true belief, informing practical conduct, another. Therefore (so the objection goes) it doesn't (really) matter if most people got to a belief in basic equality through some faulty or incorrect manner, so long as the philosopher can give reasons that the belief is nonetheless correct, and thus that practical implications drawn from it are normatively warranted. Whether or not those are the same reasons that led ordinary people to actually come to hold a commitment to basic equality is a separate question, to be handled separately. In other words, to complain that the way the belief was generally arrived at—its genesis—is not accounted for in the argument for why a belief is true, is to miss the point that what finally matters is not *how* a belief was acquired, but whether it is *correct*. Thus, the genetic fallacy.

From what I have already said, it should be evident however that I reject the claim that there is a *fallacy*—an error of reasoning—to be exposed here. This is because the way that a belief like basic equality is formed *is going to be part of what constitutes the correctness of the belief itself*. When it comes to normative phenomena, the question of how a belief came about and whether or not it is correct are *not* questions that are independent of each other. Likewise, whether we are normatively warranted in holding to a commitment like basic equality will itself have to make reference to the reasons we do in fact hold it—which means making reference to the constituting causal story about our psychologies, ethical dispositions, and histories. This takes us to the point flagged at the end of chapter 1: that rather than seeing basic equality as some prior independent fact in light of which we ought to treat each other according to the tenets of basic egalitarianism, it is more plausible to reverse matters. It is, rather, that we have over time come *to treat each other* in terms of a basic egalitarianism, and *from that* we get the notion of our each being basic equals. But as a result, the question of whether we are normatively warranted in going on this way has to examine and work from within the practice of basic egalitarianism and what it is constituted by, for there is no separate ground upon which to make an assessment beyond the practice itself. Normative justification and causal explanation thus emerge as two sides of the same coin, and hence a proper account of the former requires taking serious note of the latter—although, as I will argue below, what we need here is best construed in terms of a *vindication* of our commitment to basic equality as conducted by the lights of our existing web of values and practices, rather than hoping for a justification that somehow lies outside of what we ourselves bring to bear.

Again, the difference with scientific cases is important and illustrative. In the case of DNA, precisely how Crick and Watson came to acquire the belief that DNA has a double-helix structure cannot itself condition the truth of whether DNA does in fact have a double-helix structure, let alone what we might think appropriate in the light of that. (We can imagine a world in which they hit upon that finding by accident, through some faulty method, and which later scientists corrected.) But with basic equality, precisely because this is something constituted by the values and commitments (and therefore, the specific histories) of the agents who subscribe to a belief in it, how they came to that belief *does* make a difference, because it is what gives the belief the very content that we are trying to explain and understand, and in reference to which any judgement about whether or not such belief is not only true, but in turn also provides normative warrant for various practical implications, has to be made. Thus the question of whether or not commitment to something like basic equality is normatively warranted *cannot* operate independently from the explanation of how that commitment came to be and is sustained by the very agents who actually hold it. (I say more about this in chapter 5 below, after introducing the crucial role that psychological essentialism plays in my account.) It is thus not a fallacy to think that the "genetics"—the "how it came to be so"—of something like basic equality matters. On the contrary, it is essential that we pay attention to precisely these factors, and try to account for them, if we are going to understand what is in question. Failure to do this is a common feature of the accounts surveyed in the previous chapter; paying the required attention is by contrast the aim of what follows.

4

Essences

THERE IS OVERWHELMING evidence from psychological research,[1] powerfully corroborated by careful philosophical reflection on the matter,[2] that human beings are *psychological essentialists*. That is, we believe there to be "natural kinds": the most basic class of things, of which the natural world is believed to be constituted, and in reference to which nature (in Plato's famous phrase) can be "carved at the joints." But in turn, we believe there to be underlying, hidden, and determinative essences that *make* those natural kinds what they are. John Locke captured the idea perfectly in *An Essay Concerning Human Understanding* when he wrote that an essence is "the very being of anything, whereby it is, what it is. And thus the real internal, but generally . . . unknown Constitution of Things, whereon their discoverable Qualities depend, may be called their *Essence*."[3] However, he also claimed that if you demand to know what those essences are, "'tis plain Men are ignorant and know them not." Yet "though we know nothing of these real Essences, there is nothing more ordinary, than that Men should attribute the sorts of Things to such Essences."[4] Locke, it turns out, was right. Human beings intuitively believe that natural kinds have something "inside them," some essence, that makes them what they are.[5] We are psychological essentialists.

Yet this pervasive folk psychology is *mistaken* in ascribing essences to putative natural kinds. In most cases, and indeed perhaps all, there simply are no essences to be discovered underlying whatever putative natural kinds we suppose there to be: psychological essentialism is the "psychologically plausible analog of the logically implausible doctrine of metaphysical essentialism."[6] However—although the evidence on this matter remains limited— there are strong indications that psychological essentialism is a human universal: it both begins early (it is evident by four and five years old, and perhaps even younger[7]) and appears to be found across all human cultures. The most plausible explanation for this is that psychological essentialism is the result of evolved adaptations in the human brain, and is thus shared by all members of the species.[8] Even if there is cultural variation in the extent and degree to which, as well as localised inflection of how, it manifests in practice, the available evidence indicates that essentialist thinking "is not a local phenomenon, but rather is a pervasive aspect of human psychology."[9] In this chapter, I draw on the established philosophical and psychological research to lay out the basics of psychological essentialism. I then suggest that the persistence of a belief in essences—specifically, that each of us has a *human essence*—is key to making sense of basic equality.

I must therefore beg the reader's patience. What follows in this chapter may initially appear like something of a detour, or a tangent. But the material is crucial for the positive account of basic equality that the rest of the book goes on to advance. It is only by understanding the central role that essences play in our psychology that we will be able to make sense of basic equality. Specifically, that basic equality can be understood as the normatively desirable reverse of one of the very worst things we are capable of: dehumanisation. To see why and how this is so will take some time—but it is time worth taking.

Psychological Essentialism: The Physical World

What makes gold *gold*? A modern, scientifically informed respondent is likely to reply: "having the atomic number 79, and thus being the element Au." Anything that has the atomic number 79 *just is* gold; anything that doesn't, *just isn't.* Fool's gold (iron pyrite) may look like gold, but an appropriate analysis by a trained expert will reveal that appearances are deceptive: it appears to be gold, but it is really something else.

This example neatly captures the logic of essentialism: two things can *look* identical, yet really be different, because some (hidden, underlying) quality about them is different, and that (hidden, underlying) quality is taken to be what determines correct classification. Initially the example of gold appears to bear out the case for thinking that at least *some* natural kinds have essences: is not the essence of gold "the atomic number 79," and do our intuitions therefore not, at least in this case, correspond to physical reality? In fact, the answer turns out to be (much) more complex than it seems, for the physics of elements is not so straightforward as the layperson tends to believe.[10] But even granting, for simplicity's sake, that "having the atomic number 79" *just is* what makes something gold, it is vital to realise that this scientific fact (which most people, myself included, utter as a mantra without any serious understanding, for most of us are not competent regarding the physics being invoked) is not the *reason why* we believe that gold has an essence, that is, something that *makes* it gold. After all, many (in fact most) people in the world have no awareness of the idea of atomic numbers whatsoever—and yet they would all confidently tell you that gold is not the same thing as (say) lead, and they would steadfastly refuse to budge on the possibility that they might "really" be the same thing, unless some explanation—one making appeal to a shared underlying quality (i.e., an essence)—were supplied. Likewise, prior to the advent of modern chemistry and physics, people presumably had firm beliefs that gold was and could only be gold, and not something else.[11] These people had no recourse to the explanation "atomic number 79," because that way of thinking wasn't yet possible. Nonetheless, they still believed that gold was gold *because there was something about it that just made it gold.* What this shows is that our intuition that gold has some underlying property—some essence—that makes it gold comes prior to any knowledge (no matter whether learned and sophisticated, or, more typically, mantra-like) of elementary physics. Saying "gold is gold because it has the atomic number 79" is intuitively satisfying to us *because we already believe* that there is some essence that makes gold, gold. When a physicist tells us that "it has the atomic number 79," this confirms what we thought we already knew: gold has an essence. Happily, that essence even turns out to have a special name: atomic number 79! What is driving the process here is not scientific discovery, but a preexisting psychological disposition towards essentialism, which in such cases happily absorbs the scientific discovery precisely because it gels so smoothly with what we were already convinced of anyway.[12]

In the case of gold, or of a chemical compound like water (which most people would want to say *just is* H_2O; that "H_2O is what makes water, water"), it seems that our prescientific intuitions happily map on to, and are supported by, physical reality.[13] In fact, it turns out to be much more complex than that (although we need not get into the details of why here).[14] But for present purposes, and for simplicity's sake, we can take gold and water as cases that nicely illustrate the logic of essences, as follows.

Something can, upon superficial inspection, look like water: a clear, odourless liquid. And yet it might *not* be water, because it is in fact of a different chemical composition. Likewise, something can, upon superficial inspection, look like gold, and yet not be gold, because it is in fact iron pyrite. We are entirely comfortable with this distinction, because in both cases we believe the essences of the relevant items to be different, even if the appearances are the same. It can go the other way too. Two gold bars may *look* very different (because one has been treated with a chemical dye), and yet our belief that both are *really* gold will be unshaken if we learn why they now don't look the same. Similarly, the block of ice and the glass of water *look* very different, but if we are told that they are both H_2O manifested in different states, we accept that they are both the same kind of thing, even if they look very different (children grasp this by around the age of four[15]). Essences, that is, are taken by human psychology to be determinant of true ontological status. In turn, essences are taken to ordinarily determine outward appearance: the uninterfered-with gold bar is shiny and yellow *because* it has the essence of gold; the unmolested glass of water is clear and odourless *because* it has the essence of water (at room temperature). However, this determination is also in practice *defeasible*: the gold bar can be made to look like a lead one by clever chemical tricks; the water can be turned blue and given a smell by adding food colouring.[16] Nonetheless, the essence is most basic, and although it can be defeated in its determining outward effects, by being most basic, it determines final classification. However, if the essence *itself* is fundamentally changed, then the thing itself is necessarily changed, too. If this lump of gold ceases to have the atomic number 79, then it is no longer gold—even if it somehow continues to look, superficially, like a shiny gold bar. If water is subjected to chemical change and the bonds of the H_2O molecules are broken, then it ceases to be water, and becomes something else, even if it remains to the naked eye a clear, odourless liquid.

If all of this seems blindingly obviously, that is the point: this kind of thinking appears to be hardwired into human beings. Yet we apply this kind of thinking far beyond the (putative) natural kinds that constitute the physical world of elements and chemical compounds. In particular, we apply our essentialist psychology to the realm of living creatures. Here, however, there is no question that our essentialist psychological intuitions generate a folk biology that is decisively refuted by proper scientific understanding.[17] To this fascinating phenomenon we now turn.

Psychological Essentialism: Living Creatures

If I take a white horse, paint black stripes on it, cut its mane into short tufts, and then release it onto the plains of the Serengeti, have I created a zebra? The answer is obviously "no"—that's just a badly disguised horse somewhere it doesn't belong. And it wouldn't matter how well the disguise was made, or how long the horse stayed; it would be impossible to change a horse into a zebra by such measures. For what makes a zebra a zebra is something *inside* the animal.

It is tempting to reply here that what "makes" the zebra a zebra is "the fact it has zebra DNA" (as opposed to horse DNA). And this *sounds* like a compelling answer, to the layperson at least. But as with the case of saying "gold is gold because it has the atomic number 79," appearances are misleading.[18] First, those untrained in biological science (i.e., the vast majority of us, myself included) have no real understanding of what DNA is, or how it works. When we say "it has zebra DNA," that is just a superficially scientific-sounding way of saying "it has Zebra-ness, not Horseness, on the inside." Second, those who *are* trained in biological science know that DNA is not straightforwardly determinant of species membership, because DNA *does not* mark sharp, essential distinctions between different species (which, counter to our folk biological intuitions, are not sharply delineated and discrete categories, but complex, and often vague at the borderlines as regards final classification). For example, there are members of the cutthroat trout species which are more genetically different from other cutthroat trout (their own species) than they are from some rainbow trout (a different species). Two cutthroat trout both "have cutthroat trout DNA," but that alone does not mark out why they are members of the same species whilst a rainbow trout is not.[19] Although this is a relatively unusual example, it simply marks a point on a much wider continuum of complexity in biological classification and analysis: "DNA" does not neatly delineate species according to the intuitive classifications that ordinary people have about species, because species membership is, since the Darwinian revolution, now understood to be vastly more complex than simply "having a certain kind of DNA," or any other singular property. In fact, there is no singular, uniform, constant metric by which species are always and everywhere classified in modern biology: in practice, biologists will use a range of criteria (not all of them always compatible!) to determine species membership differently in different contexts. These include the ability for opposite-sex individuals to breed and produce fertile offspring; karyotype (i.e., chromosome composition); DNA sequence; morphology; behaviour; occupied ecological niches; or some context-specific combination of these. The discovery that in practice species classification is in part context-dependent is an intuitive affront to our notion that species are natural kinds—but that just illustrates how powerful (and how inaccurate) our essentialist psychologies are in such matters. We *think* that the natural world is divided up into neatly categorised, sharply delineated animal and plant species. But this is just false, a product of our pretheoretical folk intuitions. Vague claims about "DNA" (or the like) are really post hoc justifications for what we think we already know, due precisely to our essentialist folk biological categories about living natural kinds being so intuitively powerful. On the contrary, "Biology does not provide neat, essentialised categories of this sort, however much [essentialism] demands them. . . . There are a number of different biological routes to the phenotype, and the natural world does not label one or another of these as the genuine, true, real or normatively right one."[20] Still, the belief that it is not so is incredibly hard to shake (just try it), precisely because we are psychological essentialists.[21]

As with gold, what is going on here is that human folk biological classifications *precede* any familiarity with biological science, and we seek to bolster preexisting essentialist classifications of animal species as sharply demarcated with putative appeals to (what little we know of) biology. We treat living beings the way we treat (what our brains believe to be) natural kinds like gold and water, because we think animal and plant species *are also natural kinds*. This is scientifically unsupportable, but we all intuitively do it, from a very young age, and apparently cross-culturally.[22] And as with gold and water, the logic of essentialism is taken to apply to living natural kinds, too, as strongly evidenced by experiments asking young children whether and how an animal changes simply by altering the way it looks, or whether to change what the animal *is* one has to change it "on the inside" (children overwhelmingly support the latter, but not the former, kind of suggestion).[23]

As with gold and water, the logic of essences applies to animals too: essence dictates fundamental classification, and is typically determining of outward physical appearance, but this latter aspect is potentially defeasible in practice. Thus a tiger dyed yellow and given a fluffy golden mane remains a tiger, and has not become a lion. However, if presented with a large cat patterned with black and orange stripes, even though we would initially believe it to be a tiger, if informed by a recognised expert in big cats that despite appearances this was in fact a lion that had undergone a rare genetic mutation, we would happily defer to that expert, were we adequately convinced of his credentials and sincerity.[24] This thing *looks* like a tiger on a superficial examination, but it's *really* a lion, because on the inside it has lion-ness, which just happens (in this case) to be failing to properly manifest. We might nod sagely along with being told that this lion "has mutations in its DNA," thinking we are doing science. But what is really driving our assent that this is a lion and not (despite appearances) a tiger, is that we accept the testimony that it has a lion essence (as confirmed by the expert), whose normal manifestation is on this occasion being subverted.

Similarly, and as with inanimate natural kinds of the physical world, we also intuitively believe that species classifications are sharp and categorical. Just as gold cannot *simultaneously* be lead, so a tiger cannot *simultaneously* be a lion. It is either a tiger, or a lion, or something else, but not both at the same time. (Species classifications in folk biology are all-or-nothing matters, something again decisively refuted by modern biological science—but that doesn't alter the fact of our prescientific intuitions being the way they are.[25])

The logic of essences gets extended with living creatures, however, because we intuitively believe that essences are passed on by parental descent. Thus, a tiger is a tiger *because* it had tiger parents—and nothing that comes from two tiger parents can be anything other than a tiger. Likewise, a horse is a horse *because* it had horse parents. And part of the reason a horse and a lion cannot have a baby is (we intuitively believe, prior to any familiarity with the details of biological science and genetic reproduction, as shown by studies with children) that they are *different natural kinds*, and the essences of those two different things cannot successfully mix. Revealingly, even in cases where evidence contradicts what we take ourselves to know about the categorical, sharp, non-mixing nature of species classification, instead of admitting the (biologically true) fact that species classifications are in many cases fuzzy and noncategorical, and that some different species can indeed mix, our brains instead insist on the priority of essences, and assert a *new, sharply distinct* species as having emerged, not an ambiguous, category-upsetting blend. Hence if a lion breeds with a tiger (as is biologically possible, but an affront to our intuitive belief that they are *different species*, and thus of two different essences and hence not compatible), we do not consider the offspring to be a blend of a lion and of a tiger, some ambiguous mix of both. We instead classify it as a "liger"—a, new, third kind of entity, produced by parents with two different essences, and thus categorically different to both in turn. A liger, after all, is *a liger*—there is no question in our mind that it "might" be a tiger, or "might" be a lion. We (think we) know exactly what it is—some new third kind of big cat, not an ambiguous blend of two others. This reflects, again, that our essentialist psychology takes the essence of living kinds to be both simple and unalterable: if your parents both have tiger essence, then *you* have tiger essence, and are a tiger. But if your parents are a tiger and a lion, then by mixing those essences they have fundamentally altered them both, and what is produced is a *new* simple, unalterable (without itself being destroyed) essence: liger essence. Again, whilst this is all absurd from the point of view of proper scientific explanation, folk biology nonetheless precedes in this manner, and is typically highly resistant to the corrections of proper understanding in such areas, reflecting psychological essentialism's deep-seated presence in how we mentally process living kinds.

Finally, the attribution of essences as underlying and being determinant of species membership provides grounds for making inductive inferences about members of living kinds in our psychologies. Thus all tigers are presumed to behave alike; all horses, in their different ways, the same. If that horse ate the oats, we expect the others to do so next time, too. If that tiger ate a member of our tribe last week, we don't expect this one to roll over on its back for a belly rub. And the evolutionary adaptive explanation for why we have developed this inductive proclivity regarding species essence is compelling. As the anthropologist Francisco J. Gil-White neatly summarises it, "Species essentialism motivates inductive generalizations about hidden properties, so that we will assume that anything nonobvious learned about one beaver, say, will be true of all beavers. This is adaptive because beavers in fact do share many nonobvious properties and such generalizations reduce the costs of learning."[26] Psychological essentialism about the natural world is *heuristically advantageous*, even though it is ontologically false. This probably explains why we all do it, and why we cannot help doing it—it is the result of evolutionary adaptations to our psychology that human beings acquired a long time ago, and which bestowed significant benefits upon us in our evolutionary past.

To summarise, human beings are essentialists about putative living natural kinds: we believe that what makes an individual a member of a species is that it has, inside it, some special property—an essence—that *makes* it that species. This essence is sharply determinative of which category a living thing falls into, is passed on by descent from parents, determines (though in a defeasible way) outward appearances, and if it is changed, then the thing itself is necessarily changed also. But if the essence *is* changed, then this represents a sudden, decisive break, for we intuitively hold that species cannot be blended or ambiguous: they are to our essentialist minds sharp and unambiguous classifications. This is all false as a matter of scientific truth, as every biologist knows. But it is nonetheless how we think—and indeed, it requires a tremendous amount of effort, even from the trained biologist, to suspend this way of thinking so as to favour a more scientifically accurate picture of reality.

When doing scientific research, of course, we can and do suspend essentialist intuitions and correct them with scientific results when necessary—and this is all to the good. But it will not have escaped the reader's attention that "human being" is a species classification. Just as with tigers, horses, and beavers, so with people: a human being is, to the human brain, a living natural kind. There is therefore in human psychology (again, despite this being unsupported by biological science) a proclivity to believe in the existence of *a human essence*: of something on the inside that *makes* this individual a member of the specific group *Homo sapiens*. And from this belief, an awful lot of trouble can come. But also, I want to suggest, something altogether better.

Race and Racism

Although all human beings are members of one species, *Homo sapiens*, there is an immediate challenge to our brains accepting this truth: namely, that we often *look* extremely different to one another. Somebody whose ancestors lived in Nigeria will typically look very different in skin colour, eye colour and shape, height, bone density, and so forth, to somebody whose ancestors lived on the Mongol plains, or in Scandinavia. Superficially, the variety in outward physical appearance might indicate that these creatures are *not* of the same species—that people from West Africa and Mongolia and Sweden are rather like great ape analogues to the variety we find in big cats. So whilst jaguars, lions, and tigers all share similar characteristics (they are large felines, they are covered in fur, they may try to eat you), they are nonetheless classed by our brains as different species of animal, because each are taken to be possessed of a different underlying essence that *makes* them either jaguars, or lions, or tigers. In fact, there is evidence that the human brain *does* intuitively process different human ethnic groups, and in turn groups as sorted by phenotype (i.e., races), along the lines that it processes different animal species, although we also tend in practice to correct for this at the level of conscious reflection based on (an essentialist!) awareness that appearances can be deceptive.[27]

In any case, the logic of psychological essentialism easily enables an initial intuitive reaction that different phenotypes of human are instances of different species to be abandoned in favour of a picture of the human species as singular, despite superficial differences in appearance. Recall that we are entirely comfortable with the same essence manifesting in outwardly very different ways due to the defeasibility of essence-manifestation, and hence have no trouble saying that two things are instances of the same natural kind, even if they look very different, so long as they share the same essence. Hence, upon discovery that despite their superficially different appearances, people from Tanzania, Mongolia, and Sweden can have perfectly healthy offspring, who in turn can have healthy offspring, and that the outward characteristics of these offspring show a progressive blending of their parent appearances, the human brain can intuitively and easily process the idea that although these three great ape phenotypes *look* different, they are in fact of the same natural kind, because they share the same essence, as proved by the fact they successfully and successively pass on their outward characteristics, in blended form, to their offspring, indicating that the underlying determining essence is compatible (and therefore, identical—essences are singular and cannot mix) across phenotypes. In making this correction, the human brain in this instance comes closer to biological reality, albeit accidentally, rather than away from it: concluding that whilst individual *Homo sapiens* can look very different to each other, they are nonetheless of the same species.

Unfortunately, whilst the logic of essentialism can lead us in the direction of a more biologically correct understanding (that all *Homo sapiens*, no matter how different they look, are members of a single species), its effects do not only and always work uniformly in this direction. This is because the fact that we *do* often look so superficially different across human phenotypes is something that cries out for explanation to our essentialist psychologies. "It is not surprising, then, that when the differences are blatant, such as in facial shape or skin color, we don't brush them off as arbitrary variation; we think they matter."[28] As psychological essentialists, we intuitively infer that the reason different groups of humans look so different must be that there is some underlying difference in their essences *causing* a difference of outward appearance. This is where the idea of *race* gains strong psychological purchase on our minds (one that tends also to get vigorous reinforcement from our surrounding social structures, and from a young age). That despite all being members of one species, we nonetheless exhibit variety *within* the species due to (hidden, underlying) properties that cause us to look different from one another, and in turn (our essentialist brains inductively infer), to also *be* different in our various behaviours, those behaviours being a function of differences in more fundamental essence.

Our essentialist psychologies are strongly tempted to believe that differences in underlying essential properties must explain why we look so different—why there are different "races."[29] Of course, the idea of "race" is even more scientifically unfounded than our crude folk biological concepts of species identity: "there is little doubt that it woefully misrepresents reality."[30] There simply *are no* scientifically respectable classifications of race (whereas there are for species: it's just that these turn out to be vastly more complex than intuitive folk biology can make sense of, and do not follow the neat rules that our essentialist brains expect).[31] Nonetheless, and once again, the point about psychological essentialism is that it persists independently of scientific fact, because it is not a function of what we learn about the natural world through empirical scientific study, but an existing mental predisposition that we use as a heuristic for navigating the external world.

Importantly, however, exactly how races in practice get categorised by our essentialist psychologies is not determined at the level of basic psychological essentialism, but is culturally specific and highly historically variable. Skin colour may seem the most obvious (indeed, *the natural*—a revealingly essentialist intuition) way of doing race, at least to Westerners, at this point in history. But that is only because it is how we have tended to do race in our recent past. In fact, it is neither necessary nor sufficient to the attribution of "race" that it be indexed to skin colour: "Italian" and "Irish" were considered different races in 1900s America, whilst both would today be classed as part of the "White" race. Similarly, in 1930s Germany, a Jew was still classed as a member of the Jewish race even if he happened to be tall, blond, and blue-eyed (as many were, against the prevailing stereotypes of what "a Jew" looked like). This is precisely because race classification is a function of an essentialising psychology which says there is something *on the inside* that determines what putative natural kind (in this case, what race) an individual is being sorted into, and this is only contingently correlated with outward phenotypical appearance (because ordinary outward manifestation of essence is defeasible). It may initially seem more typical, or the default, for human brains to go from some superficial outward difference (e.g., skin colour, eye shape, etc.) *to* the thought that this is a function of a more fundamental hidden determining essence, because we find it intuitive that essences are defeasible in their outward manifestation, but nonetheless determinant of "true" ontological status. But it is equally possible for our brains to operate the process in reverse: to decouple the idea of race from simple outward appearance, and move to the thought that what "race" you are is not always and necessarily tied to what you look like. According to our pretheoretical folk taxonomies, race, like species, is determined "on the inside," and its outward manifestation is defeasible. Hence the apparently nonsensical, but entirely intuitive to our essentialist psychologies, conclusion that you can be a member of a certain race *even if you don't look like it*.[32]

This "logic" of essentialist race thinking both helps explain, and is neatly illustrated by, the commonplace notion that race is both transmitted "in the blood," coupled with the power of the "one drop" notion of racial identity in quotidian psychology. The idea that race is determined by blood is biological gobbledygook (there are no relevant differences between the blood of a "White" person versus a "Black" person to any greater or lesser degree than the differences between the blood of two "White" or two "Black" people, and the same is true of all other "races"). Nonetheless, the widespread and intuitive appeal of the idea that "White" blood and "Black" blood are somehow different is well documented, despite its lacking any scientific basis.[33] And in racist White supremacist regimes such as those previously found in South Africa, or in the pre–Civil Rights Southern United States, appealing to blood as the transmitter mechanism of racial classification was commonplace and intuitively accepted as obvious by many. This is illustrated by the so-called one-drop rule: that no matter how White a person *looked*, and no matter if they had been raised by White parents, and only ever interacted with other White people, if it emerged that they had a Black ancestor (no matter how many generations removed)—that is, if they had even just "one drop" of "Black" blood—then they *were* Black, even if they didn't look it.[34] The reason people took this to be true appears to be because the idea of a Black essence—as transmitted in the blood—was taken to be the dominating and determining one, such that its presence automatically overwhelmed any "White" essence, and negated it (remember that, according to folk biological essentialism, essences cannot mix, and they issue in sharp, determinate classifications). Clearly this attitude reflected the racist assumptions, fears, and paranoias of the societies it manifested in (why, after all, should it not be the "White essence" that overwhelmed the Black, unless a racially dominant group was projecting its fears and anxieties about a despised and subjugated racial other?). But no matter how biologically preposterous and repellent such a notion now correctly strikes us as being, it neatly illustrates how quickly essentialist psychologies both generate the idea of race, and in turn construct a "logic" for how race is sustained and determined. (In this regard, I suspect most people still share the intuitive reflex of American

GIs in WWII, who were painstakingly assured that measures were firmly in place ensuring that blood transfusions would only be given from donors of "their" race, even though medical science by that point had conclusively determined that there was no difference between "Black" and "White" blood.[35])

It is not difficult to see how this aspect of our essentialist psychology can lead to severe problems. If we look different "because" we have different essences, and if essence determines behaviour, which can itself be inductively attributed to all other members of that kind (as with animal species), then we have not just the idea of *race*, but the foundations of *racism*—that is, of believing that certain individuals act a certain way *because* they are members of a "race." (And why are they members of that race? *Because they have the essence of that race.*) And if the behaviour attributed to the race is viewed in a normatively different way by members of another "race," we have the makings of racial stratification, discrimination, prejudice—and in turn all of the evils that typically follow from those.[36] This is not to say that thinking along lines of race necessarily leads to racism, or that all human beings are racists "deep down." But it is to say that an essentialising psychology makes us vulnerable to falling into not just the attribution of race, but in turn the normative weaponisation of race classifications—that is, to racism. And this probably explains why racism is something that has, over and over, to be fought against from one generation to the next, corrected by rational reflection as well as concerted attempts to dispel the myths and lies that get attached to classifications of race, using education and repeat acculturation to train our brains out of thinking that race classifications correlate to essences, and hence to homogenously manifested group-wide identities and characteristics. As Paul Bloom puts it, learning that race is a social construct is a belief that *itself* has to be socialised into us: "You need to be socialized to think about socialization."[37] It is also likely why the in-group/out-group dynamics of racial polarisation are not confined to any one culture, society, or epoch, but appear to be a permanent threat in all human cultures (though the track record of success and failure in even recognising racism as an evil, let alone taking steps to overcome it, has varied enormously in human history, and continues to vary across the globe today).[38] And yet humans are capable of something even worse than racism (though it typically manifests as the end-point of the most virulent instances of racism): *dehumanisation*.

Dehumanisation

The most compelling account of dehumanisation is that of David Livingstone Smith.[39] As with other accounts,[40] Smith argues that psychological essentialism is central to understanding dehumanisation, which appears to be a universal precursor to, and perhaps even a necessary condition for, genocide. Central to the process of dehumanisation on Smith's picture is the convincing of members of an in-group (typically via sustained campaigns of propaganda, fear-mongering, and blame) that members of a specific outgroup may *look* human, but are in fact, on the inside, something else. This is not difficult for our essentialist brains to conceive: after all, the horse may *look* like a zebra, but it's really a horse (on the inside). Likewise, that creature may *look* like a human being, just like you. But what if it is really something else, on the inside? What if it is really harbouring the essence of, say, a parasite, or vermin, or savage beast? What would *that* make it?

Well, for a start, it wouldn't *really* be a human (or so our essentialist psychology is liable to conclude). It would be something that looked human, but wasn't, because lacking a human essence. It would, in a word, be a *subhuman*. But subhumans are potentially dangerous, for a whole host of reasons, and are deeply alarming to our minds. First, if something looks like a human, but has the essence of a vermin (a rat, say) or a parasite (a bloodsucking flea), or a dangerous animal (a rabid dog), then it is doubly threatening. First, because vermin and parasites and dangerous beasts attack human bodies and can also spread disease, and hence are a threat to you and your group. Second, because *disguised* vermin and parasites and wild beasts are especially worrisome: they may be causing you harm without you even realising it, or be about to attack you at any moment. They could be anywhere, right now. Perhaps in this very room, or the house next door. And you wouldn't even know it until it was too late.

But it gets worse. For if something looks like a human, but in fact has the essence of a different natural kind (a rat, or a flea), then its existence is a violation of our strong intuitive ban on mixed natural kinds. Rats, recall, are supposed to have *rat* essences; humans are supposed to have *human* essences—and never the twain shall meet. But if we are confronted with something that we have come to believe is simultaneously rat *and* human *at the same time*, that is a violation of the proper ontological order. It is not how the world, consisting of natural kinds determined by tightly demarcated underlying singular essences, is fundamentally supposed to *be*. The presence of this outwardly human, inwardly rat, creature, is a wholesale affront to our intuitive way of dividing the world up into ontologically separate natural kinds, and the mental effort of switching between viewing this as a mere animal that could do us harm, back to an outwardly human creature that can speak and appears rational and thus is not a mere animal, creates a state of psychological dissonance that we find deeply unsettling (this is a case of what Freud called the *unheimlich*, usually translated somewhat inadequately as "the uncanny"). The result is that what we are confronted with appears to us as quite literally *a monster*: a violation of the natural order triggering a sense of the *unheimlich* in our brains.[41] And yet monsters, we all intuitively know, are dangerous. That's why they're called monsters, why we fear them, and why they have to be destroyed before they get us first.

As Smith convincingly argues, if one group of humans comes to believe that some other group of putative humans is *not* in fact human, that they are outwardly human-like monsters concealing a hidden essence of something not-human, this is liable to spell very bad news. For not only are these putative subhumans liable to be psychologically processed as a direct threat to the in-group—just like rats, or fleas, or other dangerous animals—but they are also monsters, and even worse, they are hidden from view and therefore not open to easy identification and control. The imperative to not just control, but outright eradicate, this threat is thus progressively amplified. Indeed, eliminating these rat-human monsters becomes more than just an act of pest-control: it becomes a piece of self-defence, of protecting one's community of true humans from the danger posed by these threatening, hidden, literally monstrous subhumans. In turn, it is not just permitted to kill these dangerous subhumans—it becomes *morally required*.

It is thus no accident that every genocide in human history appears to have been prefigured by a long period of dehumanising discourse perpetrated against the eventual victim group, which has the function of depicting them as not *really* human.[42] Nazi propaganda, for example, was replete with virulently racist imagery depicting Jews as rats and other dangerous vermin.[43] Prior to the Rwandan genocide, government radio broadcasts characterised Tutsis as cockroaches. And even regimes that stopped short of full-blown genocide have propagated such dehumanising tactics when marshalling their populations in efforts to kill members of enemy groups: the US army during WWII frequently depicted the Japanese as rodent-like; Russian political art from the 1930s and 1940s shows German and Italian fascists as snakes, dogs, pigs, apes, rats, and so on.[44] This is likely because most human beings are deeply resistant to killing other human beings, and apart from a small percentage of natural-born psychopaths, it is very difficult to convince ordinary people to kill other ordinary people.[45] In order, say, to get them to hack their neighbours to death with machetes— as happened in Rwanda—it is necessary to first convince them that their neighbours are *not* other human beings. That they are in fact subhumans, misleadingly displaying the outward form of humans, but who are thereby dangerous—indeed, literally monstrous—threats to the community of real humans. Just as it is much easier to kill a diseased rat than a human being, it is much easier to kill a human being if you think it is *really* a diseased rat.

Dehumanisation, as theorised by Smith, represents perhaps the most extreme danger that human psychological essentialism can lend itself to. It is when our capacity to believe that essences are what determine what something is, but that appearances can also be deceptive regarding what underlying essence is actually at play, is harnessed to the worst impulses of hate, violence, othering, and destruction. Indeed racism, at least in its most virulent forms, appears permanently liable to slide into dehumanisation, by taking the further step of saying that the members of some putative race do not simply have a different kind of human essence, but in fact *do not share the common human essence at all*; that they merely resemble us in outward appearance, whilst being something different on the inside. (This appears to have been the attitude of many participants in the Atlantic slave trade, and subsequently in the American South. The most committed racists denied that Black Africans were even human, claiming that despite their outward appearance, they lacked what was required to be a real human being: typically, a soul. Such motivated reasoning in turn legitimated treating Blacks with appalling brutality.[46])

Nonetheless, Smith urges that dehumanisation may well be an *extreme* phenomenon, and not one that happens always and everywhere—though when it does, we ought to be very worried indeed.[47] Whilst we are all vulnerable to being seduced by dehumanising discourse, in large part due to our essentialist psychologies, we are not necessarily determined to be dehumanisers, any more than we are determined to be racists. Resistance to the rhetoric of dehumanisation, and a refusal to attribute to out-groups and minorities the status of subhumans, is eminently possible, so long as we know how to spot the signs when such things are in the offing, and provided that we are collectively strong and brave enough to resist the siren song of dehumanising discourse when it rears its head.[48]

But might we go further than simply hoping to resist dehumanisation? Indeed, have we not evidently *gone* further, in recent history, at least in some parts of the world? I believe that we have.

That whilst dehumanisation represents the very worst that our essentialist psychologies can be put to, this aspect of our minds can also be put into the service of altogether more admirable ends. Specifically, that rather than denying the possession of a human essence to some, and dehumanising them accordingly, the great innovation in recent normative attitudes has been not only the universalisation of a single human essence to all members of the species *Homo sapiens* (such that any observable surface distinctions are categorically not to count as mattering in any meaningful way), but a correlate grafting onto that shared single human essence of a further and specific normative commitment: that if you have this human essence, then by virtue of that, *you are a moral equal.*

Human Essence and Basic Equality

If this sounds like an outlandish notion, it is worth remembering that Christian theology has possessed a version of it for centuries. Consider Saint Augustine's assuring of his fellow Christians that no matter how a person *looks*, this has no bearing on their human status and correlate spiritual worth:

> [W]hoever is anywhere born a man, that is, a rational, mortal, animal, no matter what unusual appearance he presents in color, movement, sound, nor how peculiar he is in some power, part, or quality of his nature, no Christian can doubt that he springs from that one protoplast. We can distinguish the common human nature from that which is peculiar, and therefore wonderful.[49]

Augustine is here appealing to the same idea that Locke would later make use of: that because we are made by God, in his image, there is something *special* about the status of each of us.[50] For as he goes on, "God . . . sees the similarities and diversities that can contribute to the beauty of the whole."[51] The completing thought, advanced in subsequent Christian theology at various points, is that God loves us all *equally*, despite our superficially very different outward appearances, as well as our very different talents, abilities, "powers, parts, or qualities." This is precisely because, in regards to our more fundamental essence, God knows that on the inside *we are all the same* (because he made us that way).

Augustine's reasoning is a classic example of psychological essentialism. At one level, human beings exhibit vast variety and difference in terms of their superficial characteristics. But at another—more fundamental and more important—level, they are all the same, because they all share a singular human essence (the result of their being from the same "protoplast," i.e., being made in God's image). Yet onto this standard essentialist way of thinking may in turn be grafted a normative conclusion: in virtue of having the singular shared human essence, we all receive God's love *equally* (i.e., he regards and treats us all in terms of a basic egalitarianism). In turn, we therefore are all *basic equals* as regards our fundamental status and worth.

Of course, as it stands, this is a thoroughly theistic argument, and is not going to cut any ice with someone who is not already a theist. But the *form* of the argument should nonetheless intrigue us, because if Christians can argue in this mode, why can't secularists, even if they must necessarily change the way the conclusion is reached? That is, if we accept that human beings are highly receptive to the belief that all *Homo sapiens* (despite manifest outward differences on every conceivable metric) share a common human essence, then we should take seriously the possibility that for historically contingent reasons in our recent shared past, we have made the Christian move, but within a secular worldview: of grafting a normative conclusion of shared moral equality onto the premise of a shared human essence. That is: we have come to believe that *if* you have the human essence, *then* you are a basic equal. And given that we apparently *do* believe that everyone possesses the human essence, it will follow that everyone *is*, according to our current normative schema, properly to be regarded *as* a basic equal.

This, I suggest, is exactly what has occurred in our recent history. Although we no longer consciously appeal to God and the idea of being made in his image, we have nonetheless taken over the basic form of the theistic argument for basic equality, but rendered it in a secular manner.[52] The next chapter explores what I take to be going on here, by paying particular attention to the importance of fictions in our moral and political lives.

There is, however, a large elephant in the room and which it is best to acknowledge now. For it is indisputable that *there is no such thing as a human essence*. If my argument for basic equality requires positing the existence of something that *isn't real*, isn't this entire approach to the question fatally flawed? I will argue that this is not so: that whilst basic equality is indeed reliant on a fiction (the fiction of human essence), this is something we can happily embrace once we get clear on what is involved in doing so. For fictions are capable of operating with entirely real effects, and the mere fact of our knowing that they are fictions need not necessarily undermine our confidence in continuing to use them. These matters, however, require careful discussion, which can only be properly undertaken once the account of how our current belief in basic equality operates has first been set out. I therefore delay answering these important questions until later.

5

History and Fiction

THE ARGUMENT of this chapter is that in the relatively recent history of, roughly speaking, the developed West, a secular version of the Christian ascription of basic equality has come to be adopted as the widespread default amongst ordinary people. How this came about is ultimately a historical question. How it works, however, can be explained through the role that *fictions* play for us. Once these factors have been accounted for, the succeeding chapter considers the reasons why we ought to stay committed to basic equality once we have become aware of both its historical contingency, and its underlying fictional character.

Basic Equality, Secularised

Recall that the Christian account of basic equality, as found in the work of thinkers such as Augustine and Locke, operates as follows:

A) All human beings have an *essence* that makes them human.
B) Human beings have that essence because they are *made in God's image*.
C) God loves all those made in His image *equally*.
D) If you have the human essence and are loved by God equally, *then you are a basic equal.*

What we are looking for is a secularised version of such a position. Clearly, such a version must dispense with premises B) and C). What might have replaced it? I suggest the following:

1) All human beings have an *essence* that makes them human.
2) If you have the human essence, *then you are a basic equal.*

I believe that this is the underlying structure of the outlook that has widely come to be held by (most) people in (roughly speaking) the relatively recent history of the developed West.[1] When considered in this schematic form, however, such an account of basic equality is liable to appear unintelligible, a sort of mere arbitrary assertion. Yet this is why we need to recall the importance of history when trying to understand basic equality. For the idea of basic equality did not spring from nowhere, nor was it simply discovered by disinterested rational enquirers. It instead arose over time, in the context of societies in which it could make sense in large part due to other relevant proximate ideas, as well as crucial conditioning historical experiences, that together led to its eventually widespread (albeit imperfect) adoption amongst ordinary people.

How the widespread adoption of the view that 1) if you possess the human essence, then 2) you thus *are* a basic equal, came to occupy a position of relative ascendency is ultimately a historical story.[2] I am not a historian, and this book is not a work of history, so I will not attempt to offer that historical story here. It is doubtless a complex affair. Nonetheless, any plausible account will almost certainly have to involve factors such as (at least) the following.

First, it matters that basic equality came to prominence, and became widely endorsed, only in relatively recently history. Less than a century ago, eugenicist and openly racist views denying basic equality were publicly held on both the left and right. Yet by the mid-1980s Ronald Dworkin could talk of an egalitarian plateau that all serious moral and political thought departed from, whilst by the end of the twentieth century basic equality was the default norm in polite company. This remarkably rapid expansion and uptake appears however to have taken place predominantly within Western liberal democracies. It likely matters, therefore, that these same societies were, in the relevant period, subject to significant external pressures, both militarily and ideologically, in the form of fascism (and especially its ultravirulent manifestation in Nazism) and Soviet communism. Whilst fascism denied basic equality outright—and Nazi Germany demonstrated the dire consequences of systematically following through on that denial through its murder of millions of Jews, Slavs, the disabled, homosexuals, and others deemed less than fully human—the Communist regimes claimed to give the lie to the Western democratic model of political equality for citizens in the face of mass *economic* inequality as permitted by capitalism, offering themselves as the only legitimate purveyors of human equality. (That they in practice fell far short of their putative self-understanding is, in turn, unlikely to be accidental to the self-image formed by the citizens of liberal democracies.) In the end, the Western democracies saw off both these challenges, militarily and ideologically. Yet political cultures—and hence the ideas that operate and gain ascendency within them—define themselves not only by what they stand for, but what they stand against. Accounting for the rapid historical rise of basic equality in the political culture of liberal democratic societies is thus likely to require placing it in the context of the geopolitical contestations that such states endured. Basic equality became an increasingly important part of liberal democratic self-identity insofar as that self-identity was predicated on rejecting dangerous competitor ideologies who either denied it or claimed to offer a truer path to it (but didn't).

Second, the fact that it was precisely *Western liberal democracies* that saw off these competitor regimes and their accompanying ideologies, and in which basic equality emerged as a leading presumption in ordinary people's attitudes, is also likely to be important to the historical story. On the one hand, liberalism has long been preoccupied with attempting to balance the claim of equal political rights for all citizens with the fact of mass inequality of economic resources generated by markets, that is, what came to be called capitalism. Since the nineteenth century, liberal states have wrestled with what was termed the "social question," that is, of whether and how formal political equality could be stabilised and made to cohere with severe levels of economic inequality—enabling modes of thinking about individuals and their standing towards each other that bear directly upon notions of basic equality.[3] Similarly, the rise of representative democracy also matters. Political cultures in which the principle of one man, one vote—later one *person*, one vote—became entrenched likely have considerable significance in explaining how the idea that each person somehow matters equally, or has equal standing or worth, came to be widely adopted in those same cultures. In other words, notions of basic equality did not arise in a vacuum, but in certain kinds of political context, with certain histories, which themselves included a long tradition of reflecting philosophically about equality, its basis, and what it requires.[4] Those histories, furthermore, include important political events (themselves exhibiting complex connections to ideas of equality being formulated by influential thinkers as well as more practically minded political actors) which came to shape the self-understanding of peoples within the societies subsequently informed by them. Declarations of the equal status of all human beings—in for example the American Declaration of Independence (1776), the French Declaration of the Rights of Man and Citizen (1789), or the UN Declaration of Human Rights (1948)—and the enormous political changes they in part helped to unleash, punctuate not just the history, but in turn the collective self-identity, of the Western political cultures in which the notion of basic equality now operates. Whilst there is no doubt that the actual implementation of these declarations was often deeply disappointing in practice (the eighteenth-century versions, for example, pivoted rapidly to exclude women and non-Whites from equal membership in society), nonetheless what was transmitted into subsequent popular political consciousness was an *idea* that all humans are fundamentally equal, and that political arrangements had better reflect this fact in a meaningful way—which, over time, they came increasingly (albeit imperfectly) to do. Similarly, the more recent spread of human rights discourse, and the idea that governments owe to populations certain protections and obligations simply on the basis of a shared humanity, is likely to have an important role to play in any adequate historical story of the extraordinary rise of basic equality.

Third, explaining the rapid (if still incomplete) rise of basic equality to the status of default norm in public discourse in relatively recent history will also have to acknowledge the enormous transformations brought about by previously oppressed and marginalised groups, who organised politically with remarkable success, demanding that they be treated as equals in ways that they had not been before. In the postwar period, radical changes in moral and political attitudes took place within Western societies, in large part driven by successful activist political groups, who marshalled appeals to equality as a way of overcoming existing internal social and political oppression, and in the process appear to have entrenched and solidified a general acceptance of basic equality more widely. Of particular importance here were antiracist and civil rights movements, so-called second-wave feminism, and campaigns for decolonisation and recognition of the rights of peoples to practise political self-determination. More recently, the gay rights movement has had similar impacts in terms of changing social attitudes that have pushed in the direction of further support for basic equality, whilst attitudes towards the mentally and physically handicapped have also shifted dramatically. All of these are complex social phenomena, the details of which vary significantly in different national and local contexts. But the point for present purposes is that the rise of basic equality likely owes much to the street-level successes of political activist groups who succeeded in substantially altering attitudes to race, gender, ethnicity, sexuality, and so forth, away from previously widely held presumptions of innate hierarchy or inequality, towards a prevalent belief that such differences do not matter, and that despite them, all humans are fundamentally equal. The story of the widespread adoption of basic equality in the recent history of the liberal democracies is thus likely in significant part the story of increasingly successful demands by previously unequal and oppressed groups to be recognised and treated *as equals*, thus in turn helping to ever more widely entrench the view that people *are* equals, in a basic sense.

For reasons such as these (and likely others), by the late twentieth century a secularised version of positing basic equality came to be the default for most people in liberal democratic states. The result can thus usefully be understood as the reverse of the phenomenon of dehumanisation presented in the last chapter. Whereas in certain extreme (and deeply undesirable) social and political contexts some humans come to have the essence of the human *denied* to them by another (typically, dominant) group, and are thus treated as less than human, and in turn made targets for attack and persecution, in our relatively recent history, for a variety of complex, contingent, and interconnected reasons, we have gone the other way. We have come to hold not only that everybody *does* have the human essence, but that possession of that essence means they ought to be regarded as basic equals in light of that, and treated accordingly. Again, schematically:

1) All human beings have an *essence* that makes them human.
2) If you have the human essence, *then you are a basic equal*.

However, and as clearly brought out by this schematic rendering, 2) is a normative stance, grafted onto the putatively descriptive premise 1).[5] The *philosophical* question, then, is how to get from 1) to 2): what licenses the move from believing that all humans have a shared essence (which is what makes them all the same fundamental class of thing) to concluding that, from a normative point of view, all members of that class are basic equals? Once God is removed from the picture, how can this gap be bridged?[6]

It is a mistake to think that 2) can be grounded in some further purely descriptive premise, some freestanding fact in light of which we *just are* basic equals, and that one could hope to point to absent relevant political and social contexts, expecting this to gain traction with some neutral enquirer armed only with the power of reason. On the contrary, in order to appreciate how 2) is attached to 1), we need to acknowledge the practices and histories of the kinds of agents who actually hold 1) and 2) together. In short, basic equality was (and continues to be) a moral and political *achievement*, but one that only makes sense to certain agents in certain contexts. Roughly speaking: agents like us. It was something built over time, in particular historical locales, and which required real-world political and moral transformations for it to become what it now is.

Yet because what gives sense and meaning to the idea of humans as basic equals is not some neutral descriptive fact merely as such, but the background context of the relevant framing moral and political culture—one shaped in specific historical circumstances, under various political pressures—then absent that framing context, basic equality simply will not make sense. Hence why, for example, a Genghis Khan, or an Aristotle, or a nineteenth-century American slaveholder, would not be able to make sense of it. In other times and other places, either not all humans have been credited with possession of the human essence (and thus were relegated to the status of *less* than human, and ipso facto unequal, as in the case of racist justifications for slavery denying that Black people were *really* human[7]), or else the human essence was seen as equally shared but generative of no further consequences in terms of how people were to be treated, and thus was seen as compatible with extensive inequality and hierarchy (as appears to have been the widely held view amongst most Christians prior to the early modern period[8]). In circumstances such as those, basic equality as a normative principle did not—*could* not—make sense. Likewise, if *we* abstract away from our political culture and its history, and try to understand basic equality from (so to speak) the point of view of the universe rather than the point of view that we now have, then it will not make sense to *us*, either—it will look like a mere assertion, the question of why we are basic equals simply being begged. Indeed, this is one reason why basic equality looks like such a puzzle on standard philosophical attempts to explain it: by approaching the question in purely analytical terms, absent recognition of the relevant constituting history and wider political culture in which the idea arose, operates, and thus makes sense, basic equality becomes unintelligible. By searching for some independent foundation revealed by philosophical enquiry alone, the question of why we are basic equals becomes essentially unanswerable. Yet because we *do* possess the relevant political and historical context, for us it has become the default norm to view possession of the human essence as entailing equal treatment, and thus generating the principle of basic equality. To put the point slightly differently: basic equality is not itself conceptually basic, but is rather how we (or at least, most of us) go on, now and around here, and have increasingly done so with greater consistency and collective consensus in our recent past, thus strengthening commitment to it in turn. Not all peoples in all times and places have done so (or indeed, do so today), because they do not all share our constituting history. Forgetting this about ourselves is guaranteed to make basic equality seem mysterious. Remembering it should have the opposite effect.

Of course, we do not ordinarily articulate matters to ourselves in the schematic ways just presented, nor cash out our commitments in this area in terms of essences, or of explicit acknowledgement of our shared political histories and cultures. This is precisely because commitment to basic equality has become something most of us who subscribe to it take for granted as part of the day-to-day fabric of our moral and political lives (those bigots who do remain notwithstanding). That is, it functions below the level of precise abstract conceptual reflection and conscious focus—as indeed is the case with all our moral values, at least outside the highly unusual activity of philosophical enquiry. Nonetheless, I suggest that conscious reflection is able to successfully identify what is going on: that commitment to basic equality is a historically and contextually specific coupling of a locally endorsed normative conclusion of equal standing to our default belief in the existence of shared human essence. We may not appreciate, day-to-day, that this is what we are up to. But it is, nonetheless, what we are doing.

In the next chapter, I address the outstanding question that arises in turn: why, if at all, ought we *to go on* in this kind of way, once we realise that this is what we are doing? But before turning to that important matter, we must address another: namely, what are we *actually doing* when we employ this notion of basic equality? How does this conjunction of human psychology (the belief in essences) and the ascription of normative equality operate? These are important questions, and ones where philosophical reflection can certainly help—in particular, by considering the nature and role of fictions.

Fictions

A fiction is something that is not real, but which in certain contexts we treat *as if* it were real. For example, there never was any such creature as a hobbit, but when reading *The Lord of the Rings*, I enjoy the story by suspending disbelief and going along with the idea that Frodo is on a quest that will take him to Mount Doom. Similarly, whilst fairies do not exist, when entertaining young children, we can nonetheless play games based on what the garden sprites have been up to. Illustrated in this manner, fictions can seem trivial, without much substance beyond the securing of diversionary entertainment. But they can be much more than that. For whilst fictions are in themselves inherently unreal, their *effects* can be entirely real, and of great consequence.

Take the use of legal fictions in common law jurisdictions. A legal fiction is "a rule assuming as true something that is clearly false," which is "often used to get around the provisions of constitutions and legal codes that legislators are hesitant to change or to encumber with specific limitations."[9] For example, if a legislature is constitutionally required to conclude all business by midnight on a certain date, but the work will take another five hours, it can adopt the fiction of turning the official clock back and treating the day as though it had twenty-nine rather than twenty-four hours (which is much easier than changing the constitution, and better than failing to perform the required work). Although the day really has twenty-four hours, in this context the legal fiction allows the legislature to act as if the day had twenty-nine hours—allowing it to complete its necessary business. Similarly, adoption practices make use of the legal fiction that as soon as an order or judgement of adoption has been passed a child's biological parents become a legal stranger to it, with no relevant legal rights and duties, whilst conversely its adoptive parents are treated as if they were its biological parents, accruing the relevant rights and duties. Whilst the biological parents are in reality related to the child by direct genetic descent, whereas the adoptive parents are not, the legal fiction allows everyone to proceed as if matters were the reverse. Finally, corporate entities may be treated under the law as if they were singular people for certain purposes, and assigned rights accordingly, even though they are in fact composed of a multitude of individual agents: "The general proposition that a corporation is to be regarded as a legal entity existing separate and apart from the natural persons composing it, is not disputed, but that the statement is a mere fiction, existing only in idea, is well understood. It has been introduced for the convenience of the corporation in making contract."[10]

Although these are all cases of fiction, their effects can be dramatic. The legislature passing an emergency relief bill by the end of the day may be the difference between economic ruin and salvation. Who your legal parents are is crucial to determining what, if anything, you stand to inherit from them. And as the notorious judgement of the United States Supreme Court in *Citizens United* illustrated—ruling not only that corporations can be people, but that they possess free speech rights under the First Amendment of the US Constitution, which include the making of unlimited financial donations to political parties—such fictions can have profound effects, especially in a country where large campaign contributions make the difference between electoral victory and defeat.[11]

The use of fictions, however, need not be restricted to law. A particularly interesting illustration of the wider potentials of fictions comes from Thomas Hobbes's discussion of personation in chapter 16 of *Leviathan*.[12] On Hobbes's account, a person is something whose words or actions are considered either as its own, or as representing the words or actions of another. If the person is representing itself through its own words and actions directly, it is a "natural" person. But if representing the words and actions of another, indirectly, then the person is "artificial." A paradigm case of a natural person would be myself, a biologically human adult, speaking and acting in my own name. An example of an artificial person by contrast would be a barrister, or attorney, acting in their legal capacity and whom I appoint to speak and act on my behalf when representing me. (The barrister or attorney is *also* a natural person, if speaking and acting directly in their own name, but when speaking and acting in *my* name, then they are an artificial person, whom Hobbes describes as being borne by their natural, i.e., flesh and blood, one.) The link between natural and artificial persons, Hobbes claims, is one of *authorised representation*. If I appoint you to be my representative, then I authorise you to speak and act in my name. And that means that in the relevant context in which I have authorised you to represent me, everything that you say and do as an artificial person can and should be attributed back to me, the natural person. Typically, this act of authorisation happens, as Hobbes puts it, "Truly": one natural person (i.e., a biological human being) actually does appoint another to speak and act in their name, thus owning (being responsible for) all their words and actions in the relevant context. But Hobbes also claims that such authorisation can take place "by Fiction."[13] As he goes on to say:

> There are few things, that are uncapable of being represented by Fiction. Inanimate things, as a Church, a Hospital, a Bridge, may be Personated by a Rector, Master, or Overseer. But things

Inanimate, cannot be Authors, nor therefore give Authority to their Actors: Yet the Actors may have Authority to procure their maintenance, given them by those that are Owners, or Governors of those things.[14]

Hobbes is here saying that even though churches, hospitals, bridges, and so forth cannot authorise their own representatives for the simple reason that they are inanimate objects without a will or a capacity for speech, we can act *as if* they had authorised the relevant rector, master, or overseer to act in their names, and thus represent them. Rectors, masters, overseers, and the like are thus artificial persons, who in that capacity speak and act not in their own names but on behalf of churches, bridges, hospitals, and so forth, whom it is their job to look after in various ways, but whose actions are finally attributed not to their own natural persons, but to those inanimate entities they represent (and whom we suppose, by the employment of fiction, have authorised them accordingly). This will be a very useful thing to do in many contexts, both legal and social, and allows us to construct relationships of authorisation and representation even where there is no underlying natural person, and hence where authorisation cannot happen "truly." The use of authorisation "by fiction" thus opens up a host of useful practices that we would be worse off without.

Some interpreters of Hobbes have seen in his account the resources for something even more dramatic: a theory according to which the *state itself* is understood as a kind of person, brought into being through the acts of authorisation and representation that natural persons use to escape the misery of the state of nature, thereby creating a single artificial person (in Hobbes's parlance, a "sovereign") to terrorise them into lasting domestic peace.[15] The details of these accounts need not detain us here, but what is nonetheless exciting about them is their suggestion that the fiction of state personality can help us make crucial sense of ideas such as sovereign debt held over time, as well as how to apportion responsibility in international contexts. Specifically, that the incurring of financial debts, treaty obligations, culpability for military action, or any of the other myriad responsibilities we take states to be liable for, make most sense if we attribute these to the enduring and persistent "person" of the state, rather than to either its subjects directly, or to any particular sovereign at any particular point (after all, sovereigns, like subjects, come and go—it is states that persist). The mere fact that such state personality is fictitious, however, does not according to these theorists in any way count against such an understanding.

Hobbes's views on state personality are complex and highly contested, both as a matter of interpretation, as well as of final plausibility.[16] Yet the above digression is worth making because it shows how fictions may have a pivotal role to play beyond strictly legal settings. Fictions can *do* things for us when we put them to specific kinds of uses, many of which we are either familiar with or already take for granted. As a final example, think of how easily we accept news reports saying things like "The Lawn Tennis Association censured John McEnroe for his outburst," thinking of, and intuitively treating, the Lawn Tennis Association as if it were a singular discrete agent with its own will making a direct pronouncement, when in reality it is a large organisation of many thousands of individuals, some small subset of whom have put together a statement that none of them want to claim in their own names, but to attribute to the organisation as a whole—and which we and they think of as a distinct, singular, entity. This, again, is a fiction, but a very useful one for all involved (even John McEnroe, all things considered).

Basic equality, I suggest, is another case in point: an instance in which we act *as if* some things were other than they are, and where doing so carries entirely real effects. When it comes to basic equality, we act *as if* the only thing that characterises each human being were the possession of the human essence, and nothing else: as if all of the myriad ways in which we are manifestly different—health, physical size and ability, intelligence, emotional aptitude, aesthetic capacity, skin colour, biological sex, sexual orientation, you name it—were not so. Instead, we focus on the allegedly more fundamental property of the human essence, and act as if this were the only thing that characterised all and any of us. (Note that this is something we can usually easily enter into insofar as we are already psychologically predisposed to think that essences are more fundamental—truer of what we "really" are—than superficial attributes like intelligence, physicality, pigmentation, genitalia, etc.)

Strictly speaking, however, when it comes to basic equality, we are engaging in the use of *two* fictions simultaneously. The first fiction is that every human being is constituted, and defined by, the possession of something "inside of it," an essence, that makes each a member of that putative natural kind. This is certainly false as a matter of scientific fact (as discussed in the previous chapter). But it comes naturally to us because we are psychological essentialists. The second fiction is more historically and culturally specific, and arose to the level of consistent social and moral practice in our relatively recent history: of acting *as if* the only thing that characterises each of us is the possession of the human essence, such that all of the manifest differences that we exhibit on a vast array of other metrics are to be ignored, treated as if they did not exist (even though they do).

When we employ the idea of basic equality, and treat it as a normative commitment in our moral and political lives, we are thus acting on a *double fiction*. Importantly, understanding basic equality as a double fiction helps to explain why the idea of basic equality has normative content for us. Recall that essences are taken by the human mind to be simple, unalterable (without being destroyed), uniform, and held fully and to the same extent by all entities that are constituted as natural kinds by the very fact of their having them. If engaged in the fiction of acting as if the only thing that defined each of us is our possession of the human essence, then it follows that each of us is defined by our possessing exactly the same thing, and to the same extent, and thus our fundamentally *being* the same. Yet the maxim "treat like things alike" is a good candidate for the most basic, and indeed self-evident, of normative principles: after all, why *wouldn't* you treat two like things alike? Treating them differently would be purely arbitrary, at least in lieu of some further proffered reason for doing so. Yet if treating one thing differently from another identical thing means treating it *worse*, this differential treatment cries out for some kind of justification. If a plausible justification is not forthcoming, and if the things being unequally treated are human beings, then we have what looks like a paradigm case of injustice, with such arbitrariness of treatment being *simply wrong*. Hence, understanding basic equality as a double fiction helps explain not only that it is an idea about each of us—that we have a shared human essence, in light of which we are all fundamentally the same—but that this is also a normative commitment: that insofar as these two things are fundamentally the same, and are thus properly to be treated the same, then prima facie they are properly considered as *being equal*.[17]

As a result, understanding basic equality as a double fiction dovetails neatly with the schematic rendering offered above:

1) All human beings have an *essence* that makes them human.
2) If you have the human essence, *then you are a basic equal.*

But now also in turn

3) If you are a basic equal, then (ceteris paribus) *you ought to be treated equally.*

Again, how and why this outlook came to be widely held relatively recently, now and around here, is a historical matter.[18] But recognising that we *are* now engaged in a double fiction when it comes to basic equality helps to further make sense of what is going on, insofar as employing that double fiction directly supports 2), and also in turn 3). It does so by expressly ruling out all of the differentiating characteristics that humans exhibit, and which might otherwise be thought (and indeed, in other times and places, *have* been thought) to provide grounds for viewing humans as basically unequal. Instead, because we act as if the only thing that characterises each and all of us is our shared human essence, and thus take us all to be basic equals, we are thus prima facie deserving of equal treatment, and so it follows that the status of normative equality for all becomes the presumptive default, a default which is undergirded and reinforced by the shared experience of increasingly going on in this way. And to reiterate the point made above, the fact that we are engaged in the use of fictions when it comes to basic equality does not entail anything like triviality, ephemerality, or lack of seriousness, any more than the decision in *Citizens United*, who one's legal parents are, or the apportioning of state responsibility for military conflict, are rendered less important, or less real, merely because they rely on the workings of fiction. Fictions can be powerful, and their effects on our lives profound. In this regard, basic equality is no different. Indeed, it is a case in point.

Immersion

It may rightly be objected, however, that basic equality cannot be a fiction on the model of the others noted in the previous section, because in all those cases we *consciously act* on the knowledge that what we are doing is employing a fiction. Yet basic equality is not like that. For example, when a court issues a new birth certificate to legalise an adoption, or political theorists propose that we assign responsibility for debts and reparation payments to the "person" of the state, all those party to such proceedings are (indeed, must be) consciously aware that they are employing a fiction. The way such things work *requires* that all parties knowingly engage in the fictional practice in order for it to have the real-world effects it is employed to engender. But when we think of each other as basic equals, we do not think or act such that we are *consciously pretending* that something is the case. Basic equality seems instead to be something that we subscribe to *without* conscious reflection on its fictional character, and without any explicit awareness or pretence. Indeed, if we were to actively fixate on basic equality's fictional character, that would seem to undermine and weaken, rather than support and strengthen, our commitment to it. Hence more needs to be said about how the fiction of basic equality works, and why it is not straightforwardly analogous to the fictions noted above.

That something more consists in appreciating the phenomenon of *immersion*.[19] When we are immersed in a fiction, we cease to be actively conscious, in the precise moment, that it is indeed a fiction. "Children who engage in games of make-believe and method actors are the paradigm examples of subjects who lose themselves in the imagination such that the fictional world in some way, at least temporarily, becomes the real world."[20] Another is watching an especially gripping TV show, or a very good play, such that one is emotionally affected by the drama unfolding, and engages with the events being portrayed as though they were real (perhaps later talking with others about the characters as though they were real people). Or consider being lost in an especially engrossing novel, such that one's awareness of the busy café fades entirely and one is fully "there" with the protagonists on the page. Or playing a computer game that requires a high degree of concentration as well as engaged motor-function, such that for the time one is playing one fully identifies with the role being acted out within the virtual environment. In other words, being immersed in a fiction is something that we are quite familiar with. We get immersed all the time.

Immersion in fiction can provide advantages beyond merely being something we tend to enjoy. In particular, it allows us to learn and develop. For example, when children play chasing games (something the young of many other mammal species also do), by immersing themselves in the fiction of getting away from a predator they are able to practise their motor skills more effectively. "Chase play is not only fun; it trains for events that are hazardous and costly. The more immersed children are in the game, the more they invest in the game; the more invested in the game they are, the more educational the game is."[21] When it comes to adults, immersion in fiction allows us to adopt the perspectives of others, working through the implications of their situations, learning about what we think is appropriate and how we might feel and act in scenarios we have not yet experienced (but perhaps will in the future). Immersion thus allows us to gain a far wider range of affective experiences and perspectives than if we had to experience everything directly for ourselves. Similarly, some kinds of fiction can have beneficial functions insofar as they allow individuals to access goods they might otherwise lack: Internet gaming, for example, appears to enable some individuals who struggle with real-world social interaction to experience community and friendship as realised through their digital avatars, connecting them with like-minded individuals in a way they otherwise find difficult or impossible.[22]

When immersed in a fiction, our cognitive state appears to be on a continuum between simple imagination and full belief. Somebody playing the role of a wizard in an online game, or the method actor Robert De Niro getting "in character" for his role as the young Vito Corleone in *The Godfather Part II*, or even just you or me watching an especially good play, does not *believe* that they are (really) a wizard, a rising mobster, or watching a man called Hamlet talk to a skull. At any moment one could focus one's mind on what one knows to be real, distancing oneself from the fiction. Nonetheless, when we are immersed in a fiction, we approach the condition of belief insofar as in that moment we treat matters as if the relevant fiction were real, suspending our immediate conscious disbelief in favour of the fiction. We are thus doing more than just imagining that something is the case whilst simultaneously being aware that it is not so. "In cases of imaginative immersion, the imagining subject has mental states that are belief-like in that the imagining subject comes close to taking the subject matter of her imagination to be true."[23] Indeed that is what makes immersion, precisely, immersion: for as long as the immersion lasts, although we *could* break free of it at any point (we are not *deluded*, as we would be if we really did believe, wholeheartedly, that the fiction was real), we suspend our "explicit metacognition" about the situation.[24] We instead go along with the fiction and act *as if* it were real, approaching towards a state of belief that it really is so (whilst always retaining the capacity to pull back).

Whilst immersion in fiction can have many benefits, it can also sometimes become undesirable, even harmful. The phenomenon of Internet gaming disorder—where people become unable to decouple from their online avatars and their real-world lives begin to suffer accordingly (e.g., through relationship breakdown, negative effects on employment and education, as well as the health impacts of hundreds of hours of gameplay often affecting exercise, nutrition, and sleep)—is in part a function of overreliance on the immersive state provided by the game.[25] Similarly, when angry viewers of television dramas issue death threats to actors playing villainous characters, conflating the real-world actor with their fictional role, they are exhibiting a pathological level of immersion.[26] If I were to run onstage during a performance of *Hamlet* so as to help Ophelia reach a mental health crisis center, my immersion would clearly have gone too far, and it would be I, not Ophelia, who was in need of professional help. Yet such cases notwithstanding, there is nothing inherently suspect about immersion: it is only a problem when its effects go too far, or our immersion causes us to start literally losing our sense of reality, that is, when we approach the status of fully fledged belief but in something that is not real—and hence are properly said to be deluded. Much of the time, however, fictional immersion is a powerful and useful tool in our psychological repertoire.

Commitment to basic equality is best understood as another instance of fictional immersion, though we need here to distinguish what is going on with each aspect of what I have termed the double fiction. With regards the first fiction—our intuitive belief that human beings are defined by the possession of a human essence—it is fair to say that we are usually not so much immersed in the fiction on this point, as deluded by it. That is, we all typically think and act as if human beings *really do* have essences (as, indeed, does everything else in the natural world), and hence that reality is constituted accordingly. This is scientifically false, and whilst we can temporarily shake ourselves out of the delusion when we focus on the scientific facts, we are prone to immediately lapse back into it as soon as we stop making a conscious effort to resist it. This, however, is just a psychological reality for human beings, and not something in and of itself to worry about. Not only can we not stop being this way, but it isn't anyway where the interesting action is to be found. What matters is *what we do in the light of this particular delusion,* in terms of our moral, social, and political practices, not the sheer fact that we are subject to it.

The second fiction, however, constitutes a case of immersion rather than delusion: we treat others *as if* the only thing that defines them is their human essence, and ignore all of the other myriad features that might otherwise command our attention, approaching a state of belief that this is in fact the only thing that characterised each of us. In doing so, we are thus more like a method actor playing a role, or an audience engrossed in a particularly good theatrical production, than lawyers interpreting statutes, or political theorists trying to make sense of state responsibility. We act *as if* the only thing that defines us is the human essence (coupling this with the conclusion that we are therefore normative equals), but we do so without any conscious metacognition that this is what we are doing. During the time that we are immersed, however, we approach towards a state of belief, such that we effectively treat the fiction as being true. Indeed, this is a necessary feature of the phenomenon: if we constantly reflected on basic equality's fictional status, it wouldn't be normatively compelling for us in the way that it actually is—the fiction would be self-undermining. Hence basic equality's fictionality appears to have a necessarily *self-effacing* aspect: for the fiction to work, we need to forget it is a fiction (I will return to this point in greater detail in the following chapter when confronting worries that *revealing* basic equality's fictional character may be destabilising of our commitment to it[27]).

What makes basic equality different from other examples of fictional immersion noted above is the sheer extent to which we are immersed in it when we act *as if* a shared human essence were the only thing that characterises any of us. Namely, that we are immersed in this fiction on a daily basis, and for large portions of our lives, rather than just when we go to the theatre, get in character, or boot up the gaming console. But this a matter of degree, not kind. In all these cases, when immersing ourselves in the fiction, we do not consciously think to ourselves "I am now going to immerse myself in this thing, which is a fiction"; we just *do* it: we switch into that mode, and again without metacognitive awareness of what we are doing (for to maintain such awareness would prevent the immersion). Basic equality, in this sense, is no different from being immersed in a play: once immersed, we do not reflect on the fact that we are immersed without shattering the immersion. But whereas a play only lasts a couple of hours, we tend to remain immersed in the fiction of basic equality on a more or less continuous basis.

Which leads to an important question: *how* did we get so immersed in the fiction of basic equality, such that we spend so much of our time in that state? After all, when I go to see a play, I first enter the theatre, take my seat, the lights dim, the audience hushes, and the actors emerge on stage—all of which allows me to initiate the process of immersion (which will soon be broken at the interval, no matter how good the performance). What is the story with basic equality? The answer, I suspect, depends on which generation you find yourself in. Here we must make some rough generalisations, but doing so is helpful insofar as it allows us to make sense of what is going on.

For many of us, and increasing numbers as time goes on, we were *raised* in the fiction of basic equality, and from a very young age. Our parents, as well as our teachers and other role-models, taught us that what matters is "who you are on the inside." We get strong reinforcement of the message that we are not to (mis)treat others based on the way they look, how clever they are, their race, their gender, and so forth. Instead, we are taught that these are extraneous factors and thus to be ignored. At the same time, we are also taught that each of us matters equally, and that no matter our differences in levels of skill, intellectual ability, physical prowess, attractiveness, and so forth, which might tempt us to the positing of hierarchy, these are negated by a more fundamental moral equality that we all share. Of course, children are notoriously *bad* at accepting this in a thoroughgoing way, and for quite a long time, tending to single out difference and using it as a ground to exclude. They thus need repeat correction from adult supervision, and only over time do they fully immerse themselves in the basic equality fiction. But this should be no surprise, not only because ongoing immersion requires practice, but because many adults are bad at this too, and have historically perpetrated far greater cruelties than children when singling out difference as a ground for ill treatment. Immersion requires time and a supportive context, which has not always been present in human history. Nonetheless, being predominantly raised in this mode, it is relatively easy for the psychological essentialism innate to human beings to configure itself along the lines outlined above. For those of us raised in the fiction of basic equality, we practice being immersed in it from a young age, and are able to do so with increasing consistency as we get older.

For a somewhat older generation, increasingly widespread immersion in the fiction of basic equality by both themselves and others was a phenomenon they lived through the increasing entrenchment of, and in many cases themselves helped to take root and flourish through support (with varying degrees of active and passive involvement) of movements towards equal treatment amongst previously oppressed groups (think again of the successive waves of civil rights, feminism, and gay rights, and how over time these shifted social norms towards a default presumption of equal treatment for all). For many, increasing adoption of an ever more thoroughgoing immersion in the fiction of basic equality was a natural enough progression, insofar as it marked the culmination of various historical factors pushing in this direction already, and given the political and historical contexts of their societies and how those were evolving. Importantly, many such people were young and flexible enough to adapt to and incorporate the changes they experienced as they were happening, by steadily embracing a life of increasing immersion in the fiction. Many of them went on to raise their children in this state of ongoing immersion.

Finally, and for a somewhat older generation again, the world rather changed around them, increasingly defined by altered norms and practices that they themselves were not raised in, and which they did not themselves drive forward, nor necessarily entirely understand nor fully endorse, during the period these transformations were ongoing. Nonetheless, immersion in the fiction of basic equality was increasingly demanded by wider society, and hence of them too—and they had to adapt accordingly. Some members of older generations adjusted to this changed world with relative ease (they likely harbored moral and political dispositions that leant in that direction already), but others found it more difficult to do so. This helps explain why older generations tend to be the ones who struggle most with basic equality and the fictional immersion it demands: it is no coincidence that embarrassing faux pas at the family dinner table about race, gender, and so forth, tend to be uttered by (older) grandparents. Often we know that the cause of their embarrassing remarks is not *malice*—they are not committed racists or bigots; it is rather that they are not as good as we are at immersing themselves in the fiction, and by failing to stay immersed, they say things that break our immersion in turn, engendering awkwardness and more often than not embarrassment on their behalf.[28] (The experience is somewhat akin to watching an elderly relative struggle with a smartphone.) None of which should be surprising. The more elderly were not typically raised in the fiction of basic equality, and have had to try and learn to immerse themselves later in life, as the social world increasingly shifted in this direction and demanded it of them. Yet like anything that one tries to learn, doing so tends to be harder the later in life one starts. Basic equality is no exception: the earlier you learn to immerse yourself in the fiction, the easier it is to do so, on a more or less continuous basis. The later you begin to try, the harder it tends to be.

These are of course generalisations. There are some families that raise their children poorly, failing to consistently inculcate immersion into the basic equality fiction, perhaps because of sexist, racist, or other prejudiced views harbored by the parents, and passed on through their parenting. Likewise, there are plenty of elderly individuals who are fully immersed in the basic equality fiction, and have been for decades (just as some octogenarians have no trouble using smartphones). In all age brackets, some are more thoroughly and consistently immersed than others. Indeed some, it seems clear enough, are only pretending to be immersed, perhaps for the sake of a quiet life during the periods that they find themselves in the sort of polite public company where immersion is expected of them. (Some of those who are merely pretending retreat to the toxic anonymity of social media, a venue in which to abandon the pretence and vent their real sentiments accordingly.) None of this need be denied. Indeed, it is a strength of understanding basic equality as rooted in fictional immersion that it can take such cases into account. The world is complex, and the extent to which each individual is or is not fully immersed in the fiction is influenced by many contingent factors, both personal and social. We should not expect a uniform level of immersion evenly distributed across all members of society—which is precisely not what we find. After all, some bigots evidently do persist in their bigotry (and some hide it better than others), as well as there being instances of people more innocently struggling to remain immersed in the fiction of basic equality, from altogether less malicious motives. Understanding basic equality in terms of being immersed in a fiction not only helps explain what we are doing when we adopt a commitment to it, but why that commitment is often in practice found to be patchy and uneven.

Domains and Checking

It is an important feature of the fiction of basic equality, however, that being immersed in it is not something that we take as applying rigidly to all domains of our moral and political lives. After all, there are contexts in which we not only think it is acceptable not to be immersed in the fiction, but good, desirable, and even necessary to *not* be immersed in it. As Jeremy Waldron and Ian Carter have pointed out, there are many situations in which we *don't* want others to see us as basic equals, but instead want them to pay attention to the ways in which we are unequal, insofar as that is what distinguishes us as *us*.[29] The idiosyncrasies and defining features that make us *un*equal in various ways are also what make us who we are as individuals. At times we want those things to be fully recognised, and precisely not treated as if they did not exist. Happily, this is straightforward for the fictional account of basic equality to make sense of.

There are evidently domains of social life in which we do not immerse ourselves in the fiction of basic equality, and nor would we want to. For example, we think that the winning chess player had better receive the prize money, the fastest runner had better win gold in the 100m final, and the university places had better be apportioned to those who really did perform best on the relevant examination metrics. In these sorts of situations, focusing only on shared human essence whilst ignoring specific distinguishing features would not only be entirely inappropriate, but socially disastrous. Similarly, you do not wish your husband to see you merely as one bearer of the human essence, to that extent no different from all the other humans, but as *you*, and to love *you* for all *your* distinguishing features, both of character and physical form. Likewise, that this child is *mine* means precisely *not* treating it as though it were no different to all the other children that also have a human essence, but instead recognising, valuing, and helping to cultivate in appropriate ways the idiosyncratic features of intelligence, physicality, emotional development, and so forth that *my* child happens to be possessed of and is capable of improving in various ways.

What is going on here is that the basic equality fiction is one we employ in the domain of *fundamental value*—it is a position we take when considering the ultimate worth and status of people considered merely as such. Yet in domains that are less fundamental, relating to how individuals are to be treated in a given context, and when we are not considering people merely as such, but as specific individuals in specific contexts relating to specific matters (running races, chess tournaments, personal relationships, etc.), then the basic equality fiction does not apply.

Nonetheless, basic equality acts as a sort of background limiting check on how far we may go, and in what ways, with regards the distinctions made in other less fundamental domains, and thus regarding how we may and may not treat specific individuals. Commitment to basic equality thus exercises a kind of priority to, and authority over, practices that aren't themselves making use of the fiction, in light of which these latter are checked and evaluated.

Hence when it comes to chess tournaments, running races, university examinations, and so forth, focusing on individual characteristics and deciding how we treat people in differing ways has to be *targeted*: it applies only to specific relevant criteria in a tightly defined context. Being skilled at chess, or fast at running, or good at this kind of examination, is allowed to count *only* in the context of the tournament, the race, or the admissions process. Furthermore, that you were the fastest runner or best chess player means nothing once the race is run, or the prize money handed out, as regards your standing or worth in fundamental terms. Crucially, even if some people are rewarded in specific contexts for their chess, their speed, or their educational performance, it is not legitimate to infer from this that anything follows regarding their fundamental normative status vis-à-vis others (both competitors and noncompetitors alike). You may get the trophy, or the university place, and indeed do so at the expense of others, but with regards your normative standing, we are all to remain immersed in the fiction about fundamental value: that you are still a basic equal with all the rest, even if you were the winner on the day.

The same is true when it comes to interpersonal relationships. I want my lover to love *me* for all my distinguishing features, and both to acknowledge them and act on them in myriad ways. I will see my own child as unique and special, and someone to whom I have particular responsibilities of care that others cannot discharge. But it does not follow that I am therefore more special, in my fundamental worth or status, than other people *just because* my lover treats me differently, any more than it follows that because I see all that makes my child unique and special, that therefore my child is somehow *worth more* than all the other children in the world.[30]

However, there are instances in which we deem it illegitimate to pay attention to differential characteristics, and demand that immersion in the fiction take precedence, imposing checks and limits on the acceptability of our differing treatment of others. Archetypically these relate to treatment based not on specific and relevant distinguishing features of specific individuals, as applied to specific contexts, for limited and specific purposes, and that we wish on balance to allow and even promote (chess tournaments, races, university admission, personal relationships, etc.), but instead on bare membership of some wider group, and which are invoked in ways that typically serve to undermine the immersion in basic equality as a fiction that pertains to our more fundamental worth or status. Hence calling attention to (paradigmatically) race or gender as grounds for exclusion or particular (mis)treatment is impermissible, because doing so undermines the prior and authoritative commitment to basic equality in the domain of fundamental value, which checks and limits what is taken to be permissible in less fundamental domains.

Restricting immersion in the fiction of basic equality to the domain of fundamental value, and having it operate as a background limitation on when and how it is permissible to treat people in different ways, is essential for our ability to live interconnected personal lives, as well as for our capacity for operating myriad beneficial social practices that require acknowledgement of various forms of inequality. Yet because the domain of basic equality is precisely one of fundamental value, it takes priority over, and rules out, practices that *threaten* the background presumption of fundamental value—paradigmatically, appeals to group characteristics instead of individual ones. How we have come to draw this distinction is once again partly a function of history. The core reason for drawing the distinction in this way (and we will return to this matter in the following chapter) is that we have learned over time that whereas allowing individual characteristics to count, in certain specific contexts, tends not to undermine the fiction of basic equality, or the work that we employ it to do, the same is not true of appeal to group characteristics. When human societies allow group characteristics to count, they allow influence for factors that we now consider to be either normatively arbitrary, or based on outright lies and falsehoods, and whose effect is typically to perpetrate cruelty and injustice against members of subordinated groups. Yet these are precisely the sorts of moral and political evils that basic equality has historically been marshalled as a means of combatting. Commitment to basic equality has thus become importantly self-reinforcing over time, as we have learnt how it hangs together with other aspects of our moral and political lives, and how (badly) things tend to go if left unchecked.

An important part of the reason that we have adopted the fiction of basic equality, and increasingly become collectively immersed in it over time, is because we have drawn on the historical experiences of societies (our own and others) which did not use it, or were not fully immersed in it, and we now judge that we can do better than they did, to our collective benefit. We can also see once more why it should be no surprise that basic equality is historically conditioned, and why it is unlikely to make sense to agents who do not share some sufficient part of our relevant political, moral, and cultural histories. Due to the fact that being committed to basic equality requires being immersed in a fiction, one that it helps to have been raised in and/or to have many of your peers simultaneously immersed in, we should expect to discover that those lacking the cultural practice of widespread fictional immersion are not committed to basic equality: which is exactly what we find. Basic equality requires practice—both of becoming immersed in the fiction, as well as learning which domains it applies to, and how—and such practice can only be acquired through living in a suitably hospitable political and social environment. Yet for most of human history such suitably hospitable environments have been sorely lacking. In turn, commitment to basic equality has, likewise, mostly been absent.

Conclusion

Being committed to basic equality is to be immersed in a double fiction: that each of us has a uniform human essence that makes us human, and that when it comes to questions of fundamental worth or value, the shared human essence is *the only* thing that is permitted to count. This double fiction is not a human universal, however, but a culturally and historically specific practice, learnt and honed over time, both collectively and as individuals. This explains why we do not find basic equality to be something thought of, let alone practised, in all times and places, and why philosophers who go looking for some independent foundation to basic equality outside of our history and culture are condemned to a wild goose chase.

Yet although basic equality is indeed something we have created, we did not do so ex nihilo. Nor, as Anne Phillips has recently suggested, is it something that we bring into being by (collectively) choosing to do so, by proclaiming our commitment to it as a sort of axiom which is to receive no further defence or justification beyond a recognition of previous struggles for equality by real-world political actors, an act of normative voluntarism we should now endorse as simultaneously a "claim and a commitment."[31] On the contrary, we can explain this claim and commitment in terms of its origin in our psychology—our innate essentialism, plus our use of immersive fictions—whilst recognising that it took on the particular normative configuration that it has for us due to contingent reasons bound up with our relevant political and moral histories, in particular the increasing practice of *treating* each other as equals. And whilst the ascendency of basic equality was relatively rapid in the recent history of (roughly speaking) the liberal democratic West, this did not happen overnight. It took time for basic equality to become entrenched to the point of eventually constituting the default for (most) people. In turn, however, this means that we should also reject Phillips's correlate conclusion that because the search for some foundation of basic equality is indeed a hiding to nothing, that basic equality therefore "needs no justification," and must simply be put forth as a nonnegotiable commitment.[32] That might have been true if the only sorts of justifications we could offer in this area were, precisely, foundationalist ones; if it were the case that basic equality could only be justified if it were rooted in some independent grounds, presumably accessible by any impartial observer simply through the power of reason (or some variation thereupon). But that is not the only form that justification can take, or that we might appropriately be interested in exploring. For we might instead ask: given that we (or at least, most of us) find ourselves, now and around here, with a commitment to basic equality, and having identified what it consists of, and having at least a rough sense of where it came from, what reasons (if any) do we have for *going on* in this way?

If that is the question, we no more need a foundationalist answer at this point than at any other stage of our enquiry. What we need instead is to ask whether we find basic equality to be stable under reflection. That is, can our commitment to basic equality survive critical awareness of its historically contingent and fictional nature, or does such critical awareness reveal it either to be somehow incoherent, or on balance normatively undesirable— and hence something we might be better off without? As Bernard Williams put it, in a slightly different context: is the account of basic equality offered above debunking or vindicatory?[33]

The next chapter tackles these matters. It argues that the account of basic equality advanced in this book is firmly vindicatory, and that we would do well to keep going on in this sort of way. The reasons for this rest not, however, in some external justificatory grounding, but in the plentiful reasons we already possess for opposing and resisting cruelty and injustice. Contra Phillips, basic equality *can* be justified. But that justification comes from firmly within our current political and moral practices, and not from somewhere ostensibly outside of, or somehow prior, to them.[34] To these important matters we now turn.

6

Vindication

THE AIM OF THIS chapter is to show that the account of basic equality offered in this book is *vindicatory*: that once we become aware of what we are doing, we can confidently *keep on* in this way. In order to achieve this, two matters must be addressed. First, we need to be able to say what it is about our culturally and historically located commitment to basic equality that we think is valuable, and thus to be persevered with. Why stay committed to basic equality rather than giving it up in favour of something else? Second, it needs to be shown that the theoretical account of commitment to basic equality is not *destabilising*: once we know what it consists in, can we continue to *be* committed to it, or does knowledge inhibit ongoing allegiance? This chapter seeks to lay both these worries to rest: not only do we have compelling reasons to remain committed to basic equality, but such commitment is stable under reflection. As a result, the argument of the book seeks to have both *explained* basic equality as a normative phenomenon to be accounted for, but also to have *justified* it as something that deserves our continued support, once its origins and nature are made fully transparent to us. That justification, however, comes from firmly within our existing wider ethical and political practices, not from some place outside of them.

Advantages of the Account

Before tackling head on the two outstanding issues required for vindication, it is worth first considering the numerous advantages of the account presented in the previous chapter, especially as compared to the existing rival explanations on offer (as discussed in chapter 2). Insofar as the double fiction account is able to avoid the many problems that plague alternative approaches, this reinforces the conclusion that it is the right way to deal with the matter: that the argument has succeeded in properly *explaining* basic equality as a normative phenomenon, even if the question of whether commitment to it can be reflectively justified remains to be addressed.

The first major advantage of the double fiction account is that it is not faced with the embarrassing task (noted in chapter 3) of needing to provide an *error theory* purporting to explain why most people, in most of history, across most of the world, have not subscribed to basic equality. On the double fiction account, there simply *is no error to explain*. The reason most people in most times and places have not subscribed to basic equality is not because they were in error, but because they did not share our historically contingent, and relatively unusual, coupling of innate psychological essentialism with the practice of immersive fiction to generate a norm of fundamental equality as the correct way to treat and view uniform bearers of the human essence. The double fiction account is thus *ontologically modest* in its ability to recognise, without embarrassment, a central feature of basic equality's status in the real world: that it is contingent and localised to relatively recent history, and to only some corners of the globe. Rather than this relative parochialism being an awkward outcome that has to somehow be explained away in terms of error on behalf of the vast majority of people throughout almost all of history (or, as is more typical, simply being conveniently ignored), it is instead acknowledged up front as a central aspect of the phenomenon.

Second, the double fiction account does not presuppose controversial philosophical premises, but makes recourse only to ideas that ordinary people can be expected to actually be operating with already, in a plausible way. This means it entirely avoids getting bogged down in controversial wider philosophical debates, for example about the nature of personhood, or rationality, or subjectivity, or range properties, or any other contested philosophical concept proposed as the basis for basic equality, but about which there will inevitably be severe disagreement and controversy. The double fiction approach is thus *explanatorily ecumenical*: one need not adhere to some prior sectarian philosophical theory—Kantianism, political liberalism, etc.—in order to employ it as an explanation for what is going on.

Third, and closely connectedly, the double fiction approach has the major advantage of being *psychologically plausible* as an account of what is actually going on in the real world. Rather than implausibly supposing that ordinary people are committed to basic equality because they endorse complex philosophical theories which only a handful of professional academics even know about, let alone understand, the double fiction account avoids being *implausibly intellectualist*. As noted in chapter 1, this is not the same thing as claiming that the argument of this book—relatively complex as it is—must itself be fully comprehensible to all who might cast eyes on it, nor that the explanation must itself avoid recourse to philosophically demanding ideas (which clearly enough it must make use of). But it is to say that the explanation is plausible *as an explanation* of what ordinary people (as well as philosophers who are yet to think on the issue) are actually up to when they exhibit a commitment to basic equality in their day-to-day lives. It is a core contention, and strength, of the double fiction account that its explanatory ambitions are grounded in the universally available materials of psychological essentialism, historical experience, cultural inculcation, and fictional immersion, rather than complex and controversial philosophical theories that it is not plausible to suppose ordinary people are even aware of, let alone being actively guided by in their day-to-day lives. It is not necessary for the vast majority of people to be aware of how psychological essentialism, immersion in fiction, and so forth, actually operate (or even that they are themselves employing these mechanisms) in order for the explanatory claims of the account to hold good. By contrast, the alternative extant philosophical theories in this area typically require (though they rarely admit it explicitly) that the theories themselves have been explicitly comprehended and internalised, and thus become action-guiding for ordinary agents, in ways that are not psychologically or sociologically plausible.

Fourth, throughout this book I have not cleaved to any sharp distinction between basic equality of *worth* versus *status* versus *authority*, and so forth. This is deliberate. It reflects the fact that in practice we do not distinguish sharply between these formulations when we are committed to basic equality, but emphasise some of them (or combinations thereof) as befits the contexts and purposes we find ourselves operating with. Thus whilst Nikolas Kirby is right to point out that that in the Western tradition there have been at least two broad schools of philosophical thought about basic equality (one side trying to ground it in equal *worth*, the other in equal *authority*), in the real-world practice of basic equality things have largely been much messier.[1] Commitment to basic equality in the recent history of the West has taken influence from both of these camps (and likely others) over time, and we tend to employ whichever metric of basicness seems most apt for a given purpose. Sometimes we want to emphasise the worth of individuals, at other times their standing vis-à-vis peers, at others their right to participate politically and thus their claim to a baseline level of authority. Which of these we plumb for depends on what we want to achieve in a given situation. The double fiction account thus does not try to settle the matter of the basic equality "of what" in any decisive sense, precisely because an element of vagueness and flexibility is constitutive of the phenomenon. We are often ourselves unclear whether we are precisely affirming the basic equal worth, or status, or authority, and so forth, of each of us. But the point is that we muddle by just fine this way (the flexibility afforded by the muddling likely brings advantages). Accordingly, it is a feature of the double fiction account that it attempts to impose no further precision here than is found in the phenomenon it is aiming to explain. Sometimes a commitment to basic equality is focused on status, sometimes on worth, sometimes authority. There is no one final "true" metric of basic equality to which the double fiction in practice ultimately lays claim, and so it is unwise for the theorist to try and stipulate that only one metric ought "really" to count in this regard. It all depends on what we want claims of basic equality to do for us, and in what contexts.

Fifth, as noted in chapter 2, it is an embarrassment for many foundationalist accounts of basic equality that they end up excluding some categories of human from equal consideration. If basic equality is made to depend on personhood, or rationality, or subjectivity, and so forth, then there is the awkward issue of what to say about those human beings that manifestly *lack* these attributes, or exhibit them to very differing (and normatively weighty) degrees: the profoundly mentally handicapped, those suffering terminal psychological or physical degeneration, newborn babies, and so forth. Foundationalist approaches of the sort surveyed in chapter 2 are faced with the dilemma of either including these groups despite the fact they evidently lack the attributes claimed as the basis of basic equality, or else excluding them from inclusion and thus precisely failing to establish basic equality within the human set. By contrast, the double fiction account can explain why we nonetheless take such cases to fall within the remit of basic equality: no matter how young, mentally impaired, handicapped, and so forth, a human being is, they nonetheless are taken to *possess the human essence*. When operating within the double fiction of basic equality, we act as if that essence is the only thing that marks them out, and thus they are ipso facto deserving of equal treatment, and thus to be regarded as basic equals with all other humans.

In turn, the double fiction account is not perturbed by Anne Phillips's recent worry that providing a basis for basic equality generates grounds for exclusion precisely because some will always be found to lack the basis.[2] When it comes to the human essence, all human beings possess it by definition; thus there *can be no* grounds for exclusion on *this* basis without denying the human essence to some. Which is not to say that such denial cannot happen—it manifestly can, as the horror of dehumanisation attests (see chapter 4)—but this will constitute a *rejection* of basic equality, rather than (as Phillips worries) the surreptitious use of basic equality as a way of reintroducing normative hierarchy through the back door.

Sixth, a major advantage of the double fiction approach is that it neither ignores nor denies the fact that commitment to basic equality is in practice far patchier and more inconsistent than many scholarly discussions of the topic would lead one to suppose. As noted in chapter 1, whilst it is true that in polite company the presumption of basic equality has become the only permitted stance, there is still plenty of garden-variety bigotry around, as well as the more thoroughly committed rejection of basic equality to be found on the fringes of political respectability (even if, for the most part, the opponents of basic equality hide their true views in public, or at least do so when running for major office). A quick glance at the more dispiriting parts of social media is enough to confirm that many people are *not* fully and consistently committed to basic equality, at least when hiding behind the screen of anonymity. This however is something that the double fiction account is well situated to explain. Whilst many people now really are sincerely immersed in the fiction, some are less good at staying consistently immersed than others, whilst some are merely pretending. The reasons for these varying levels of immersion are themselves various. Age and cumulative experience of being immersed are likely to be important factors, as suggested in chapter 5. Upbringing will also play an important role (bigoted parents are more likely to raise bigoted children). Likewise, levels of sincerity will vary amongst different people, and amidst different groups, for different reasons. Christian fundamentalists, for example, will typically have a harder time immersing themselves in the fiction of basic equality than secularists and the moderately religious, given what tends to be taught within fundamentalist groups about

the "proper place" of women, the "permissibility" of homo-
sexuality, and so forth. By contrast, committed racists and proud
xenophobes, whilst far more politically marginal than they once
were, for different reasons again are going to be at best only pretending, strategically, to be immersed in the fiction of basic equality, at least when appearing in public (but often finding an outlet
for their true voices on social media platforms such as Twitter or
4chan). All of this is straightforward for the double fiction account
to make sense of. That real-world adherence to basic equality often
falls short of Dworkin's egalitarian plateau isn't surprising given
the real-world variability in the level of fictional immersion we
ought to expect to encounter—and do in fact find.

Likewise, when there is a conflict between people's personal
interests and remaining immersed in the fiction, we should not be
especially surprised if it is immersion that gives way to interest,
which helps explain why this is an area rife with hypocrisy and
inconsistency. We are all familiar with those individuals who talk
a good game about basic equality until it is *their* promotion, or
their child, or *their* neighbourhood that is on the line. Likewise,
it shouldn't be especially surprising that historical figures who
affirmed basic equality—John Locke, say, or the American Found-
ing Fathers—often pivoted rapidly from declaring a general commitment to basic equality to almost immediately denying meaningful inclusion to some groups of humans. In the competition
between the private interests of socially dominant White men in
remaining wedded to prevailing ideological orthodoxies which
subjugated (in particular) women, non-White racial minorities,
and indigenous peoples to their power, versus becoming fully and
consistently immersed in the fiction of basic equality (of which
they themselves had only very limited lived experience), it is not
surprising that private interest and adherence to the status quo
typically won out, at least in the short term. Nonetheless, it is also
the case that in the longer term the balance was gradually, painfully, but ever more consistently, tilted in favour of the immersion, rather than towards the private interests of the originally

dominant group. In large measure this was due to the heroic efforts of the historically excluded themselves to secure real-world inclusion, in line with the self-professed ideals of the societies they lived in. There is no denying that the process has been slow, and often extremely painful, and is in many ways still far from complete. But there *has* been change—of an astonishing order of magnitude when viewed in the *longue durée*—and this is something the double fiction account can explain, but also celebrate the reality of.

Seventh, and as a result, we therefore again do not need to conclude, as Phillips appears to, that because the real-world performance of basic equality often falls short of the ideal, and because historical figures who professed basic equality often failed to live up to it in practice, that therefore the ideal is itself suspect.[3] On the contrary, the double fiction account acknowledges the *increasing success over time* of commitment to basic equality becoming the default norm in society, and the real and significant success of immersion becoming the only acceptable public stance by this point. And even if some people are still only faking that immersion, *getting* them to fake it is itself a meaningful political victory, as well as an effective way to drive further change. The more socially unacceptable it became to deny basic equality, the more that the normative force of basic equality took over and became the social default—sincerely accepted—by increasing numbers of people in successive generations. That the process is not yet complete means only that the project is ongoing, and that we ought to guard against complacency, not that basic equality talk in the past is exposed as fraudulent, or that it was necessarily inherently self-defeating, as Phillips appears to suggest.

For these reasons, I take it that the double fiction account of basic equality is *explanatorily powerful* as regards the target phenomenon, and considerably more so than the currently available alternatives. But even if so, this still leaves the matter of vindication outstanding. Why, if at all, are we justified in adhering to this practice? Why ought we to *go on* in this way?

Against Cruelty and Injustice

On the account presented in this book, our commitment to basic equality consists in the coupling of innate psychological essentialism with widespread immersion in the fiction of treating the human essence as if it were the only thing that defined any of us, and which in our historical and cultural locale now issues in a norm of basic equality. Yet it is evidently the case that it is *not true* that human beings possess any shared and uniform "essence." We are, technically speaking (and as noted in chapter 5), *deluded* about this matter: we have a belief in something that is false. Similarly, when we immerse ourselves in the fiction of treating the (itself fictional) human essence as if it were the only thing that defined any of us, we adopt a mental state in which we act as though we believed something that is not in fact the case (that all of the myriad ways in which human beings are unequal do not obtain). Given the manifest failure of our belief in basic equality to track the truth of how things really are, ought this not to be of grave concern to the reflective enquirer?

I believe not. The answer lies in asking what our commitment to basic equality *does* for us. We must ask: what needs and ends are being served by our going on this way, and are those needs and ends sufficiently important such that it *doesn't matter* if the process that delivers them is one that employs fictions, such that we frequently fail to directly track the underlying truth? Here we do well to appreciate the strong and significant connections between basic equality and the reduction of cruelty and injustice.[4]

A good way of seeing what is at stake is to ask: how do we think the social and political world would likely go were we to abandon commitment to basic equality, giving it up in favour of something else? Here we do not need to merely speculate from our armchairs but can employ a basic awareness of history to make an informed judgement. Absent norms of basic equality, human societies tend to the formation of explicit hierarchies that draw distinctions within the human set regarding the worth, status, authority, and so forth, of some group of humans as compared to others. And those hierarchies are typically not benign or neutral in their effects, but serve to enable a dominant group to exploit and subjugate those deemed "lesser," whilst typically providing a legitimation narrative for why it is permissible to dominate the subordinated. Indeed, such domination is standardly recast as not being domination at all, but as putatively rightful rule, thus neatly eliminating even the conceptual possibility of injustice as regards the subordination of the inferiors. Yet what follows from this—as attested to by the experiences of (for example) women, colonial subjects, ethnic, racial, and religious minorities, and the sexually "deviant," over several millennia and around the globe—is more often than not *cruelty and injustice*. When some group of humans is denied basic equality by another which wields power over it, whilst the local dominating group might claim the mantle of paternal benevolence in its actions, we can be sure that this is not, in fact, how things are most likely to go. The historical record is painfully clear that those denied basic equality can be expected to bear the brunt of repeated cruelty at the hands of their "superiors," be it physical, psychological, economic, or indeed on pretty much any other available metric. In turn, the "inferiors" are also standardly faced with institutional structures (legal systems; forms of government; prevailing ideological narratives) that not only systemically fail to recognise the claims of the subordinated to not be mistreated by their "superiors," but which tend to affirm that their subordinated treatment *is the proper order of things*. This, though, is ultimately injustice of the worst sort: not only the denial of any possibility of redress to those who suffer at the hands of their oppressors, but a denial even of any recognition that what they are being subjected to *is injustice at all*.

We now know, all too well, just how horrific the denial of basic equality is liable to turn out to be in practice. In its most extreme manifestations, denial of basic equality is a crucial staging post along the road that leads to Auschwitz, apartheid South Africa, the Japanese occupation of Korea, the Atlantic Slave Trade, the mass extermination of indigenous peoples, and other such (sadly all too numerous) human catastrophes. But even the more mundane and less spectacular denials of basic equality available in the historical record, and which cover most of human history, amply illustrate the rampant cruelty and injustice that standardly go along with it. Mary Wollstonecraft's *A Vindication of the Rights of Women*, for example, remains a searing testament to the ubiquity of cruelty inflicted upon eighteenth-century women by patriarchal suppositions of inherent male superiority. (As her own life story shows, some of the most vicious treatment was reserved for those women who, like her, dared to challenge the status quo.) Black Americans living under Jim Crow intimately understood their status as lesser humans to be bound up directly and purposefully with the systematic infliction of cruelty and injustice by the Whites who degraded them physically and psychologically, at the level of both individual treatment and institutional ordering. Black South Africans under apartheid knew the same. Jews have known it for thousands of years, in many parts of the world, living beneath the spectre of the pogrom as well as the day-to-day indignity of routine anti-Semitism. Homosexuals in countries such as Saudi Arabia, Qatar, and Uganda know it today. Endless further examples could be cited. This is the sorry and depressing story of most of the human race, for most of its history.

What the ideal of basic equality provides is a rejection of the politics of cruelty and injustice as being (falsely) legitimated through (false) claims about the inherent superiority of some kinds of humans compared to others. The history of basic equality is in significant part the history of *opposing* the kinds of cruelty and injustice that standardly accompany the denial of basic equality. By contrast, the more successfully a widespread commitment to basic equality has been established, the more successful it has in turn become as a preemptive *block* to the kinds of cruelty and injustice that have been the rule, rather than the exception, in human history. This is not to say that societies where basic equality has become widely entrenched as a presumed default have thus finally succeeded in eliminating cruelty and injustice (or even that they consistently adhere, in practice, to the stated commitment to basic equality). Far from it. Plenty of cruelty and injustice remains, now and around here, and a good deal of it is the stubborn legacy of earlier historical denials of basic equality. But the wide-ranging and relatively rapid ascent of basic equality has been far from nothing, and there is every reason to suppose that were we to abandon commitment to it, the world would rapidly again become a far worse place than it already is. Insofar as we care about trying to reduce cruelty and injustice, however, and insofar as we know that immersion in the fiction of basic equality is an important and historically proven way to help achieve this, then we have good reason to *stay* committed to it. That the commitment to basic equality is constituted by the use of fictions, functioning through aspects of our psychologies that are not primarily truth-tracking in their operations, is ultimately not what is most important here. What matters most is what basic equality *does* for us: its function in reducing and blocking the human tendency to cruelty and injustice. *That* is why we should go on being committed to it.[5]

Does this, though, not fatally beg the question? After all, if we want all human beings to be free from cruelty and injustice, then doesn't it look like we are *already* committed to basic equality for all human beings, on at least this metric, which informs our aversion to their suffering cruelty and injustice in the first place? Is this not to reason in a circle?

If the aim of the preceding were to try and offer a *foundation* for basic equality, then the charge would indeed hold good: it would be assuming what needed to be proved. But the aim at this stage of the argument is not to explain what the commitment to basic equality itself consists in. It is instead to explain why we, who *do* now find ourselves with the commitment to basic equality constituted by the double fiction rooted in our psychological essentialism, ought to feel confident *going on* with that commitment. The reasoning here is thus not viciously circular, but self-consciously self-reinforcing by drawing on mutually complementary aspects of our normative outlook. Insofar as we do care about cruelty and injustice, and insofar as we do recognise as rightful the claims of other humans not to experience nor be subjected to these evils, then we should recognise in turn that our historically contingent and locally developed practice of according basic equality to all humans is an excellent and proven way of averting and combating these evils (and furthermore that this is not some thin coincidence, but a historically significant and normatively robust connection). Thus, whilst it is indeed true that *for us* combating cruelty and injustice is in part constituted by who we already take the basic equals to be, and thus who we recognise as being wrongly subjected to these things in the first place, and hence who is entitled to such redress accordingly, this is a feature, not a bug, in the account. By this point in our history, and given the normative values that we now find ourselves with, what counts as cruelty and injustice will make reference to our extant beliefs about basic equality. Yet because the aim here isn't to ground the latter in the former, but rather to show why on reflection we ought to keep holding on to the latter given our aversion to the former, acknowledging that the two interact in various and important ways is not a problem. Indeed, quite the opposite: it illustrates the depth of commitment in the area, by showing how our values coherently hang together.

Furthermore, it is surely the case that the commitment to basic equality emerged when and where it did—roughly speaking, in the developed West, over the last century or so—because it served certain needs possessed by the agents who came over time to espouse it. That is, appealing to claims about basic equality was *useful* in various ways. On the one hand, the notion of basic equality provided a common rallying point which enabled it to serve as a foundational political notion around which various groups could coalesce when attempting to advance various causes of social reform. (Think in particular of the activist groups of the mid- to late twentieth century who instigated widespread change with regards to attitudes and, crucially, social practices around race and gender, as noted at the start of chapter 5.) On the other, basic equality was useful for the advancement of various further ends, in particular (and again as indicated at the outset of chapter 5) constructing a liberal-democratic self-understanding in opposition to fascism and communism during the twentieth century, reconciling claims to political equality with the reality of considerable economic inequality under conditions of capitalism, and reforming attitudes towards oppressed and marginalised groups. Basic equality was thus useful in helping to meet certain needs of both collective self-understanding, as well as facilitating the active reduction of persistent cruelty and injustice: it *did something for us* (and indeed, continues to do it today). There is thus an aspect of basic equality which is amenable to what Matthieu Queloz has termed pragmatic genealogical analysis: locating the origins of a concept in its functional usefulness.[6]

I will return below to the question of functionality and the importantly self-effacing nature of functionality in the case of basic equality, but for now the point to note is that the connections between basic equality and an aversion to cruelty and injustice run deep: it is not simply that, now that widespread commitment to basic equality is up and running, it has the happy downstream effect of helping to reduce cruelty and injustice. It is that *part of the reason* widespread commitment to basic equality successfully got up and running was that appealing to it as a commitment was motivated by an aversion to cruelty and injustice, which itself went along with, and also deepened, a shifting collective moral and political self-understanding, which in turn had the effect of helping to actually deliver the goods on these scores, in a process that was spontaneously self-reinforcing over time.

Yet what if someone asks in response to all this: "why, though, should we care about cruelty and injustice?" At this point, we reach a kind of normative bedrock in the account. For there is likely nothing we can say to get a grip on someone asking such a question, unless they in fact already see (or rather *feel*) what is wrong with those things. In this case, the honest answer is ultimately "if you really have to ask, you'll never know." Fortunately, most people asking this question *do* know; they are merely playing sceptical devil's advocate and pretending that they don't, or else have spent too much time doing philosophy, and would do better to go and read some history, or even just a newspaper, to (re)calibrate themselves. And what really matters here is not our ability (or otherwise) to convince some philosophical sceptic who intransigently denies the value of opposing cruelty and injustice. What matters is what we, who *are* committed to basic equality already, can confidently say to ourselves and each other about why basic equality is a value for us, given the wider values and commitments we presently find ourselves with. And in this regard, the historical record provides overwhelming reasons in favour of keeping the commitment.

As a result, we need not worry unduly about what we might say to some committed bigot who sincerely claimed that there *was no* cruelty or injustice in, for example, the treatments meted out to (for example) eighteenth-century women, or Blacks under Jim Crow, or any other subordinated group, because their subordination was allegedly "the proper order of things," and therefore that whatever was done to them was by definition done with propriety. For what we need here is not some argument that could (somehow) compel those outside our ethical perspective to see it our way, but rather to be confident in what we can say *to each other* about the reasons that *we* have for going on in this way, rejecting the views of the bigot and committing to fighting them (politically, and if necessary, perhaps even literally) should the need arise. Insofar as we already care about resisting and reducing cruelty and injustice (and I take it that we do), then we have plentiful reason to continue in our commitment to basic equality.[7] If that leads us into severe political conflict with those who do not see it our way, so be it. May we have the courage of our convictions, if and when the confrontation comes.

Again, this emphasis on cruelty and injustice is not guilty of introducing a foundationalist claim via the back door. My argument is not that basic equality is itself *grounded in* the capacity for humans to experience cruelty and injustice.[8] Whilst it is certainly true of all human beings that they are vulnerable to cruelty and injustice, it is also the case that they vary considerably in the degree to which they are indeed vulnerable (both as a matter of personal calibration and experience, as well as this being heavily conditioned by historical and political context). To appeal directly to the capacity to suffer cruelty and injustice as the basis of basic equality would reintroduce the sorts of problems surveyed in chapter 2. Accordingly, I do not maintain that it is via direct reference to the capacity to suffer injustice and cruelty that the commitment to basic equality operates. Basic equality works via the double fiction, centred on our innate psychological essentialism combined with fictional immersion. Upon reflection, however, we can see that this double fiction is one we ought to continue employing, in large measure because it promotes and supports other values that we hold dear: principally, the reduction of cruelty and injustice. Furthermore, it is important that this is not an *accident*: it is not some coincidence that basic equality does this, but one of its primary effects in real-world moral and political practice, that itself helps to explain why it has been increasingly adopted and entrenched over time, garnering greater political allegiance from many quarters in the process: basic equality has *done* something for us in our collective recent history, insofar as it has helped advance the cause of reducing the amount of cruelty and injustice in our world and thus helped meet a perceived need amongst those who seek to change things in that direction (think again of the historical factors and movements noted at the outset of chapter 5). Yet the fact that basic equality has an important functional component insofar as it reduces the scope and opportunity for the cruelty and injustice that humans are vulnerable to experiencing, and hence that is why as reflective agents we ought to be confident in continuing in our adherence to it, does not mean that it is itself directly *grounded in* the human capacity to be so-vulnerable. These are two distinct things. They interact, but do not collapse into one foundationalist story.

This completes the first stage of vindication. We have good and strong reasons to go on being committed to basic equality due to the strong and non-accidental connections between basic equality and the reduction of cruelty and injustice, which the historical record is an unambiguous testament to. Insofar as we care about the latter, we have abundant reason to remain committed to the former.[9] What remains, then, is to consider whether the account offered is *stable under reflection*: can normative commitment to basic equality survive critical awareness of its own nature?

Stable under Reflection

It is important to understand that the argument for basic equality offered in this book does not take the form of a "noble lie" account. In *The Republic*, Plato infamously suggested that in order to establish the rule of philosophers in his ideal city-in-speech, the people would have to be divided into classes and told a legitimation story about *why* they were assigned to some class rather than another (especially as their biological parents might well be in a different one). Accordingly, citizens would be told that they were all born with either bronze, silver, or gold in their souls, and were assigned to different classes, and thus radically differing educations and social roles, on that basis. This would be, plainly, a lie: no such prior and independent division of souls existed. Nonetheless, it was "noble" because it was used to secure something of greater overall value: a rightfully ordered and therefore just city, in which rightfully ordered and therefore just souls could hope to exist.

The account of basic equality offered here is not like that. In the first place, this is because a fiction is not the same thing as a lie. Whilst our immersion in the double fiction of basic equality means that we proceed *as if* the only thing that defines each and all of us is the possession of a shared uniform essence, we need not affirm—nor try to persuade others, let alone indoctrinate them into thinking—that human essences *really do* exist when we (or some special elect group) know this to be false, but conceal that fact for an instrumental purpose. Whereas a noble lie is a calculated deceit perpetrated by those with more power and knowledge upon those who are to be denied that knowledge so as to bring about some end, basic equality as immersion in a fiction is not a *deceit*. Rather it, is a collectively enacted way of going on *as if* something were the case (even though it is not) that allows us to achieve desirable results by acting in a counterfactual manner, yet without deliberate suppression of the truth.

The difference between a lie and a fiction does, however, raise some delicate metaethical issues regarding the claim that we *are* each other's basic equals, as I take it that we do typically want to say.[10] One initially tempting response is to say that we *truly are* each other's basic equals once the practice of treating each other as such is consistently up and running, because we have *made* it so through that very practice itself. The problem with taking such a stance, however, is that it looks incoherent given that the practice is, precisely, rooted in the use of fictions. For consider: if I were to say "It is *true* that Sherlock Holmes lives at 221B Baker Street," there is a sense in which this is readily intelligible, for within the world of Arthur Conan Doyle's novels, that *is* where Holmes is identified as residing. But if someone were to press me, I would of course have to concede that it isn't *really* true that Sherlock Holmes lives at 221B Baker Street, because he is a fictional character and thus does not (cannot) truly live anywhere. The same seems to be the case with basic equality: insofar as it is founded in fiction—of acting *as if* certain things are the case, when in fact they are not—it is surely incorrect to insist that we *truly are* basic equals, at least if that utterance is intended as registering some thick, metaphysical, claim. Fiction and truth do not sit well together here.

The alternative, and it seems to me preferable, option, is to understand claims about our being basic equals as not marking any strong metaphysical commitments at all. If we insist that, unlike in a noble lie account, we really *are* basic equals, that is not to be taken in a metaphysically strong sense, such as we might intend when saying something like "there *truly are* electrons," or "there *truly is* a God." Instead, it is better understood as something more modest: a kind of shorthand for saying "in this context, where the available historical and psychological materials have been put together in this particular way, and now issue in this kind of practice, with people having these kinds of robust dispositions to treat each other in terms of a basic egalitarianism, we have constructed matters such that each person is accorded the status of an equal, and for us now and around here, that is what they count as, and they couldn't count as anything else."[11] Of course, for agents who find themselves (for whatever reason) outside of this context and practice, it *won't* be the case that we are basic equals. But as argued in chapter 3, that is just how it is with normative values—there is an irreducible degree or relativism (more on this in a moment).

Understanding matters this way allows us to navigate between the Scylla of a noble lie account, and the Charybdis of an incoherent metaethical fictionalism making strong metaphysical truth claims. Insisting that we are in fact basic equals (because we have *made* it such that we are; see above for the shorthand made long) is not the same as insisting that all are equal even though we know that they are not (really), say because it is useful to get others to *think* such a thing. Yet doing so does not require that we insist upon strong, and metaphysically suspect, truth claims about the nature of reality beyond our practices, either. Between those two poles lies a more modest understanding: that we become basic equals when we consistently treat each other as such, and that is all there (really) is to it. Of course, were we to *stop* treating each other as basic equals in the consistent and robust ways the practice both depends upon and consists in, then we would necessarily stop being basic equals. That would certainly be a loss, for the reasons outlined above to do with the prevention of cruelty and injustice, but also insofar as we are now normatively committed to there being something valuable about basic equality in and of itself (more on this momentarily). We thus have good reason to try to prevent that from happening. But whilst the practice *is* up and running, there need be nothing incoherent, nor metaphysically extravagant, associated with thinking and referring to each other as being, truly, basic equals—so long as we remain aware that should we lose the undergirding practice, that fact about us would itself necessarily cease to obtain.

Another way to put the point is that it is precisely an effect of the well-entrenched disposition to treat each other as basic equals that generates a syntactic tendency towards stating things as though claims of basic equality are primarily fact-stating about some independently true order. After all, if the disposition to treat each other as basic equals is well entrenched, it is to a large extent a *behavioural* disposition. Yet a crucial dimension of that behaviour is how we *talk* about each other: one of the core ways in which we manifest a disposition to treat each other as basic equals is to talk about each other as *being* basic equals (and hence, ultimately, to think of each other as being such). Thus, the behavioural disposition is also a discursive one, and in this case the discursive tendency is to talk as if, when we claim that people are basic equals, we are making a claim about something independent of our social practices: that people *just are* basic equals, and that our disposition to treat them as equals is downstream of that prior fact. Indeed, if the disposition to treat each other as basic equals is especially well entrenched, it is likely that this apparent independent priority of the putative fact of basic equality is precisely how things will seem to ordinary practitioners who have not critically reflected on what is going on. But this critically unreflective tendency to see basic equality talk as making fact-statements about an independently true status is readily confounded by the revelation that there are apparently *no good reasons* for adhering to such a claim: that on all available metrics we are not equal, but manifestly unequal. And this leads directly to the collapse of all the strategies for finding a "basis of basic equality" discussed in chapter 2.

By contrast, the account advocated here attempts to *deflate* the superficially fact-stating discourse of basic equality, whilst reversing the order of conceptual fit between disposition and principle. So whilst it may look like we are making statements about independent fact when it comes to claiming that each of us is a basic equal (and to the critically unreflective practitioner, that may even be what they think they are doing), this is best understood not as making a claim about some independent metaphysical status that is supposed to be true of each of us, independently, and which is prior to and informs the validity of our disposition to treat each other as equals, but rather as the *effect* of those very practices: a constructed truth that obtains only when the disposition to treat each other as basic equals is robustly up and running (as, for most of us in the developed West, it now is).[12]

Seeing things this way helps to address an important challenge. This is the objection: "but surely we would remain basic equals *even if* everybody tomorrow stopped thinking we were?" (And relatedly: "surely people in the past, and in other societies, *really were and are* basic equals, even if their local practices meant they weren't, or still aren't, being treated as such by their relevant peers?") The key here is to see that what *look* like second-order claims about metaphysical reality are better understood as first-order claims about our own moral practices: they are instances of *moralising*, of demonstrating the depth of our commitments to the disposition to treat each other as basic equals. After all, part of what it is to be fully immersed in the double fiction of basic equality is for the question of the foundations (or indeed, lack thereof) of this practice never to occur to the average practitioner. And if the question *is* raised, the most intuitive and spontaneous response is to deny that the practice is in any way relativised, and to think of it as responsive to an independent prior fact about our being basic equals—something which obtains regardless of whether or not anybody actually thinks that it does. That, indeed, is what it *means* to be fully immersed in the fiction, and fully committed to the disposition to treat each other in terms of a basic egalitarianism. Yet once we calm our moralising and engage in more dispassionate critical reflection, we come to see that, at the second-order (or metaethical) level, the above story of the disposition generating the principle is the most plausible way of understanding what is really going on. And this takes us back directly to what was argued in chapter 3. That on the one hand, *for us* it will be true that all people are basic equals, both now and around here, but also in the past and over there, precisely because they all have the human essence, and we are immersed in the relevant fiction-based practices that generate the disposition to treat people as equals in light of that (wherever and whenever such people happen to be found). Yet on the other hand, we will also have to admit that for people who *lack* this constituting history, and thus the necessary practices of treating each other as equals, it *won't* be true that all people are basic equals: indeed, the idea won't even (can't even) make sense to them. This realisation need not, however, diminish *our* commitment to basic equality, because that commitment can be reflectively stabilised in terms of what the practice of treating each other as basic equals *does* for us: its tendency to reduce cruelty and injustice, and which we have important reasons to go on caring about and thus reflectively endorsing, as outlined above. Acceptance, at the second-order level, that basic equality is necessarily relativised need have no impact on our first-order disposition to go on treating each other as basic equals. Nor does it preclude us from thinking of all others as *truly being* basic equals, so long as the latter is properly understood as a shorthand for the state of affairs that is generated by the practice, and not a thick claim about some supposedly independent reality.[13]

In clarifying that the argument for basic equality offered here does not take the form of a noble lie, and does not commit us to extravagant or incoherent metaphysical truth claims, we can in turn alleviate the worry that it might nonetheless be a "government house" account, incapable of openly acknowledging its own true nature without collapsing in on itself. The charge of being a "government house" account has most famously been attached to a particular species of so-called rule utilitarianism, which reasons that if the goal of morality (and thus, on the utilitarian view, of all social policy) is to maximise utility, then the best way to do to that will be to *conceal* the truth of utilitarianism. This is because if ordinary people constantly try to maximise utility directly, the strain this puts on them, coupled with their poor individual calculations, plus the impact of myriad unintended consequences and various coordination problems, is liable to impede rather than advance the overall maximisation of utility. Better for a government of informed utilitarian calculators to make the necessary calculations for them, and simply tell the ignorant citizenry to follow various rules that the cognoscenti have devised, and which are calculated to best maximise utility. Indeed, better for ordinary people not to even know that these calculations are being made at all, or that the rules are ultimately utilitarian in nature. After all, knowledge of the existence of this secret cabal would be liable to decrease, rather than maximise, utility, insofar as ordinary people would presumably begin to question—and quite possibly fear, and maybe even resist—the decisions made by their utilitarian overlords. On this guise, the truth of utilitarianism is a secret that must be withheld from the masses, for the very knowledge of what is really going on would defeat the goal of maximising utility. Accordingly, such a species of utilitarianism *cannot* truthfully and openly acknowledge its own existence, let alone its rationale or calculations, or else it would fail to maximise the utility that was its very raison d'être.

Whatever the merits (or rather, considerable demerits) of "government house" utilitarianism, the account of basic equality offered here is not structured in this way. This is important, because whereas the rule utilitarian is only interested in maximising utility—and thus any problems associated with a "government house" version are assessed by the utilitarian solely on that metric—for those committed to basic equality there is a crucial dimension in which basic equality must be transparent to itself. That is, we cannot really treat each other *as equals* if central to doing so is the practice of some deceiving others in order to manipulate them towards ends, the very nature of which they are kept deliberately unaware of. Doing so would directly undermine genuine commitment to the value that is purportedly being promoted. Happily, however, this is not what is going on. In the first instance, and as with the case of the "noble lie" charge, the argument for basic equality in this book does not posit any kind of manipulation or deception by an elite, perpetrated against the masses who are kept deliberately ignorant. Crucially, it likewise does not lead us to the conclusion that we *ought* to manipulate or deceive people into believing it, say because of the good consequences such manipulation might be presumed to generate. Basic equality is not something that needs to be imposed on ordinary people by a secret cabal, and furthermore also not something that must in turn be *kept secret*, at pain of self-refutation and collapse should the truth about it get out. Rather, commitment to basic equality has been spontaneously developed over time as a response to the historical circumstances of recent Western societies, and as a result the truth about its constructed nature is not something that needs to be hidden upon pains of self-refutation or destabilisation. This is a crucial feature that distinguishes its structure from that of a "government house" view: it is, so to speak, bottom-up rather than top-down, and not committed to systematic deception about its own nature, in a way that would be especially damaging (because essentially self-refuting) in the case of basic equality. These are simply different sorts of accounts.

Nonetheless, it might reasonably be objected that if everyone came to be fully aware of the account offered in this book, then such awareness would itself fundamentally change the way in which people were committed to basic equality. Indeed, could they even remain committed to basic equality in the way that they (or at least many of them) had previously been, once they knew what it really consisted in? Surely, truthful reflection in this instance cannot leave everything just where it was. Whilst basic equality might not implode by the light of its own internal logic were the truth of it to become widely known (as would be the case for "government house" utilitarianism), it is surely implausible to presume that *nothing* would change were the truth of what is going on to become widely appreciated.

This is an important charge, and indeed it is in some measure correct, so the answer to it must be handled carefully. Accordingly, we do well to first draw a distinction between what is *realistically going to happen*, versus what is a mere *conceptual possibility*, but which we can be sure is never actually going to happen. The answers required differ in both cases, and seeing why helps us to handle the relevant issues with the requisite care, and in turn to reach a reflectively stable assessment.

As regards what is *realistically going to happen*, we can be sure that a critical mass of ordinary people is not going to acquire this book, read it, understand it, come to reflect critically on its attitudes towards basic equality, and hence alter its normative outlook as a result. Even if I am right in the account I offer here, my merely offering it in this form is extremely unlikely to have any discernible effect on commitment to basic equality as it is currently encountered. Indeed, in terms of the practical likelihood that the account offered here will have any real-world destabilising consequences, that likelihood is so vanishingly slim as to be functionally zero. My merely making the argument is not going to destabilise anything *out there*, because academic philosophy simply does not have that kind of power (and this is something we should on balance be grateful for, but also not in the least bit surprised by).[14]

Nonetheless, it is still a *conceptual possibility* that all of those currently immersed in the fiction of basic equality should tomorrow read this work, come to agree with the correctness of its argument, and go from a state of relatively unreflective immersion in the double fiction, to a more critical, detached, reflective perspective vis-à-vis what they are doing, and why, when they hold all humans to be basic equals. If *this* were to happen, would the account remain stable under reflection, or would it collapse under the weight of its own self-awareness? My sense is that commitment to basic equality *could* continue under such (highly improbable) circumstances, though the nature of such a widespread revelation would certainly not leave everything where it was. What we would presumably see would be a much less *spontaneous* commitment to basic equality being persevered with than had previously been the case, with individuals having to go through the relatively laborious process of reminding themselves of the complexity of the phenomenon, where it comes from, how it works, and why on balance it is good to keep on with it. This would certainly be inefficient from a societal, as well as an individual, point of view, and I suspect that it might well undermine the immediate normativity of basic equality generated by the instantiated practice itself (as described above), serving to reduce it to something valued for merely instrumental reasons to do with the reduction of cruelty and injustice. In such circumstances, widespread critical reflection might well undermine normative commitment, at least along this particular (important) axis. Nonetheless, it would not negate the value of basic equality entirely, nor would it lead to the conclusion that we would be better off without it: on the contrary, the reasons given in the previous section about reducing cruelty and injustice would still continue to apply, and likely remain decisive in favour of maintaining ongoing commitment.

What this helps us to see, however, is that whilst it is bad news for my future royalty payments, it is rather good news for everybody else that the above is a mere conceptual possibility and will not come to pass. In turn, we can here appreciate that basic equality in the real world (i.e., absent a mass critical reflection on the origins and nature of this commitment that is never actually going to happen) importantly exhibits what Matthieu Queloz has described as a *self-effacing* aspect to its functionality, and that it works all the better for it.[15] As Queloz puts it:

> Where functionality is *self-effacing*, it is a functional requirement on the practice's functionality that participants not be primarily motivated by awareness of that functionality, but when they acquire awareness of it, this awareness is fully compatible with— and may indeed encourage—confident engagement in the practice on any reasonable conception of it. This last qualification is required because one's conception of what the practice must look like to merit confident engagement may be so demanding as to exclude its performing such mundane offices as the

satisfaction of human needs if it is to be worthy of respect. . . . A self-effacingly functional practice is thus functional, but only insofar as it is sustained by motives that are autonomous, i.e. not conditional on the practice's functionality in any given case. The practice must outrun its functionality in order to be functional. When this condition is met, the functionality of the practice will tend to show up, if at all, only as a secondary consideration among the contents of the participants' deliberation. But this, crucially, will be so for purely functional reasons, and not because the function is objectionable to the participants. The functionality is not just *effaced*, but *self*-effacing.[16]

Take, for example, the case of loyalty to a group or cause:

> [Loyalty] is functional (let us assume) in that it stabilizes cooperative behaviour in ways that ultimately benefit most participants; but our motives in being loyal are not conditional on its fulfilling that function, and it is only because they are unconditional in this way that loyalty can fulfil its function. If loyalty is understood in purely instrumental terms, it will be mere window-dressing where it aligns with individual interest, and irrelevant where it does not: where the interests of the individual anyway align with the interests of the group, loyalty is functionally redundant; where they diverge, loyalty thus understood will not bring the individual to forfeit personal gain for the sake of the group and pull his or her weight in the cooperative venture; free-riding will be more attractive. And since the same is true for every individual in the group, the benefits of loyalty will be lost altogether. Hence, loyalty is unable to make a useful difference so long as it is understood in purely instrumental terms. To be functional at all, it must be more than just functional.[17]

Commitment to basic equality operates similarly. It is functionally beneficial due to the fact that widespread commitment reduces cruelty and injustice, but it serves that function far more effectively when it is treated by those who are committed to it *not* as a merely functional, instrumental value, but as something that is *valuable in and of itself*, a normative commitment in its own right (which, for those engaged in the practice of treating each other as basic equals, it really is). This may seem paradoxical, but it is not. Insofar as treating people as basic equals is going to most effectively reduce cruelty and injustice, it will do so not by ordinary people *reasoning* that they *ought* to *pretend* that people are basic equals *merely so as to bring about* a reduction in cruelty and injustice, but rather by ordinary people *just treating* others as basic equals, because that is what they sincerely hold to be the appropriate disposition to adopt, and which regulates their attitudes and actions in turn. Genuine normative commitment to basic equality in its own right (i.e., rather than seeing it as a merely functional mechanism) means ordinary people are both more likely to adhere to this norm, and more likely to do so spontaneously and without conscious direction (from within or without), which in turn will be the most effective way of delivering the social results—i.e., reducing and blocking cruelty and injustice—that the practice of widespread commitment to basic equality functionally promotes. The best way to promote the functional end (reducing cruelty and injustice) is for individuals not to focus on the functional outcome at all, but to treat basic equality as a normative commitment in its own right, which is most effectively done if it *is* a normative commitment in its own right—as I have suggested that it now indeed is for us. Hence the functionality component is, as Queloz terms it, *self-effacing*: it is best secured when reference to it is eliminated from the conscious motivations of those engaging in the practice.

Yet appreciating this importantly self-effacing aspect to the functionality of commitment to basic equality in turn allows the phenomenon as a whole to be rendered stable under reflection. This is because although the functionality of basic equality is importantly self-effacing, becoming *aware* of that self-effacing functionality does not by itself give us reason to give up on our commitment to basic equality (whereas a noble lie, or a government house account, necessarily cannot be transparent about its own nature to all who might encounter it). We can quite happily go on viewing basic equality as normative for us (people *are* basic equals, and ought to be viewed and treated accordingly), whilst also appreciating that this normativity itself has a functional benefit in the aggregate: it helps reduce cruelty and injustice. Indeed, upon being subjected to critical reflection, we see that these aspects *reinforce* each other: they are complementary, rather than being in competition, or somehow mutually undermining. Thus, not only can we explain *why* basic equality is a normative commitment for us (the double fiction account), we can in turn stabilise and reinforce that commitment by reflecting on the desirable things that this commitment *does* for us (its functional usefulness in reducing cruelty and injustice), but without claiming that the normative commitment collapses into a narrowly or reductively instrumentalist story. The advantage of a self-effacing functionality account is thus that it avoids a regress whereby a value is understood *only* in terms of its functionality—which in the case of basic equality would certainly mischaracterise the phenomenon, insofar as we plainly do not value it on merely instrumental grounds, but take it to be a genuine normative commitment in its own right. As a result, we can therefore upon reflection remain committed to basic equality, even once the phenomenon has been made fully transparent to us: knowing that this is what the phenomenon consists of need not undermine our commitment to it. Indeed, it may *increase* our commitment. For example, if one previously felt assailed by sceptical doubts as to the apparent lack of good reasons for subscribing to a commitment to basic equality due to the sorts of problems outlined in chapter 2, then the considerations offered here ought to *alleviate* such worries, increasing rather than undermining confidence.

The above process of critical reflection thus cannot promise to ultimately leave everything exactly where it was. If somebody previously held a strong, but largely uninterrogated, belief in the basic equality of all humans as rooted in (say) some strong intuition that they had about our equal inherent fundamental worth as some descriptive property to do with personhood, but came to agree with the argument of this book that basic equality is rooted in a process of socially learnt and historically contingent fictions predicated on quirks of human psychology, then it cannot be denied that they will now value basic equality *differently* to how they did before. Yet that is inevitable for anyone who thinks seriously about what is at stake (though precisely how and why they change the way they come to think about what is at stake will depend on where they took themselves to be starting from in the first place, as well as where they end up). What is *not* inevitable, however—and as I have tried to show above—is that one should feel compelled to give up on basic equality. Quite the contrary.

Furthermore, even if my answer does not leave everything where it once was, it is important to realise that there was already no going back to what "once was" anyway. The question of why we are basic equals has now been asked (and not only by me), and so *some* answer needs to be given if we are to proceed as critically reflective agents. Yet once the question of why we are basic equals had been raised, the possibility of everything remaining just where it was before was thereby negated. As soon as the question was raised, reflection was initiated, and we were always going to have to see where it ended up taking us. The vindicatory account given here could thus never have been a promise that *nothing* would need to change, precisely because such an eventuality was rendered impossible by the relevant questions having already been posed. Happily, however, we can now see that what needs to change in this regard is our perspective on the status and nature of our continued normative commitment to basic equality, not the fact of there being, for us, any such commitment at all.

Conclusion

This chapter has sought to establish that the account of basic equality put forward in this book operates as both an effective *explanation* of what is at stake, whilst being something which on balance deserves our continued allegiance: it can be *vindicated*, so long as we recall that the grounds for such vindication are internal to our wider existing values, in particular an aversion to cruelty and injustice. Finally, the account is *stable under reflection*: we are able to go on endorsing it once the reasons for where our commitment to basic equality comes from, and what it is ultimately constituted by, are made fully transparent to us as reflective critical agents. As a result, we are entitled to be confident that we are *normatively justified* in continuing in this way—so long as we recall that the materials of such justification are drawn from within the practice itself. Yet there remains an outstanding challenge to the account as it stands. This is the charge that in restricting basic equality only and exclusively to human beings, the argument is unacceptably *speciesist*, and hence must ultimately be rejected. The next chapter considers this important objection, but suggests that it fails.

7

Speciesism

IF THE ARGUMENT of the previous chapter is successful, then the case for basic equality offered in this book is amenable to vindication, whilst remaining stable under reflection. But there remains an important challenge to confront, one purposefully postponed until this point. This is the charge of *speciesism*: that whilst my argument might well secure basic equality within the human set, it is nonetheless unacceptable because it continues to exclude *nonhuman animals* from equal consideration. And insofar as it does that, the objection goes, my account must be rejected. This chapter considers the objection from speciesism, but argues that not only does it fail, it ultimately gives us reasons to increase, rather than withdraw, our commitment to basic equality within—but only within—the human set.

Unpacking the Objection

To properly understand the objection from speciesism, it first needs unpacking. This might go as follows.[1] Whilst the argument for basic equality given above has provided reasons for ruling out discrimination within the human set, it nonetheless arbitrarily excludes nonhuman animals in a way analogous to the arbitrary exclusion of (say) Blacks or women under conditions where basic equality is denied to *them*. The arbitrariness lies in the fact that nonhuman animals are bearers of interests, and these interests ought to be fairly weighed in the balance along with the interests of human beings. Failing to do so threatens to constitute an arbitrary exclusion, on a par with racism, sexism, or other forms of intrahuman bigotry.

On the one hand, there is the point that some animals are in some cases bearers of greater interests than some humans, at least when comparing pair-wise individuals. For example, a normal adult dog may have a greater interest in being able to access open green spaces than a three-month-old infant; an orca may have greater interests in being able to communicate with others of its kind than does an adult human in a vegetative state. These, however, are exceptional and for the most part atypical cases. In the ordinary run of affairs, it will usually be such that the interests of the average human are weightier and more extensive than the interests of the average nonhuman animal, given the typically more sophisticated and complex needs and abilities of the former. *However*, the thought then goes, even if it is true that the average human has greater and more extensive interests than the average animal, and that it is therefore usually correct to accord an individual human greater moral weight than an individual animal, this does not tell us what to do when considering all the creatures that have interests *in the round*. So, for example, all can agree that the interests of a normal chicken are less extensive, and ultimately less morally demanding, than the interests of a normal adult human. But chickens still have interests: for example, in not being intensively battery-farmed in ways that clearly cause them suffering. Yet given that there are literally tens of millions of chickens being battery farmed every year, the *cumulative* effect of this is a gross violation of the interests of the chickens (and a huge quantity of suffering is thus taking place). The sheer scale of this interest-violation ought to be of serious concern, and to command our moral attention. For whilst nobody need make the outlandish claim that the interests of an individual chicken are on a par with those of a normal individual human adult, it is surely wrong to say that the interests of chickens should somehow not count *just because* they are chickens, and to conclude in turn that (for example) battery farming is fine so long as it marginally benefits the interests of humans (e.g., by making cheap eggs widely available), and regardless of the impact upon the chickens themselves. On the contrary, the interests of chickens *should* count, morally speaking, and especially when we are talking about what to do vis-à-vis the tens of millions of chickens whose interests are being severely violated en masse. Now, what particular stance we take towards various animal-related practices (battery farming, etc.) will depend on each specific case, as will the question of how much weight to accord to which interests and when, and for what reasons. But what the advocate of animal interests centrally seeks to claim is that to exclude the chickens *just because* they are chickens is morally unjustifiable. Specifically, it is morally unjustifiable because it is an instance of *speciesism*: it is to exclude based on arbitrary criteria—species membership—when what *ought* to matter is not what species a creature happens to be, but the fact that it has interests which are deserving of moral consideration. On this view, speciesism is revealed as a prejudice on all fours with sexism or racism, which likewise exclude the fair consideration of the interests of some individuals due to arbitrary and irrelevant criteria to do with race or sex.

If one takes this stance, then basic equality's being taken to apply within—and *only* within—the human set may appear to be worryingly morally problematic. Given that nonhuman animals are bearers of interests, how is it anything other than arbitrary to exclude their interests from consideration, and say that basic equality applies *only* to human beings? Isn't this just rank prejudice? The objection from speciesism is thus ultimately that basic equality, by restricting membership only to human animals, *doesn't go far enough*. Instead of advocating for basic equality within (and only within) the human set, and arbitrarily excluding nonhuman animals, we should abandon basic equality within the human set as itself a vehicle of injustice: the injustice of disregarding the interests of animals based on the arbitrary criteria of species. We should instead recognise animals, when it comes to the crucial dimension of their being bearers of interests, as entitled to having their interests weighed in the balance with those of humans, and thus being deserving of equal basic moral consideration accordingly, not excluded on the (arbitrary) grounds of their being a different species. Insofar as basic equality arbitrarily excludes non-human animals—the charge runs—it is speciesist. Insofar as it is speciesist, it is to be rejected.

What to say in reply? It will certainly not suffice to point to the possession of a "human essence" as the grounds for including all human animals (whatever their cognitive, emotional, physical, etc. capacities) but excluding nonhuman animals. This is for the straightforward reason that such an essence *does not exist*. Whilst the double fiction of proceeding *as if* it does, and as if it were the *only* thing that marks us humans out, can operate successfully as grounds for *inclusion* as regards all human beings, because in such cases it operates in a way that benefits all (human) comers, and out of the materials of which we have constructed a norm of fundamental equality, it cannot work analogously as a means of *excluding* nonhuman others. Appeal to essences as a means of excluding nonhuman animals will rightly be pointed to by proponents for the animals as no answer at all, because rather than this being a fiction which benefits those included, and thus can be rendered legitimate by their own lights, it now becomes the appeal to a falsehood used precisely to justify some group privileging itself at the expense of those they place themselves in positions of superiority and power over. Here the charge of speciesism as analogous to something like racism really has bite: to say that animals don't get to count because they "lack the human essence" would be to propose as a reason for exclusion something that is no good reason at all, precisely because we know that *humans* don't have the human essence, either. It would be to trade on an untruth, in the way that racist or sexist or otherwise bigoted views paradigmatically trade when coming up with "reasons" for excluding some kinds of human, such as the false claims that "Blacks are less intelligent than Whites" or that "women are by nature fitted for obedience, men for command." Insofar as these "reasons" are simply false, they cannot function *as* (genuine) reasons at all. Regarding nonhuman animals, an appeal to the "human essence" as legitimating their exclusion could only function in the same way, and thus cannot be the basis of a successful answer.

Furthermore, the opponent will be apt to point out that if the proponent of basic equality genuinely cares about preventing cruelty and injustice (as argued in chapter 6), then the best way to live up to *that* commitment is to pay more serious and sustained attention to the way that billions of animals are being treated by humans at present: not just their industrial farming in often abject conditions, but their being hunted for sport, poisoned en masse, their natural habitats destroyed, and so forth. The degradation of animal interests at the hands of humans represents perhaps the most colossal locus of human-induced cruelty and injustice of all, and an emphasis on the ways in which animals are bearers of interests, and how it is usually *we humans* who are massively violating those interests, focuses attention on this point dramatically. If basic equality is supposed to be reflectively buttressed by reflection on its acting as a block to cruelty and injustice amongst humans, then it is surely a mistake to stop reflection there. If we extend our reflection consistently, we ought to see that it is *nonhuman animals* who suffer cruelty and injustice the most—and insofar as basic equality is applied only to the set of human animals, it not only blinds us to the wider cruelty and injustice that is going on in the world, but provides illicit ideological cover for us to privilege our own species at the direct expense of the others. Again, the structural parallels with sexism or racism seem to emerge with compelling force.

Furthermore, it will be no reply here to point out that by appealing to capacities for suffering amongst the animals that the accusation of speciesism reopens the Pandora's box of problems for explaining and justifying basic equality of the sort surveyed in chapter 2—for that is rather the point. If the capacity to bear interests is made the metric of principal moral concern, and if paying attention to interest-violation regardless of whether it is occurring in a human animal or a nonhuman animal is what really counts, then we will be forced to see that the precise locus of any particular interest is not what matters, as that locus is merely contingent, and ought not to be normatively relevant.[2] Hence if we observe that (say) a chimpanzee is a bearer of more complex and weighty interests than a profoundly mentally handicapped human, then it is the chimpanzee that ought to be accorded priority—not *because* it is a chimpanzee (which fact, by itself, is irrelevant) but because its particular interests are weightier than those of this particular human. Attempting to relegate the chimpanzee to a status lower than the handicapped human would be *morally the wrong way around*. If this in turn means that enacting basic equality within the human set, but *only* for humans, is therefore ruled out by the same logic, well then so much the worse for basic equality within the human set. Better to do away with this self-serving arbitrary restriction of normative concern and focus on what really matters: paying attention to the interests of sentient creatures wherever those happen to be located. Basic equality for humans, the charge again runs, does not go far enough: we need basic equality *within the set of all those creatures who are capable of bearing interests*. This is a radical position, to be sure—but basic equality for all humans was radical once, too. Why stop there? Onwards, upwards, towards further moral progress.

Interests, Species, Relationships

When presented in this manner, the argument from speciesism can seem powerful. But I do not think that it is—indeed, I do not think that it is ultimately even coherent. The reasons for this have already been given in a pair of brilliant articles, first by Cora Diamond, and later by Bernard Williams, and which I adapt here with specific reference to defending basic equality within (and only within) the human set.[3] The essence of the reply as I (re)construct it is to *accept* that our preference for humans is, indeed, a form of prejudice. But unlike racism or sexism, it is a prejudice we are justified in going on with, not least because it constitutes the very grounds for making any relevant normative judgements in this area whatsoever. Insofar as the accusation of speciesism fails to appreciate this, it fails to appreciate the incoherence of its own position.

Before getting to these points in more detail, however, it is important to stress that the gap between the advocate of animal interests and the proponent of basic equality need not be as wide as the above has presented it as being. For there are really *two* objections worth distinguishing here. The first is the general plea that *we ought to take the interests of animals more seriously than we typically do.* The second is that *commitment to basic equality for humans (and only humans) rests on speciesism, and for that reason it is to be rejected.* Regarding the first point, the proponent of basic equality need have no profound quarrel with the proponent of animal interests. For whilst it is true that the defender of basic equality says that this sort of commitment applies only within the set of human beings, this leaves entirely indeterminate what might then be thought about the interests of animals outside the set. It in no way follows from being committed to basic equality within the human set that one must somehow view those who fall outside of that set—i.e., nonhuman animals—as somehow being *without* any claim to moral consideration whatsoever, that they somehow simply do not count.[4] To think that this must follow is just a mistake. After all, there is no contradiction in somebody affirming, on the one hand, that human beings are each other's basic equals, whilst *also* thinking we should seriously concern ourselves with (say) the appalling suffering perpetrated by battery hen farming, insofar as the interests of chickens are also deserving of some important level of moral consideration (and so on with other animals, in other cases). Being committed to basic equality for humans entails *nothing* about what to say and do with regards the moral claims of animals, which the proponent of basic equality certainly need not deny, and which they may take a wide range of possible stances regarding. We will come back to this point later, but making it explicit here helps us to see that the real challenge to the commitment to basic equality as argued for in this book is the specific claim that it rests on *speciesism*—i.e., the use of arbitrary prejudice—and that insofar as it does that, it is therefore normatively compromised.

In order to address this much more serious charge, we can begin by putting pressure on the idea that "speciesism" is indeed straightforwardly akin to prejudices like racism or sexism. As Diamond points out, if this were really so, then there ought properly to be no meaningful difference between, say, a funeral held for a dog versus a funeral held for a person, other than a regard to the relevant interests involved in each case (the strangeness of that formulation ought already to alert one to the fact that something is going wrong here). Or more dramatically, if the only thing that really matters, normatively speaking, is which creatures' interests are being looked after and how, then what is "the difference between miscegenation and *chacun à son gout* with consenting adult gorillas"?[5] The point being that we *do* think there is a difference in these cases, yet it is not to do with merely the interests of the relevant parties. A prohibition on interracial coupling within the human set is *not the same kind of thing* as a prohibition on interspecies coupling. Yet this is not (or at least not only) because of the interest that are or are not involved in either case. Our objection in the case of human-gorilla sex is *substantively different* from the case of miscegenation, not because of the interests involved, but because the ethical relationships we stand in towards gorillas (and other animals) are not of the same kind as relationships we stand in towards other human beings (whatever race they happen to be). An objection to sex with gorillas is *not* a prejudice akin to the prejudice against miscegenation, and thus likewise to be overcome.[6] The reason for this lies in the fact that human beings have complex and nuanced understandings of *how we behave towards them*, which are not the same as our complex and nuanced understandings of *how we behave towards each other*—and neither of which reduce to the metric of weighing interests, wherever those just so happen to be located.

The point here is that making the weighing of interests normatively fundamental, with animals and humans in the final instance
featuring as essentially nothing more than receptacles for such
interests, profoundly mischaracterises the nuance and complexity
of human relationships to the animal world, flattening and simpli-
fying those to the point of serious ethical distortion. We can see
this better by recalling that we stand in multiple, complex, and
sometimes perhaps even contradictory, relationships to different
kinds of animals in different ways. Consider the following cases.

With regards to the gorilla, we have complex ethical responses
to this kind of being. It is not simply a case of "do not have sex with
that kind of thing," but also "do not eat that kind of thing, either,"
and similarly, "don't hunt it for trophies" (though matters have
certainly been different in the past in these regards). Contemporary sensibilities, at least for those in the (relatively fortunate and economically secure) West, are highly attuned to the
similarities between gorillas and ourselves: we share a common
ancestry, and so the fact that they look quite a bit like us is no accident, or mere superficiality, and that *means* something to us, in
a way that isn't the case with (say) geckos or toads. Neither is it a
coincidence or mere incidental fact that it is *we* who are destroying
their habitats and putting at great risk the continued existence of
this variety of natural wonder, with whom we share an unusually
close biological link. A gorilla is much more than just a particular
locus of interests, and thus what we think the appropriate ethical
response to it should be is both more subtle and more complex
than simply working out what its interests are and weighing those
in the balance with other interest-bearers (though actually, given
how much of a mess we've made of things, that will often be a
pretty good place to start).

But now take another example: a cow raised for slaughter. We
understand that "do not have sex with this kind of thing" applies
also in this case, but we (or at least, many of us) *do* eat this kind of
thing—unless it's a dairy cow, in which case we do not eat this
kind of thing *yet*. And some cultures have strict rules about *how*

this kind of thing gets properly killed in order to be eaten, as in the Jewish and Islamic traditions, where specific means of slaughter is often part of an understanding of how that creature is shown respect at the moment its life is taken. Modern Western industrial farming is often, in fact, much *less* preoccupied with showing respect—but we (i.e., the mass-consuming public) shield ourselves from confronting what that means for the cows and for ourselves by having somebody else do it for us, out of sight, such that we don't have to think too much about it. We might of course sincerely prefer for cows not to be made to suffer at the moment of their death, and likewise for their various other interests to be promoted as much as is feasible whilst they are still alive, all the while knowing they are nonetheless ultimately destined for our table. But even so, far more is afoot here than merely the interests that a cow happens to bear. A cow is not merely a receptacle of interests in principle interchangeable with any other sentient creature on the planet: it is *a cow*, and that means certain stands and attitudes apply to it that will not be the case with regards other kinds of animal. And to recall another point of Diamond's, we readily understand why the vegetarian might adamantly refuse to eat the cow that had lived a blissful life free from suffering and only died because it had been hit by lightning. The cow's interests don't, in this case, come into it: for the vegetarian, the cow may remain something that she does not eat, for reasons that may well still apply for her, just as deeply, regardless of the fact that it was a lightning strike rather than a bolt gun that caused the fatal outcome. For her, the cow is *a thing she does not eat*.

Consider, now, a different class of animal: the pet. These are creatures we take into our homes, and indeed our lives, and extend towards them a much greater degree of companionship than we do with wild animals (e.g., gorillas) or food animals (e.g., cows). It is categorically central—and we expect children to grasp this from a young age, and for the most part they grasp it very easily—that the family cat *is not for eating*. And that it is not for eating is not to do with how good or bad it might taste, nor with whether its interests were violated by us killing it for food. It is not for eating *because it is not that kind of thing*. Of course, what counts as a pet, and thus at the very least what is not for eating, varies across cultures. In the West, dogs are very much not for eating; in South Korea, it is not always so. But that this thing is a pet establishes a very different set of ethical relationships between humans and the animal in question than if it were one of the other classes of animals. My mother tells the story of when she was a little girl, growing up in rural 1960s France, and how she fed and loved what she believed to be her own pet rabbit. When she came home one day, was served dinner, ate it, and then went out to feed her rabbit only to find the hutch ominously empty, her disgust and trauma— which she remembers vividly to this day—were about far more than what interests the rabbit did or did not bear. Or consider these varying scenarios. A family's beloved pet Labrador passes away, and they hold a funeral for the dog, so that the deeply upset children (aged eight and ten) can say their goodbyes. This is readily intelligible to us. Now consider the same family, but instead of holding a funeral for the dog, they butcher it so that its flesh can be fed to the neighbourhood crows, with the rest of its remains used as fertiliser for the garden. Things now seem radically different; was that ever even a pet at all, if that is how they treat it in death? Now consider the same family, but this time whilst they do hold the funeral for the dog, they don't bother holding one for granny, who happened to die the same week ("we loved her, of course, but it was just too expensive"). Now imagine that the family not only does not hold a funeral for granny (yet does for Rover), but turns *granny* into crow food. Clearly, there is much more going on here, in our range of attitudes and responses, than simply a regard for interests.

Take, now, another important class of animal: the *pest* or *vermin*. These include vectors of disease, like rats, or destroyers of our assets, like locusts or woodworms. Such classes of animals we characteristically see ourselves as, so to speak, at war with. To be sure, it is a war in which we are for the most part overwhelming winners. We trap, poison, and generally exterminate these "enemies" in huge numbers. And insofar as we consider this legitimate, we do so, it seems, because we think of it as a form of self-defence. In turn, we tend to think that the interests of these perceived assailants *don't count*, or at least, that they count a lot less than do ours, those of our pets, and even of animals who will be our future meals.[7] But if all that matters is the fair weighting and consideration of interests per se, and if there are so many rats in the world whose interests are being seriously harmed from the effects of our poisonings and trappings, such that it is determined that this properly outweighs *our* interests in killing them, and hence that we should make way for the rats, then it would seem that we are doing something profoundly wrong as things stand.[8] (The intuitive implausibility of *that* conclusion speaks, I think, for itself—but more on this below.)

Similarly, there is the class of animal that we might think of as the temporary enemy: the man-eating tiger, or the great white shark that has recently developed a taste for surfers. We don't *normally* kill this kind of thing (we've shifted, for the most part, to a mindset of trying to preserve the remaining ones, after we wiped out so many of their forebears), but in special circumstances, we might. Then there is the *game animal*, whom we hunt for sport as well as for the table. Not all animals count as game (deer do, in the right circumstances, but horses don't; trout is game in the UK, but carp is categorically not—although it is in Poland). Furthermore, there are *rules* for how you hunt game properly, which typically means doing so "fairly," that is, according to agreed-upon conventions that provide a "sporting chance" for the quarry. The deer on the Scottish Highlands may be shot, but it must be shot well, by a good marksman, ideally through the heart so that it dies quickly, whilst it is impermissible to first capture it by holding it in place with a leg-trap. The salmon must be caught by rod and line, and only in the lower reaches of the river, not dynamited when it has reached the spawning grounds. Whilst the opponent who alleges speciesism in the name of promoting animal interests will likely be horrified by such examples, they will nonetheless be getting something wrong if they think that the only issue at play in these cases is (or should be) the fair weighting of animal interests. Human lives—and thus, human ethical relationships to animals— are vastly more complex than that.

As the above cases have sought to establish, ethical considerations vis-à-vis animals are replete with complexity, and are not properly characterised as being simply about animals having the capacity (as indeed they do) to bear interests. Furthermore, if it were as the proponents of speciesism claim, and the only thing that mattered were the interests of animals per se, then presumably we ought rightly to concern ourselves not only with the impacts upon animal interests that people cause to animals, but which *animals* cause to animals, and also which animals experience entirely independently, absent any human involvement at all. My suggestion here, following Williams, is that to adopt such a view is plainly absurd: that to go about trying to prevent the lions from eating the gazelles, or to insist that vaccination drives for alpine marmots be weighed in the balance with those for human children, is to go quite severely off the rails.[9] And not simply because these things would be impractical, or because, for example, human children are assumed to come out first when it comes to scarce resource allocation due to their usually weightier interests, but because to even *think* like that evidences a deep distortion of well-regulated ethical thought.[10] But if so, this in turn means admitting that what actually matters to us isn't animal interests per se, but the kinds of animal interests that become germane with regards to questions about what *we* do to *them*. Yet if so admitted, this leads to a dilemma for those alleging speciesism, who can respond either of two ways: either by taking a hard-line stance of extensive revisionism regarding our values in this area and saying that we *should* embrace such radically counterintuitive conclusions, or accepting the reality of the nuanced complexity of our relationships to animals and their interests and proceeding accordingly. In either case, however, both ought properly to end up in the same place: the realisation that affirming basic equality within the human set is *not* tantamount to a prejudice like racism or sexism, and thus that we need not give it up on the alleged grounds of needing to avoid "speciesism." The reasons are as follows.

The Soft Reply

Let us take the softer response first, which fully accepts the evident truth of the matter that our ethical relationship to the animal world is not characterised simply by a preoccupation with animal interests per se, but is far richer and more nuanced. Once we see that there is more afoot here than merely aggregating interests, and once we see that animals (like people) matter to us not simply because they happen to be loci for interests, but because they are complex creatures that we have developed complex ethical relationships to, and all of which are embedded in rich histories and extensive cultural practices, then the analogy between (say) racism and sexism on the one hand, and "speciesism" on the other, simply breaks down. Animal interests *do* matter to us, but not all animals matter to us to the same degree, and in the same kinds of ways, and what matters to us about them is not simply their interests. We care differently about cats than we do about cows than we do about gorillas than we do about rats. But by the same lights, we care differently about *human beings* than we do about (other things being equal) animals. It is thus *true* that we have a prejudice in favour of humans over the many different kinds of animals. But this prejudice is not arbitrary and without good foundation (as in the case of a prejudice based on race, or gender, which make appeal to lies and falsehoods so as to illegitimately entrench domination). It is rather a function of the complex ethical relationships we really do stand in towards each other *as humans*, and which are not on a level with the (highly variable) relationships we also have towards (different kinds of) animals. It is, so to speak, a deep fact about us that we think humans matter more than animals, and that we think some kinds of animals matter more to us, and in different kinds of ways, than do others. Part of what is deep about this fact is, furthermore, that to an important degree we learn what it is to be a human, and why that has especial ethical significance, by learning why we are *not* animals (of the many varying sorts), and why we treat them differently to how we treat each other.

Given that this is how we are, however, there is nothing inherently wrong with drawing a boundary around the set of specifically human animals and saying: *this kind of thing is special to us, and accordingly it is going to be treated specially.* Basic equality is a way of doing that, and doing it powerfully, and to that extent it reflects the preexisting fact about us that interests per se are not the only thing that matter in our ethical lives, and that whilst we manifestly care about animals in important and various ways, we ultimately care *more* about human beings—both about their interests, but also and more fundamentally about them as a class of being. Insofar as we care more about human beings, and if, as per the arguments above, we also believe that according them basic equality is a good way of not only affirming that we care, but making good in practice upon that caring, then we have good reason to go on supporting basic equality, coherently denying that it is normatively on a par with sexism or racism. Crucially, we can here usefully recall the point already made above: that *nothing follows* from the mere fact that we accord basic equality (only) within the human set regarding how we should treat nonhuman creatures. This latter matter is left entirely open. Anybody who concludes "well, if the animals are not our basic equals, then anything goes as regards them!" is not only making a logical error, but is failing to appreciate that it is *not true* that "anything goes" with regards the animals. The fact that we accord basic equality within the human set does nothing to change this. It merely says that when you are dealing with a human animal, certain very special conditions apply. What conditions apply when dealing with a nonhuman animal are left undetermined by the ascription of basic equality to humans.[11] And we may well, as it happens, in fact want to do much more to promote the interests of (various kinds of) animals than is typically done at present. Thus the vegetarian who opposes animal testing and avoids using pesticides, yet does so whilst continuing to affirm basic equality within (and only within) the human set, is not making some mistake, not running afoul of any sort of contradiction or inconsistency or inability to follow through on her own principles. She is *not* a self-deluded parallel to the benevolent racist, or the paternally restrained sexist, unable to see that her preference for her own species is a mere arbitrary distinction that should carry no normative weight. On the contrary, her preference for her own species is anything but arbitrary, whilst her having it does nothing to preclude her from also caring about other species (albeit in different ways, and often with lower priority and lesser intensity). A preference for one's own species is not the same thing as a preference for one's own race or one's own sex, because the relationships we stand in towards animals are quite properly not of the same kind, nor of the same ethical significance to us, as the kinds of (themselves highly variable) relationships that we stand in with regards our fellow humans. Accordingly, the charge of "speciesism" being a form of illegitimate prejudice on a par with racism or sexism simply fails to obtain.

The Hard-Liner

This answer, however, will not satisfy the hard-liner, who says: this is nothing more than yet further rationalisation of the unjustified prejudice for human over nonhuman interests. Rather than capitulating in the face of the nuance and complexity of human ethical relationships to animals, they will say, the point here is to be *radically revisionary*: we must *abandon* the currently existing way of going on, and this is the radical upshot that correct philosophy delivers in this area. Interests, they steadfastly insist, are what *should* really matter most, and the fact that our existing practices and values don't realise this, and don't accord the impartial weighting of interests regardless of where those are located priority, merely illustrates the inadequacy, the corruption even, of our existing practices. Perhaps we *should*, when on balance we think it will do more harm than good, stop the lions eating the gazelles, and set out to vaccinate the marmots, and so forth[12]—and that my dismissing this as absurd merely shows how deeply entrenched the prevailing speciesist worldview currently is. Failure to see this is as ideologically motivated and self-serving as racism or sexism, the hard-liner insists. For would not the racist likewise say: "but giving ethical priority to Whites is simply our ethical practice; we have complex relationships to Blacks which are not the same as to Whites, and we learn what it is to be a White by learning what it is to not be a Black, etc., etc.—and that's a deep fact about us we should simply accept as our starting point"? Hence does not the charge of speciesism hold good after all, because what really is the difference here? In turn, the hard-liner will claim, the point is to get rid of *any* such appeal to "local ethical practices," and focus instead on something universal and nonparochial—which is what the emphasis on interests, wherever those happen to be found, precisely provides.

Alarm bells should sound, however, at the demand for such radical revision to our ethical sentiments. For on what basis does the philosopher claim to overrule all our existing ethical practices and values, replacing them with the alleged absolute and singular priority of interests above all else?[13] Why should we believe them when they tell us that we are wrong in all the ways we view and relate to animals, and that animals (as well, indeed, as people) are at root nothing more than nexuses of interests, the weighing and balancing of which has final normative priority? We are surely owed some story here. They are, after all, asking rather a lot from us.

Yet what could that story possibly be? As Diamond and Williams have pointed out, it is *not true* that (for example) suffering—a typically paradigmatic instance of the violation of a creature's interests—is a self-evident normative phenomenon that we must automatically be motivated to respond to, and thereby seek to reduce or eliminate merely as such, wherever and whenever it happens to be found.[14] On the contrary, suffering is something that matters *to us*, given where we are starting out, that is, due to our existing lives and the values we have inherited from our upbringings and wider cultures. It is categorically not the case that suffering matters "from the point of view of the universe," because there *is* no such point of view (and even if there were, it wouldn't be ours). In order for an appeal to the badness of suffering to get a grip on us, it needs to appeal to *our* values—and those, ultimately, are human values. The same is true of interests generally: we care about interests (both animal and human) because of *our* values, that *we* bring to bear, not because interests are themselves somehow normatively basic, self-evident, or invested with automatic moral force.[15] Yet one of the central human values is that humans stand in different kinds of ethical relationship towards each other than they do towards (different kinds of) animals. The extent to which we care about interests is thus *predicated upon* the values that we are already operating with. The normative salience of interests, let alone our proper ethical response to different interests in different circumstances, does not (as the hard-line opponent above needs to presuppose) act as something *prior to*, or *independent of*, the human values we necessarily operate through and make appeal to. In order for interests to be able to get a normative grip on us, we need our human values to be up and running in the first place. But then, it is a constitutive feature of those human values that we do not think that interests are the only things that have value, nor that human and animal relationships are constituted only by reference to interests. Hence it is ultimately incoherent to suppose that our complex ethical relationships to animals (as well as to each other) could be revised by an appeal to the priority of interests, for that priority can only make sense when first presupposing the existence of the very ethical relationships that it is being proposed we overturn. But that ultimately means starting from, rather than overcoming or abandoning, what Williams fittingly calls "the human prejudice."

Once this is understood, we can see why the charge that the "speciesist" is on a level with the racist or sexist when appealing to existing ethical practices as justification for grounds for exclusion is incorrect. The defender of basic equality as obtaining only within the human set points out that we have to work outwards from the human values that we already have. They are thus correct when they say that as things stand, on questions of value *there is only the human perspective.* Animals do not have normative values, and this systematically conditions how we interact with them, and view them in relation to us, something itself heavily inflected by the fact that they are always more or less in our power, and we are only ever rarely and fleetingly in theirs. As Williams reminds us, this means that when it comes to the different kinds of animals, it will always be a question of *how we are to treat them.*[16] It is just not like this, however, when it comes to (say) racist or sexist differentiations and exclusions. For it is simply false that there is "only the male point of view" or "only the White point of view." The normative points of view of, for example, Black people and women *do* exist, and certainly matter, at the very least to those individuals themselves.[17] To suppose otherwise would be another of the lies that bigoted arrangements use to (fraudulently) legitimate the local arrangements for domination. Likewise, it is not only ever a question of "how the Whites will treat the Blacks" or "how the men will treat the women" (even if, for sociological reasons, that is how it tends to go in a particular locale as a brute function of who wields power). Oppressed humans can—and if enabled to do so, most certainly will—speak for themselves, and demand that *their* point of view be taken properly into account. And one of the first things they will typically demand is an end to the condition whereby their dominators are able to view them merely as objects subject to whatever treatment they deign to dole out. Or to put the same point in a different way: the oppressed will demand that their oppressors *stop treating them like animals.* For they are not animals, and everybody, when they are being truthful, damn well knows it. The oppressed will in turn typically call for the chance to have a say in controlling their own destinies, and that the prevailing normative attitudes be (re)arranged in turn so as to make central the essential rightness of their claim to do so.[18] There is simply no parallel here with animals, for when it comes to animals, how "we" should treat "them" is "the only question there could be."[19] "Speciecism" is thus not on a level with intrahuman bigotries like racism or sexism.[20]

Here the account comes full circle. For basic equality, we can now add, is one of the most powerful and historically striking *success stories* in making central this fact about previously oppressed human beings: that they are, precisely, not animals—that they have their own normative viewpoint and a rightful claim to a say in controlling their own destiny. It is for this reason a grave mistake to think that basic equality is merely another bigoted prejudice, this time introducing a rank speciesism in place of a rank racism, or a rank sexism, or any other form of intrahuman exclusion. Basic equality just is not like that. Not because it isn't speciesist. It *is* speciesist. But the speciesism it rests upon is not a rank bigotry, but a principled and defensible ethical position, which is furthermore the grounds for a coherent normative assessment in this area *tout court*, due to the underlying fact that there is only ever the human perspective to take in these matters. Rather than giving up on basic equality, we have every reason to continue to commit to it as fully as possible.

Animal Rights?

The above has sought to respond to the charge of speciesism as manifested from a fundamentally *welfarist* perspective on animals, which suggests that what matters is the promotion or interests wherever those happen to be found (regardless of species). By contrast, proponents of *animal rights* may eschew a welfarist perspective and insist that animals—just like humans—have a moral status sufficiently important such that they can only be properly respected and defended by our according rights to the animals, and which impose duties on us in turn, albeit with the specifics depending on the class of animal in question, and the situation at hand.[21] Ought proponents of animal rights object to basic equality for humans? I think not.

First, and as emphasised above, nothing necessarily follows from the according of basic equality only to human animals regarding how we should view and treat nonhuman animals. One can be a proponent of basic equality within (and only within) the human set, and yet still hold that the animals' interests in various regards are sufficiently important such that we ought to conclude that certain animals have certain rights. Basic equality need not be zero-sum: just because we view human beings as a special class of creature, it does not follow that other classes of creature don't matter and simply get nothing. On the contrary, they evidently *do* matter, and we can reflect that in various ways, for example by according them certain rights when we find that to be appropriate. The proponent of basic equality for humans can also be a proponent of rights for animals.[22]

What the proponent of basic equality denies, of course, is that animals and humans will always have *the exact same* rights, and to the same extent. Yet this is something that, presumably, most proponents of animal rights themselves already agree with. For we do not typically think that all animals get the same rights as each other, either. One may well think that the interests of a cognitively sophisticated creature like a chimpanzee are so significant that the chimpanzee ought to be accorded certain rights to protect those interests, such as the right not to be tortured psychologically, even if left physically undamaged. By contrast, we may not accord such rights to less cognitively sophisticated creatures—hamsters, say— and yet insist that in both cases the hamsters and the chimpanzees have sufficiently weighty interests that both have a right not to be subjected to physical cruelty, as well as other rights such as to be fed and looked after by humans that have them in their power. By contrast, we tend to withhold this right from creatures like urban rats, which we perceive as a threat to us due to their being vectors of disease (there is little doubt that the slow death-by-poisoning inflicted on millions of rats each year is cruel), whilst thinking them less applicable to creatures like wild sea fish, which we capture for food (and so on, in different kinds of cases).

Yet it does not follow that because we typically think that the rights of humans are of a weightier sort than those of animals (and that different animals also have different kinds of rights), that we always and uniformly privilege the rights of a human over those of an animal, regardless. Questions of trade-offs between the rights of animals and humans are complex, and that is part of the point.[23] The proponent of basic equality for humans will say (as presumably would most of those who do not support basic equality even for humans) that in a choice between saving the life of a human child and that of an adult chimpanzee, it is the former that ought to take precedence over the latter. Yet she could also say that the right of the chimpanzee not to be subjected to psychological torment is sufficiently weighty that it defeats the interest that a scientist has in whatever might be learnt from subjecting the chimpanzee to torture. It is, in other words, no part of a commitment to basic equality to insist that human interests (let alone whims) defeat animal interests every time, and automatically. Instead, we need to recognise that precisely because the relationships between humans and animals are complex—and in turn, so are the questions about what rights different creatures have, and what to do when those rights potentially come into conflict—that no straightforward story can be extracted about what an affirmation of basic human equality entails about the rights of animals. Absent specific examples that would need to be assessed on their own merits relative to particular and precise circumstances, insisting on the rights of animals carries no determinate normative force: we always need more information before deciding what to say. Thus, for example, a person who claimed a right to torture chimpanzees just because it amused her to do so, and when pressed on the legitimacy of such behaviour replied "well, I'm a human and this thing is not, so I have a right to abuse it if I like" really would be violating the rights of the chimpanzee, and would be offering an illegitimately speciesist "justification" to boot (scare quotes appropriate, because in this instance, such a response would indeed amount to nothing more than rank bigotry). But the proponent of basic human equality can readily agree with advocate for animal rights that what this person is doing is wrong, and that they ought to stop doing it (and if necessary, *be stopped* from doing it). Somebody who thinks that because a chimpanzee (or any other animal) is not a human, *therefore* it has no rights, and indeed perhaps therefore has no moral standing at all, is making both an ethical and a logical mistake. Yet neither of these mistakes is licensed, let alone entailed, by a commitment to basic equality within the human set. What rights animals have, in what circumstances, and how those rights measure up vis-à-vis the activities and interests of humans in given cases, is a complex, open question, which the commitment to basic equality itself is radically underdetermining of any answers to.

It may well be the case that, as some proponents of animal rights allege, our current practices display such a level of inconsistency and hypocrisy regarding our treatment of animals as to constitute a kind of moral schizophrenia.[24] It may also be the case that the more we reflect on what we do to animals, the more we come to feel the need to revise and change our practices in ways that benefit them (perhaps even at some sacrifice to ourselves). But the proponent of basic equality within (and only within) the human set is not precluded from engaging in such reflection or revision, nor is the commitment to basic equality itself the primary source of any such moral schizophrenia, and nor is giving up on basic equality a necessary prerequisite for improving our treatment of the animals. Insofar as how to treat the animals is indeed a live question, it is a question orthogonal to the matter of basic equality obtaining within (and only within) the human set. It ought thus to be viewed and handled accordingly.

Of course, if a hard-line proponent of animal rights insists— against the considerations above—that animal rights *should* be treated as normatively equal with the rights of humans (and indeed, that all animals should get exactly the same rights, regardless of species), then the charge of speciesism appears to resurface once more. But really, this is just the welfarist conception in disguise. For if the charge is that *all creatures should have the same basic equal rights,* and that according basic equal rights only to those within the set of human animals whilst excluding all the nonhuman animals is "speciesist," we need to ask: on what grounds ought these equal basic rights to be apportioned between all species (or rather, between all creatures capable of experience, regardless of species)? Presumably, it will have to be some metric universally shared by all creatures—and so presumably, the metric is the capacity to have interests. But if so, we are back to the arguments considered and rejected above.

Conclusion

This chapter has attempted to show that the accusation of speciesism does not undermine allegiance to basic equality, but when properly worked through, reinforces it. This concludes the main argument of the book. What remains is to close by briefly considering the relationship between basic equality and the substantive ways in which people are treated, and why this connection likely matters if basic equality is to survive as an important normative value for us. Precisely because basic equality is historically contingent and relatively recent in its provenance, we ought to be especially sensitive to the possibility that it may prove fragile, and in need of particular care, if it is to go on doing the work that we want from it.

8

Conclusion

IN HIS GROUNDBREAKING 2008 samizdat paper on basic equality, Jeremy Waldron began by drawing a distinction between "(a) a discussion of equality as an economic or social aim, and (b) a discussion of the basic equality of all humans as a premise or assumption of moral and political thought."[1] As Waldron noted, a "tremendous amount of energy has been devoted to (a) in recent political philosophy." By contrast, regarding (b), "Analytically, the state of this discussion is a disgrace compared to that of the philosophical literature focused on (a)." Given the growing body of literature on basic equality that has since emerged, the verdict of things being a "disgrace" on this front has happily already been overcome. The hope of this book is to have gone further: to have both explained and justified our commitment to basic equality, vindicating it at the bar of critical reflection given the wider histories and commitments we currently find ourselves with.

Yet this leaves open the further question of what, if anything, the connection *between* Waldron's (a) and (b) is taken to be. What does a commitment to basic equality mean for the "economic and social" concerns that have more centrally animated egalitarian (and indeed, anti-egalitarian) thinkers in both the recent and more distant past?

It would be pleasing and neat if a tight, uncontroversial, and straightforward connection could be drawn here: if I were able to say that *because* we are basic equals (as explained and justified on the above terms), *therefore* certain specific conclusions follow about who gets precisely what, how much, and why, when it comes to things like economic resources, social standing, access to employment, educational opportunity, the materials of dignity, and so forth. But alas, it is not going to be like that.

The reason it is not going to be like that is inherent to the very basic-ness of basic equality. In order for it to *be* basic, basic equality needs to be sufficiently broad such that all humans can be included *without substantive controversy*. Yet questions of substantive distribution in economic and social affairs—of who gets what, why, and whether what they get should be equalised on some metric (and what metric that should be)—are inherently, and necessarily, going to be controversial in any cases that matter. This is because in any cases that matter people's interests, as well as their normative commitments, will come into conflict, given the fact of finite and scarce resources, coupled with the multiplicity of judgement and interpretation by different actors whom the relevant questions affect. Claims of equality on substantive matters are bound to be rejected by at least some of those they are addressed to, and for a wide variety of reasons. Any conception of basic equality that took a definite and prescriptive stance about what *follows* from basic equality in terms of economic and social distributions would thus also itself be controversial. It would in turn no longer function as a basic universal commitment, because it would be taking a partisan stance. To put the matter another way: it is a baked-in feature of Dworkin's "egalitarian plateau" that in order for the plateau to accommodate so many different and competing political and philosophical outlooks, it has to be compatible with all of them—and the only way *that* is possible is if the plateau is inherently indeterminate about what follows from being on it. If a right-libertarian like Robert Nozick, a left-liberal like John Rawls, and a socialist like G. A. Cohen are all going to inhabit the egalitarian plateau simultaneously, it is going to be necessary for the plateau to determine nothing beyond the mere fact that they all start from *there*.

Yet being on the plateau—being committed to basic equality—is not merely trivial, nor is it empty, just because at this point in our history it accommodates a wide range of substantive distributive outlooks, and by itself cannot settle further debates between those outlooks. The first reason for this is to recall that being on Dworkin's plateau is a relatively recent, historically unusual, and yet very much to be valued, political achievement. Taking an unduly narrow perspective, it might seem disappointing to discover that getting clear on the commitment to basic equality does not help contemporary political philosophers settle complex questions about who ought to get what and why. But the correct response here is to broaden out the perspective. What basic equality rules out is the converse: of saying that these people *definitely don't* get the same amount as these other people, say because of their race, or their gender, or their religion, or their caste, or their intelligence, or their physical prowess, or their virtue, or any of the other myriad bogus rationalisations humans have all too readily employed in the past to treat some as inferior to others. Again, the important work that basic equality does is primarily negative: it might not tell us what to equalise, and how, but it does tell us on what kinds of grounds we are forbidden from imposing *inequalities* on each other. Again, this is not the default state of affairs in human history, and having gotten to this point is far from nothing. To be disappointed because basic equality does not help us definitively answer substantive distributive questions is to misunderstand the kind of work it does for us, and hence the reasons we have for continuing to value it. And even here, the work basic equality does is not entirely negative, for it imposes conditions on what plausible answers to distributive questions will have to look like in terms of being intelligible to us vis-à-vis a commitment to basic equality. Historically, by no means all answers have started out from Dworkin's plateau. But ours now must, and that already begins to determine their structure, even if many different and incompatible answers may be forged in due course.

Second, as Waldron and Anne Phillips have both emphasized, the connection between economic and social equality on the one hand, and basic equality on the other, is likely to be more significant in terms of how they interact with each other dynamically over time, rather than basic equality simply informing distributive questions in a straightforward or unidirectional sense.[2] Our primary worry here should not be that basic equality offers little guidance in terms of what to do in terms of the precise settling of contested questions about distributions in social and economic affairs, but that prevailing social and economic conditions may serve to undermine commitment to basic equality, and then potentially vice versa, in an ongoing vicious cycle. As Waldron puts it:

> Indeed, we have to consider the possibility that massive economic inequality may leach into our commitment to basic equality, seeping through to undermine our adherence to fundamental principles of equal worth and equal dignity. I have argued elsewhere that how things look in society from the point of view of justice is important (even if it is not as important as how things actually are). I think we need to be concerned about whether our commitment to basic equality, deep and pervasive as it is supposed to be, is actually visible on the face of our society. How we look is partly a matter of how we have treated one another, how we have cooperated, and how we have shared the burdens and benefits of social interaction. Do we look as though we have treated one another as equals? Inequalities may be entrenched even when they are not justified; if they become well-established and visible, then we may begin to look like a society which does not accept basic equality because we are evidently not prepared to follow through on its justificatory implications.[3]

As Waldron goes on, the problem in fact cuts even deeper: "worse, the fact of economic inequality may come to be written in the visible lives of those who are most deprived. It may look not only as though they are not being treated as equals but as though they are *not* the equals of other prosperous members of society."[4]

It is not clear, however, that Waldron's emphasis on *economic* inequality is quite the right focus, or that the danger here takes precisely the form that he indicates. In the first place, the evidence of the last half-century in countries like the United States and Great Britain is that material economic inequality has exploded,[5] whilst at the same time a commitment to basic equality for racial minorities, women, homosexuals, and so forth has gone from strength to strength.[6] Whilst Waldron is surely right to draw attention to the possibility that economic inequality may leach into and undermine basic equality, the sociology of recent decades appears to tell in another direction. That *ignoring* vast disparities of wealth and income, whilst continuing to affirm basic equality, appears to be part of what is involved in adopting a commitment to it now and around here. That is, indeed, part of what being immersed in the double fiction of basic equality requires.[7]

Furthermore, whereas Waldron focuses on economic inequality and its capacity to "leach into" basic equality, this is to draw the scope of the threat too narrowly. For economic inequality is not the only way that basic equality can be severely undermined, and potentially even destroyed, by the relevant social conditions. Imagine a racial minority that is disproportionately harassed, beaten, and intimidated by the police at far higher rates than other racial groups, which is ghettoized in poor neighbourhoods, denied access to education and opportunity, and routinely treated with disdain and contempt by other sections of society whenever it ventures beyond its imposed confines. If treated in this manner, on a consistent and long-term enough basis, it is hard to believe that affirmations of the basic equality of all humans in such a scenario will come to seem anything other than at best a hollow façade, and at worst a deliberate piece of disingenuous hypocrisy adding only insult to further injury, itself part of the unjust and unequal coercive apparatus of domination being exercised over the dominated minority. And if things get bad enough, then that's what a stated commitment to basic equality will in fact really be. Yet economic inequality will be only one of the many sources of the undoing of basic equality in such conditions. Insofar as parts of different Western societies currently approximate the scenario just described, difficult questions are raised about the extent to which a commitment to basic equality, in those contexts at least, is indeed fully sincere, or whether at times its function is more perniciously ideological. Conversely, however, it is also important to remember that core institutions of Western states have surely had the opposite effect, and with oftentimes great success: of bracketing the differences between us and helping to focus attention on what we have in common, and that in turn facilitate our treatment *as* equals. The rule of law, representative democratic institutions, and the existence of a social safety net appear especially important in this regard. Maintaining these things, and ensuring that they operate as successfully into the future as possible, may thus turn out to be crucial to maintaining a sincere and truthful commitment to basic equality. This, however, is both an empirical *and* an ideological matter. Such matters cannot be settled by conceptual fiat but are open to question and contestation by those already on the egalitarian plateau.

In light of these considerations, the true nature of the danger here is revealed as being even more severe than Waldron indicates, and is structured differently. For on the account given in this book, basic equality is not a fact about us that exists independently of our contingent social practices. Instead, we are basic equals because of the complex ways in which we have come to treat each other in our recent history. Yet this is not a fixed or necessary feature of the normative possibilities available to creatures like us. If we collectively stop viewing and treating each other as basic equals, *then we will stop being basic equals*. Likewise, if we live in social conditions that persistently and severely interfere with our ability to treat and regard each other as basic equals, then basic equality will not simply go unrecognised—it will (eventually) be destroyed.

These considerations are especially important because of the centrality of being immersed in a fiction when it comes to the practice of, and ultimately the commitment to, basic equality. If we are trying to act *as if* the only thing that marks each and any of us out is our shared human essence, this fictional immersion will be very difficult to sustain if we repeatedly witness (say) one particular racial group being routinely and viciously beaten by the police; or being constantly characterised as of a criminal nature and subject to viciously dehumanising propaganda; or if women are perpetually portrayed as suited only to child-rearing and housework, and incentivized accordingly; or if an ethnic group is endlessly depicted as inherently stupid, or as living in ghettoized poverty due to congenital laziness; or if certain minorities are denied fair access to the social safety net, or not treated fairly under the rule of law—and so forth. The social conditions in which we live—not just the distribution of material assets, but the standing and status of individuals and groups in terms of how they relate to each other, as well as how the state relates to each of us individually as well as in terms of group membership—will necessarily affect our ability to remain immersed in the fiction. The more that such immersion is shattered by social conditions that draw attention to putative differences within the human set and invest those with meaning, claiming them to be relevant features of distinction and difference, the harder it will be to sustain a commitment to basic equality in terms of immersion in the fiction of a shared human essence. At the limit, such a commitment can and will be lost, if the social conditions in which we live make it impossible to consistently maintain the immersion.

Having said that, immersion is itself a complex phenomenon, not yet particularly well understood, especially when it comes to basic equality. To return to the example of going to the theatre, we all know how immersion-shattering the sound of a ringing mobile phone (especially if it is pulled out of a pocket, screen glaring) is to the experience of watching a play. On the other hand, I can attest that it is possible to immerse oneself in a story about a boy being adrift on the Pacific Ocean in a lifeboat with a Bengal tiger— even though the "tiger" is quite clearly a puppet being operated by three adult humans on a stage in London. Human imagination is rich and complex, and so also is our capacity for fictional immersion. What breaks our immersion, and what doesn't, is not a straightforward or always obvious matter. Similarly, in the social realm, we clearly *are* able to balance knowledge of sometimes enormous inequalities of material distribution with an ongoing immersion in the fiction that the only thing that defines any of us is our shared human essence. The extent of differences in treatment, status, dignity, and so on that we are prepared to countenance as compatible with commitment to basic equality seems to be different, however, and to vary considerably across contexts, and depending on what exactly is at stake. Nonetheless, whilst it is impossible to specify in advance what the limits and degrees of compatibility between basic inequality and various forms of distributive inequality are, it is vanishingly unlikely that such balancing is without limits: grossly unequal conditions and treatments will eventually undermine commitment to basic equality, if pushed sufficiently far. There is, clearly, a lot we don't know here. But given what is at stake, that gives us ample reason to be cautious, and to be disinclined towards finding out where the breaking points lie.[8]

Waldron's (a) and (b) thus can and do interact, in important ways. We have reason to worry about both, and reason to worry about them in the light of each other. Of course, that does not by itself provide the answers regarding what a commitment to (b) requires in terms of (a). Disagreement here is inevitable, and experience shows that it will be profound and protracted, even when rooted in good faith (and let alone when it isn't). But insofar as we are indeed committed to basic equality, and insofar as we recognise that the normative justification for this commitment rests primarily in its negative value in preventing (or at least mitigating) cruelty and injustice, that ought to focus our attention on whether the social conditions in which we expect basic equality to go on being a meaningful commitment are truthfully conducive to that end. At the very least, being honest about these matters is a good place to start. Having said that, however, there is also something important to be said for keeping (a) and (b) apart. Remaining immersed in the fiction of basic equality is likely to be easier if most people see it as entailing almost nothing about (a), not least because this enables us to disagree vigorously about what (a) requires, without this either undermining our commitment to (b), or the belief that our interlocutors at least share this common ground with us, if nothing else. For as emphasised above, that common ground is a major historical achievement, and one not to be undermined lightly. Alas, nothing here is likely to be easy or straightforward. But that is just how it is going to be in these matters, and it would be foolish to pretend otherwise.

I have emphasised repeatedly in this work that basic equality is not the norm in human history, and that even for us it is a remarkably recent development (and even then, with the large caveat that beyond the confines of polite company its victory is by no means complete or fully secure). It is something we have developed as a contingent response to our recent ethical and political histories, but one that, given those histories, and the values we currently hold in light of them, we have excellent reason to go on adhering to. I have however said nothing in this book about, broadly speaking, *non*-Western political societies, for two principal reasons. First, I do not know enough about them, and second, telling a relevant story about the presence or absence of basic equality in other societies, on the kind of account given above, *requires* knowing something substantive about them. Nonetheless, it is part of my position that something like the above explanatory matrix (or if one prefers, genealogy) is in principle generalisable to other contexts: explaining how (and if) basic equality can successfully come to take hold in non-Western locales will need to employ the above materials, though in precisely what manner they are assembled—and hence what story ultimately gets told—will necessarily be different, because of the differences that exist out there in the real world in the rich and complex histories of different regions and peoples.

Yet precisely because the rise of basic equality as enjoyed in the developed West is contingent and recent, such a commitment might also turn out to be easily lost. There are likely many routes by which this might happen (and it would be very unwise to attempt to predict the future on this score). But there is every reason to believe—and history makes this plain—that if this commitment is indeed lost, things will become significantly worse as a result. There is no arc to the moral universe, let alone one that bends towards justice. Things can deteriorate, as well as improve, and it is up to us to try and ensure that they go one way rather than the other. Judgements about how best to remain committed to basic equality—and what social conditions are needed in order to extend this into the future—will inevitably be controversial, dispute about them eternally ongoing. For these reasons, such judgements really do matter, and are worth treating with the utmost seriousness, no matter how hard the task proves. Indeed, a genuine commitment to basic equality demands of us precisely such seriousness.

NOTES

Preface

1. Acetaminophen, for North American readers.

2. There is a not unrelated question about whether Mountain Rescue should pick up foolish climbers (etc.) *at all*, given the expense of doing so incurred by society at large, and the fact that foolish climbers (etc.) have chosen to put themselves in harm's way. But that is a separate question: I take it that even those sceptical as to whether Mountain Rescue teams should indiscriminately assist those in distress are focused on the need for individuals to take responsibility for their actions, rather than it being a question of the characteristic features of distressed individuals that determines whether or not they should get help in the first place.

3. It is significant, however, that the discourse around the migrant crisis is *not* conducted in terms of the fundamental status of refugees as being somehow lesser than that of (e.g.) UK citizens: nobody is claiming that it is OK to let migrants drown *because they are somehow worth less, or of a fundamentally lower status*. When the commentator Katie Hopkins began to venture down this path, comparing refugees and migrants to "cockroaches" in a 2015 column for the *Sun* newspaper, the response was one of near-universal condemnation, and this seems to have begun the subsequent implosion of her media career. See, e.g., John Plunkett, "Katie Hopkins: Sun Migrants Article Petition Passes 200,000 Mark," *Guardian*, 20 April 2015, https://www.theguardian.com/media/2015/apr/20/katie-hopkins-sun-migrants-article-petition-nears-180000-mark.

Chapter 1. The Basic Problem

1. Dworkin 1983, 25.

2. For example, and representing only the very tip of the iceberg, Sen 1992; Dworkin 2000; Temkin 1986; Parfit 1997; Frankfurt 1997; O'Neill 2008.

3. On there being two distinct strands of thought about basic equality in the Western tradition—equal worth and equal authority—see Kirby 2018.

4. Waldron 2003, 2005, 2008, 2012, 2017.

5. Arneson 2015.

6. Williams 2006a, 155; see also Williams 2014.

7. Waldron 2008, 7.

8. Our thinking here reflects a still-strong commitment to the idea of there being a "Great Chain of Being," which is found across many human societies, albeit with variations. In the Western Christian tradition, the chain posits God at the top, creatures like angels below him, ourselves below the angels, and then all of the other animals below us, who are ranked hierarchically in turn. As David Livingstone Smith puts it, "The Great Chain is considered by historians to be a moribund artifact of the neoplatonic synthesis of Platonic and Aristotelian ideas that disappeared in the wake of the Darwinian revolution. But even a cursory examination of the sorts of moral distinctions that come naturally to us shows that the idea of a normative hierarchy is still very much alive in our moral psychology. All of us, it seems, attribute different degrees of intrinsic value to different kinds of things. We regard our own kind as having the greatest value and think of animals as having greater value than plants. We esteem 'higher' animals like primates more than 'lower' animals like invertebrates (notice that terms like 'higher' and 'lower,' which roll off the tongue so easily, are hierarchical and ultimately normative notions that are inconsistent with a scientific conception of the biosphere)" (Smith 2014, 821). Indeed, as Smith also points out, the very term "primate" is Latin for "of the highest rank" (2021, chap. 6).

9. This claim is shared by those animal rights activists who object to us drawing a distinction between humans and nonhumans; indeed, one way of construing the claim of some animal rights activists is that the equal consideration extended within the human set be expanded outwards so that equal consideration be accorded to, e.g., all living creatures capable of experiencing pain, or all creatures that can be construed as having interests, and so on. In chapter 7, I will cast doubt on the likelihood that we do indeed have good reason to expand the set of equal consideration to human and nonhuman animals alike.

10. Kant 1996, 82–98, 143–60.

11. Hoekstra 2012 for detailed discussion.

12. Waldron 2003, chap. 2.

13. Locke 1960, 271.

14. Waldron 2003, 241–43. For scepticism about the claim that theism will help us resolve issues around basic equality, see Kelly 2010, 62–68; Sangiovanni 2017, chap. 1. On the important connection between belief in basic equality and earlier Christian morality, as refracted through Nietzsche's searing analysis, see Leiter 2019—though my hope in this book is to resist Leiter's sceptical (Nietzschean) suggestion that we ought to give up on basic equality insofar as we've given up on God.

15. And even *within* polite society, there is a difference between publicly affirming a claim and sincerely believing it in private. As Judith Shklar reminds us, hypocrisy

in public performance can often be conducive to equality in political practice (Shklar 1984, 77). Anne Phillips (2021, chaps. 1 and 2) has recently drawn attention to the ways in which we frequently fail to live up to the ideal of basic equality in practice, though I believe she goes too far in claiming that this somehow gives the lie to the ideal itself; more on this at various points in what follows.

16. Johnson 2013.

17. Rosenblatt 2018, 235–37; Misak 2020, 229.

18. On the complexity of "racial priming" effects in politics, however, see Stephens-Dougan 2021, who notes that amongst a not insignificant proportion of White Americans, *explicit* racial cues remain entirely effective. As noted above, there remain plenty of people who are not signed up to basic equality.

19. For example, the Anglican clergyman Morgan Godwyn, an early civil rights activist and abolitionist, reports hearing those who defended the slave trade proclaim that Blacks are "Unman'd and Unsoul'd; accounted and even ranked with Brutes," nothing less than "Creatures destitute of Souls, to be ranked among Brute Beasts, and treated accordingly" (Godwyn 1708, 3, quoted in Smith 2014, 815).

20. Rashdall 1924, 237–38, quoted in Waldron 2008, 7; 2012, 68; 2017, 25.

21. Which isn't to say that philosophers never play any role whatsoever: the eighteenth-century declarations of the rights of man were clearly in part indebted to the ideas of philosophers, and the affirmation of these rights is part of the history that leads eventually to a belief in basic equality (more on this in chapter 5). But that history is complex, and the causal efficacy of philosopher's and their ideas is far from straightforward in trying to understand it (see, e.g., Moyn 2012).

22. Though what we mean by "justified" will itself need to be subjected to reflection: later I will suggest that vindication, rather than justification, is what we need in this area.

23. This will raise worries about relativism, and also objections regarding the so-called genetic fallacy, i.e., the worry that I am here conflating justification with explanation—I return to these matters in chapter 3.

24. Anne Phillips has recently put forward a version of this kind of argument, suggesting that basic equality be treated as "a claim and a commitment," something we bring into being precisely by holding it to be true of ourselves and others (2021, 53–57). In this, she echoes an earlier argument put forward by Margaret MacDonald (1947) and which Waldron labels "decisionism," although "collective voluntarism" might be a better label: the idea that we are basic equals because we decide, or (perhaps better) *choose to make it such*, that we are. Whilst I am sympathetic to Phillips's rejection of the sort of foundationalist accounts that I also reject (see chapter 2), her own solution requires us to shut down reflection on the key point of *why* we are basic equals, and this will not do. For more details, see my review of Phillips in Sagar 2022.

25. For more detailed replies on why we do need to account for basic equality, see Kelly 2010, 58–62; Nathan 2011; Leiter 2019, 396. However, some—notably Joseph

Raz (1986, chap. 9) and Peter Westen (1982)—have suggested that equality-talk may be a sort of wheel that doesn't turn, and that we might lose nothing important if we do not include it as one of our normative commitments. I agree with Waldron (2008, 11–12) and Nathan (2015) that this is unlikely to be so.

26. This is why the "claim and commitment" thesis offered by Phillips (2021) will not do: we can ask *but why?* are we all unconditional equals (as she puts it), and an answer here is required once the question has been asked. Although she does not put it this way, Phillips might be read as treating basic equality as what Wittgenstein (1969) called a "hinge proposition," i.e., something which we simply have to accept as being the case in order to even begin to make sense of anything else we are trying to understand. The problem, however, is that basic equality is *not* a hinge proposition. In the first place, most people in most times and places have gotten along without it. Second, even if it were true that *for us* basic equality is a precondition of our other normative commitments working together coherently (which is highly questionable), this wouldn't change the fact that asserting that basic equality is a hinge proposition comes *too late*. Once basic equality has actually become the target of sceptical doubt (as it now has), it is too late to affirm that the fact of our basic equality is something it is impossible to doubt. Basic equality is not plausibly akin to, for example, Descartes's claim "I am thinking," or (on some accounts) that when one understands that $2 + 2 = 4$ there is no way to genuinely doubt the truth of this. Hence whilst I agree entirely with Phillips that commitment to basic equality does not need to be justified by recourse to foundationalist accounts of the sort surveyed in chapter 2 (which she and I concur in rejecting), it does not follow—as she appears to suggest—that basic equality needs no justification simpliciter. More on this at various points below. For discussion of Wittgenstein on hinge propositions, see Pritchard 2011.

27. See also Sangiovanni 2017, 68–69; Sher 2014, 87.

Chapter 2. Answers That Don't Work

1. On this view, at least given what we currently know about the state of life in the universe, all persons will therefore be humans, though in the case of, e.g., the profoundly disabled, not all humans will be persons, say if they lack sufficient rational capacity to qualify.

2. Arneson 2015, 34. As Arneson also points out, this however leaves open serious complications about humans that are not *yet* persons—i.e., children—because they have not yet achieved personhood status, because lacking rational agency, as well as those who have *lost* personhood status, e.g., perhaps because they have become brain-damaged, or are suffering from senile dementia. On this view, furthermore, basic equality is accorded in light of being a person (defined as being a rational agent), and is entirely separated from biological considerations: not all human beings

will be persons, but equally rational aliens from Alpha Centauri would be. Arneson thinks it is a strength of the rational agency account that it is entirely separated from questions of biology; as will be clear following chapters 4 and 7, I suspect the opposite to be the case.

3. Arneson 2015, 36. For a recent reply to Arneson that tries to establish that rational agency is indeed enough for basic equality, see Parr and Slavny 2019. This hyperintellectualist account is the sort of answer I judge to be implausible precisely because of its extensive theoretical demands. How could we have come to believe in basic equality if we first need to subscribe to something as complex as *that*?

4. Williams 1973, 232.

5. This is the path taken by Jeff McMahan (2001, 245), who as a consequence abandons commitment to basic human equality, instead arguing for a "two-tiered" view whereby certain human beings lacking features of personhood are relegated to a lower status, more akin to animals. For discussion, see Cochrane 2018, 21–23.

6. Rawls 1971, 504–12.

7. Carter 2011, 548.

8. Rawls 1971, 505–6.

9. For example, Waldron (2017, 196) proposes "personal autonomy, reason, the capacity for moral thought and action, and the capacity for love" as being the kinds of things that a relevant range property will appropriately include.

10. For more detailed critiques, see Arneson 1999, 2015; Cupit 2000; Beillard 2013; Friday 2004; Pojman 1992; Carter 2011, 549–50; Sher 2014, 76–78.

11. Carter 2011, 549–50; Arneson 1999; Cupit 2000, 110–12.

12. Kant 1996, 169.

13. Kant 1997, 36–37.

14. In fact, the picture is even more complicated than this. As Kirby (2018) points out, it is plausible to read Kant as primarily making a claim about equal *authority*, with equal *worth* being derivative of that.

15. On this, see especially Williams 1985, chap. 4.

16. Waldron 2008, 38.

17. This point still holds even in light of Kant's infamous suggestion (1997, 20) that due to the power of "inclination" in human psychology, it may be an empirical fact that *nobody* has *ever* performed a truly good moral action, i.e., out of pure respect for the moral law alone. Indeed, given such upshots of the Kantian picture, we might question whether a theory that produces such astonishing results can possibly end up giving us what we need in any other area of moral life.

18. Kant 1997, 36–37, emphasis in original.

19. Waldron 2008, 40–41, n. 130. For a detailed critique of Kantian attempts to ground basic equality in a notion of dignity and concomitant respect owed to persons, see Sangiovanni 2017, chap. 1.

20. For example, Beillard 2013; Parr and Slavny 2019; Christiano 2015.

21. For a much more promising way to think about personhood than the standard criterion-driven accounts that dominate the philosophical literature at present, see Chappell 2011, whose approach is highly congenial to what I will argue later in terms of accounting for basic equality.

22. In the next chapter, I address the concern that I am here committing the so-called genetic fallacy, i.e., that it doesn't matter *how* people come to hold a belief, so long as that belief in fact turns out to be *true*—a truth which philosophers might independently reveal through, for example, complex analytic argument.

23. Carter 2011.

24. For further detailed critiques, see Arneson 2015; Beillard 2013; Christiano 2015; Husi 2017; Sher 2014.

25. Shklar 1989.

26. For example, Pettit 1997.

27. For example, Nozick 1974, 45–51.

28. Arneson 2015, 46.

29. Arneson 2015, 47.

30. Williams 1973.

31. Sher 2014, 82.

32. Sher 2014, 83, emphasis in original.

33. Sher 2014, 83.

34. Sher 2014, 84.

35. Husi 2017, 392.

36. Arneson 1999, 122.

37. Sangiovanni 2017, chap. 1.

38. Sangiovanni 2017, 74.

39. For more detailed critique, see Floris 2019, 2020.

40. Rozeboom 2018, 168.

41. Sagar 2018a, chaps. 4 and 5; Sagar 2018b.

42. Charvet 2013, 91.

43. Charvet 2013, 97.

44. For a more detailed critique, see Schuppert 2016.

45. Arneson 2015, 52.

Chapter 3. The Basis of an Alternative

1. My argument here is heavily indebted to Williams 2005a, 2005b.

2. It may be objected that there is an important difference here, between (say) Genghis Khan on the one hand and Aristotle on the other—and not just in the fact that the latter might be prepared to sit down and have a conversation about these matters were we to emerge from our time machine at the right moment, whereas the

former would probably just disembowel us. The important difference is that Aristotle (we can safely assume) was a reflective enquirer interested in establishing the best explanations, and thus open to all the relevant available evidence, whereas Genghis (we can probably safely assume) was not. Thus, whilst Genghis won't listen long enough to change his mind, Aristotle might—and thus if we can make Aristotle fully aware of the facts as we know them supported by all the best reasons, *he* would come over to the side of basic equality, so long as he was being fully coherent and honest about how things are (whereas Genghis would by this point have added us to his pile of skulls). Yet for reasons that will become clearer as we go on, I find this deeply implausible as a claim about Aristotle: insofar as he did not share the history and constituting sociological features in which our idea of basic equality has come to make sense, then basic equality *could not* make sense to him, no matter how patiently and carefully we explained our reasons to him. The only way he could come to see it our way would be if he were in fact one of us—but then he wouldn't be *Aristotle*.

3. Hume 2007, 301.

4. To put the matter slightly differently, we can note that Bernard Williams is absolutely correct to observe that once "we become conscious of ethical variation and of the kinds of explanation it may receive, it is incredible that this consciousness should just leave everything where it was and not affect our ethical thought itself" (Williams 1985, 159). But (as Williams himself was keenly aware) what does *not* necessarily follow from such consciousness is universal scepticism about, nor serious doubt about the authenticity of, our ethical values. Acquiring such consciousness means we will indeed have to think about our ethical values differently to how we may have done before—but how we go on from that point is indeterminate.

5. Williams 2006b, 193–94.

6. I am thus in close agreement with what Matthieu Queloz and Damian Cueni (2021) label "Left Wittgensteinianism," and agree with their reasons for adopting such an outlook. One way to read the argument of this book is as an exercise in this kind of approach; another, as will be seen in more detail later, is to see it as a species of vindicatory genealogy.

7. With Hume, I wonder what could possibly account for *that*, until one turns one's gaze "into your own breast." If the answer turns out to be some sort of Kantian claim that practical reason merely as such demands it, on pain of rational inconsistency, then we are back to the severe problems with Kantian accounts noted in the previous chapter. A different, non-Kantian, form of metaethical realism, of the sort associated with John McDowell, would have much less to disagree about here: I take it that a McDowell-style realism would happily concede that only those who have been appropriately brought up and trained to be receptive to the fact of basic equality would indeed be able to appreciate it, but insist that the truth of basic equality nonetheless stands *independent* of whether or not suitably reared observers happen to be around to appreciate (perceive?) it. The problem for such a view, however, is its

metaethical quietism: what is the explanatory story for why basic equality is a fact about us, and how do we come to know this fact, and what is the connection between knowing this fact and its being a normative value for us, specifically, at this point in history? On these matters, the case I advance in the rest of this book is clearly at odds with something like a McDowell view, as will be seen in chapters 4 and 5, even if McDowell-style realism is not wedded to the *rationalism* (and thus, the self-enacting ex nihilo normativity) of Kantian realist accounts. See the essays collected in part 2 of McDowell 1998. For a helpful discussion of McDowell's quietist approach more generally (though without using that term), see Ahmed 2006.

Chapter 4. Essences

1. E.g., Gelman 2003; Gelman and Wellman 1991; Keil 1989; Springer and Keil 1989; Medin and Ortony 1989; Bloom 2011; Solomon and Johnson 2000; Rips 2001.

2. Leslie 2013; Griffiths 2002.

3. Locke 1975, 417, emphasis in original.

4. Locke 1975, 378–79; cf. Smith 2014, 816.

5. Gelman 2003, 7–8.

6. Medin and Ortony 1989, 183.

7. Gelman 2003; Keil 1989; Bloom 2011, 14–18.

8. Exactly what those adaptations consist in and are constituted by is a matter of controversy, however: Smith 2014, 817.

9. Leslie 2013, 119. For evidence and argument that psychological essentialism is a product of our evolutionary heritage and culturally universal, see especially Gil-White 2001 (but also the replies that follow); Hirschfeld 1996; Atran 1998 (see also Leslie 2013, 118–19, for further supporting references). For scepticism based on countervailing experimental data, see Hampton, Estes, and Simmons 2007. On the philosophical difficulty of using the idea of "innateness" to capture whether psychological essentialism is something necessary to all human beings, see Griffiths 2002.

10. Leslie 2013, 152–55.

11. Although many people tried to *transform* other things into gold; for a long time, alchemy was a serious business, taken seriously by learned scholars, Isaac Newton included. But what they were doing was, precisely, attempting to alter *essences*: to transform base metal into gold, something more valuable. More valuable, in part, because it was something fundamentally different.

12. Jerry Fodor (1998) argues that it was the other way around: that we only became essentialists after the advent of modern science. Like others, I find this implausible: psychological essentialism has likely been around far longer than modern science, as indicated by, e.g., the prevalence of essentialist thinking in young children who know nothing of science (e.g., Gelman 2003, 15; Keil 1989; Griffiths 2002; Bloom 2011, 15).

13. The examples of gold and water are standard in the philosophical literature, in large part due to the work on natural kinds done first by Sauk Kripke (1980) and then especially Hilary Putnam (1975), in particular the latter's conclusion that because "water" would only refer correctly to water if the substance *really was* H_2O (and not some other substance, XYZ), and thus it follows that "meaning just ain't in the head" (1975, 227), but is to some degree determined by external reality. For a powerful refutation of the Kripke-Putnam view, showing that it fundamentally begs the question precisely because its authors (being human) are psychological essentialists, see Leslie 2013, and also Gelman 2003, 16.

14. Leslie 2013, 142–58.

15. Stavy and Stachel 1985.

16. Rips 2001.

17. Hull 1986; Griffiths 2002; Leslie 2013; Smith 2014.

18. Leslie 2013, 121–24; Smith 2021, 77–78.

19. Leslie 2013, 132–33.

20. Leslie 2013, 136 (and 132–42 for the support for this claim); Griffiths 2002, 72.

21. As Smith (2021, 70) puts it, summarising Leslie (2013): "the essentialist mindset can be suppressed, but it probably cannot be overcome."

22. See note 9; Griffiths 2002, 76.

23. Keil 1989; Gelman 2003.

24. Deferring to expert opinion appears to be an important feature of psychological essentialism. When it comes to natural kinds, we are willing to believe that a thing is not as it appears if we are told by somebody who is an expert that it is in fact otherwise. This is presumably because essences are *hidden*, so we are sometimes happy to rely on the judgements of others about the hidden thing, allowing this to trump the evidence of a superficial inspection, as a way of accessing what our brains take to be a deeper reality. Interestingly, this appears to be much more robust for natural kinds than artificial ones. Whilst people are happy to defer to the biologist who tells them that this lion is *really* a tiger, they are much less likely to defer to, e.g., the librarian who tells them that this book is *really* a magazine. Artificial kinds seem to be viewed as areas where opinion may legitimately differ (because there is perceived to be *no underlying fact of the matter*, precisely because there is *no underlying essence*), whereas natural kind classification disputes are resolved by expert judgement (because we believe that there is a definite right answer, determined by the underlying essence, and which the expert is taken as knowing about): Gil-White 2001, 521; Malt 1989. However, this appears to manifest differently in adults as compared to young children, the latter of whom tend to treat artificial kinds more like natural kinds: Bloom 2011, 16–18.

25. Smith 2014, 816.

26. Gil-White 2001, 530. Or as Douglas Medin (1989, 1477) puts it, psychological essentialism is bad metaphysics but good epistemology. See also Smith 2021, 139–43.

27. Gil-White 2001.

28. Bloom 2011, 12–13.

29. Evidence of this being intuitively basic to human beings comes from studies with young children: Hirschfeld 1996. For discussion on the difficulties regarding whether essences can mix according to folk essentialism, and the implications of this for species and race classification, see Smith 2014, 818–19.

30. Gelman 2003, 10.

31. Smith 2020, 53–62; Smith 2011, 304–5, n. 3. That there may nonetheless be *socially constructed* categorisations of race, ones that we can meaningfully employ in appropriate contexts even if they are not determined by underlying biological facts, is a separate issue, on which see Shelby 2012, 337–38.

32. For an excellent discussion of what can be termed the metaphysics of race, see Mills 1998, although I suggest that his analysis requires supplementing with psychological essentialist considerations, of the sort outlined in this chapter, in order to be fully satisfactory.

33. Smith 2011, 182–86; 2021, 61–67.

34. See as illustration the long-standing racist trope of the "tragic mulatto," a "White" woman who is found to "really" be Black, and loses everything accordingly: Leslie 2013, 129–31. Revealingly, the "one drop" rule reverses in different historical and political locales: in Brazil, having "one drop" of "White" blood traditionally made you *White*, no matter how Black you looked: Smith 2011, 184.

35. Smith 2011, 182.

36. For a more detailed overview of theoretical accounts of racism, see Shelby 2012, 338–41.

37. Bloom 2011, 17.

38. Smith 2020, 43–52, for the implausibility of the claim that racism is a specifically Western, and relatively recent, invention, as is sometimes maintained.

39. Smith 2011, 2016, 2020, 2021.

40. E.g., Leyens et al. 2001; Haslam 2006; Haslam and Loughnan 2014.

41. Smith 2016; 2020, 156–64; 2021, chap. 12.

42. Smith 2011, 142–54.

43. With, it seems, grim success. Consider Primo Levi's account of being looked at by a German concentration camp doctor: "When he finished writing, he raised his eyes and looked at me . . . that look was not one between two men; and if I had known how completely to explain the nature of that look, which came as if across the glass window of an aquarium between two beings who live in different worlds, I would also have explained the essence of the great insanity of the third Germany. . . . The brain which governed those eyes and those manicured hands said: 'This something in front of me belongs to a species which it is obviously opportune to suppress. In this particular case, one has to first make sure that it does not contain some utilizable element'" (Levi 1959, 122–23).

NOTES TO CHAPTER 5   191

44. Smith 2011, 21.

45. Grossman 1995.

46. Smith 2014, 815; 2020, 29–33.

47. Smith 2014, 821.

48. Smith 2020, 184–90.

49. Augustine 2009, 479; see also Smith 2011, 36.

50. See chapter 1.

51. Augustine 2009, 479.

52. Although it certainly matters that the Christian mode of thinking was already available, and had set down a precedent and way of thinking that a later secularised version could draw upon and take over. For wider studies on the Christian origins and foundations of many (putatively) secular ideas, see Gillespie 2008; Siedentop 2014; Holland 2019.

Chapter 5. History and Fiction

1. Furthermore, that it has come to be held *coherently*, in a way that can be reflectively endorsed. An alternative suggestion—as made for example by Brian Leiter (2019)—is that basic equality is a legacy of a collapsed Christian tradition which no longer makes sense given that the old metaphysical assumptions have been repudiated (or as Nietzsche would put it, now that God is dead). Whilst the fact of a Christian inheritance is no doubt causally important in the story of how a nonetheless secular conception of basic equality emerged, the aim of this book is to resist the Nietzschean inference that without God, basic equality is revealed as incoherent because lacking its necessary foundations. On the contrary, I aim to show how a secular account can nonetheless be vindicated, in part precisely by repudiating the appeal to foundationalist explanations.

2. Importantly, the causal (historical) story—as I have tried to indicate above, and will expand on below—likely centred on practices of treating *as* equal, and from which the idea of *being* basic equals emerged over time. Nonetheless, once that process is up and running (as it now is), the rationale for basic equality obtaining follows the schematic form in this ordering.

3. On liberalism as centrally preoccupied with the problem of securing political equality in the context of economic inequality, see Hont 2005; Sagar 2018c. On liberalism's long involvement with ideas of basic equality, see Fawcett 2018, chap. 4.

4. On the long (and internally contested) history of thinking about basic equality in Western political thought, see Kirby 2018; Bejan 2022.

5. Leaving aside, for now, the fact that it is false that human beings share an essence, what matters is that we intuitively *think* that they do.

6. Although it is worth noting that it is not even clear that God *does* bridge the gap. If one is not already a theist, then obviously premises B) and C) cut no ice, and do not

help get one from A) to D). Yet even if one *is* a theist, there is an evident gap from the claim that God loves us all equally to the conclusion that we are *therefore* basic equals. Could God not love all his creatures equally, whilst holding some of them to be intrinsically superior to others? Here, I suspect, the Christian argument for basic equality ultimately becomes one of asserted faith—that is to say, it is in the final instance not an argument at all, but an affirmation of normative belief without further support.

7. Smith 2014, 815–16.

8. Bejan 2022, 607–8.

9. Britannica 2018. For a helpful overview of different kinds of legal fictions and some illustrative examples, see Miller 1910.

10. From the case of *Ohio vs. Standard Oil* (1892), as quoted in Miller 1910, 627.

11. On one legal interpretation, property might also best be understood as a sort of fiction, given that it appears inherently impossible to define in terms of any "property-ness" one might allege it to consist of: Gray 1991.

12. Indeed, Kinch Hoekstra (2012) has convincingly argued that for Hobbes basic equality is also a kind of fiction, one we need to affirm because although it is not true that we are all by nature equal (even in his much-vaunted and oft-referenced suggestion that we are all equally able to kill each other), by acting *as if* this were true, we are thereby better able to exit the misery of our natural condition. Hobbes's argument thus resembles the (Rousseau-inspired) account of Rozeboom (2018). I do not think that Hobbes (at least as Hoekstra reads him) put the materials together in the right way, for reasons discussed in the rest of this chapter—but suffice to say that I am not the first person to suggest, as I do below, that fictions are crucial to making sense of basic equality.

13. Hobbes 2017, 131.

14. Hobbes 2017, 133.

15. Skinner 2009; Runciman 2000; Fleming 2020.

16. See, e.g., Fleming 2020, chap. 2; Sagar 2018d.

17. It is important to note however that the basic principle "treat like things alike" is not, by itself, enough to generate a normative commitment to basic equality, but needs to be located in a supporting political and moral context to achieve that end. Aristotle, for example, makes it a central point in *Politics* that the definition of justice is treating equals equally. The problem, however, is how to decide who and what gets to count as an equal. Women, on Aristotle's view, were defective men, and barbarians were inherently of less worth than Athenian male citizens, and so he thought it self-evident that these groups were not to be treated equally—and such inequality of treatment was just, for it would be precisely unjust to treat unequals equally. Thus we cannot hope to build basic equality simply out of the axiom "treat like things alike," because who and what gets to count as "alike" is contested, and varies according to the moral and political context the question is being raised in.

18. In the historical story I suggest that it was the practice of increasingly *treating as* equals that led to the widespread adoption of the belief that individuals *are* equals. Note, however, that once that practice is up and running, it gets reinforcement from the apparently self-evident principle that if two things are indeed equal, then it is right to treat them equally, as just described.

19. For discussion of immersion in fictions, see Schellenberg 2013; Stock 2021, chap. 6; Kampa 2018; Nilsson, Nordahl, and Serafin 2016; Wolf 2004.

20. Schellenberg 2013, 507.

21. Schellenberg 2013, 508.

22. Przybylski et al. 2012.

23. Schellenberg 2013, 509.

24. Kampa 2018, 692.

25. Laconi, Pirès, and Chabrol 2017; Sioni, Burleson, and Bekerian 2017.

26. For example, see the story in *The Guardian* about actor James Norton receiving death threats following his role in the TV series *Happy Valley*: https://www.theguardian.com/tv-and-radio/2017/dec/29/james-norton-got-death-threats-after-playing-happy-valley-baddie-mcmafia.

27. For more on how concepts can have important self-effacing components with regards their functional usefulness, focusing on the cases of blame and truth-telling, see Queloz 2018, 2021a.

28. Of course, if we suspect that they really *are* motivated by malice—by some form of bigotry—then our reaction will typically be one not of awkwardness and embarrassment, but of morally offended anger.

29. Waldron 2017, 155–74; Carter 2011, 552–53.

30. Of course, my child is the most special and worth more *to me* (and any good parent will act accordingly). But that is quite compatible with acknowledging that one's own child is a basic equal in relation to all other children in their fundamental standing. Indeed, holding both these thoughts simultaneously is a good example of being successfully immersed in the fiction of basic equality.

31. Phillips 2021. As noted in chapter 1, important questions are now there to be asked about basic equality—about what it is, where it comes from, why we should believe in it now and in the future—and we cannot simply refuse to engage in critical reflection on these points. The same reflection that gave rise to critiques of previous presumptions of inequality and hierarchy must also be applied to basic equality, at least if we are being fully truthful about both our self-understanding and our normative commitments. Phillips's stipulation that we ultimately close down reflection on this matter, in favour of activist political commitment, will not do.

32. Phillips 2021, 41.

33. Williams 2002, 35–38.

34. Seeing things this way also avoids Phillips's other worry: that offering a justification for basic equality inevitably provides grounds for exclusion, insofar as some

always fall outside the scope of justification, and thus are relegated to a normatively inferior standing because hierarchy is thereby inevitably reintroduced. This is a fair worry about foundationalist accounts, but as I show in the next chapter, there is no reason to think that the antifoundationalist view put forward here need generate the exclusionary effects Phillips worries about. On the contrary, basic equality as immersion in a fiction is a good bet for facilitating the widest possible inclusion of all members of the human species—all of them being, by definition, holders of the human essence, and thus none may legitimately be excluded. A fiction this will certainly be, but a good and useful one for us to hold, and to try and promote as widely as possible.

Chapter 6. Vindication

1. Kirby 2018.

2. Phillips 2021, chap. 3.

3. Phillips 2021, chap. 2.

4. My argument in the following section is heavily influenced by the "negative" approach championed by Judith Shklar, who urges us to focus on the prevention of injustice and the need for a politics of damage control as our priority. Whilst less edifying than utopian political visions for enacting justice, this "negative" approach is far more urgent in a world, such as ours, that is centrally characterised by a contrast between the weak and the powerful, and the ongoing need to protect the former from the latter. See Shklar 1984, 1989, 1990. Furthermore, I agree with Shklar (1990) that injustice is not simply the absence of justice—it is its own particular normative phenomenon, associated with suffering wrongs at the hands of others whom one perceives to be responsible for the sufferings and the wrongs. This matters in what follows, because it is no reply to my account to say that it begs the question because injustice *just is* denying people basic equality, so preventing injustice cannot therefore be what constitutes basic equality (for such reasoning would evidently be circular). This complaint is a misreading of the argument advanced. It is not my claim that basic equality is *defined by* the provision of justice, but rather that avoiding the horrors associated with injustice (which is not simply the absence of justice) is crucial to our understanding both why a commitment to basic equality has historically emerged, and why upon reflection we ought to *go on* being normatively committed to it. More on this below. The account offered here bears certainly similarities to the account of human rights famously put forward by Richard Rorty (1998)—though as should be clear by now, I agree with Williams (2006b) that we must go both further and deeper than Rorty acknowledges when it comes to ensuring the stability under reflection of our normative commitments.

5. It is also significant that commitment to basic equality is now up and running, and has a proven track record of success in this regard. If someone were to object that

we might do *better* in terms of reducing cruelty and injustice by swapping out basic equality for something else, then we need to ask: Are you sure? How sure? On what evidence? The point here is manifold. In the first place, it is not informative to compare the track record of basic equality with some purely hypothetical alternative: a benevolent absolute monarch, say, who pledges to outlaw cruelty and injustice wherever it arises but introduces distinctions within the human set at the same time. We know that such monarchs will never actually exist (and certainly, that *we* have no hope of getting from here to there). Furthermore, the problem of unintended consequences applies with especial force when the stakes are as high as they are in this area: we now know how things tend to go when division within the human set is introduced, but it can almost certainly go even worse than we expect, and in new and unexpected ways, which there is every reason to think will be very bad indeed, and this is true even in much less fanciful scenarios than that of an imaginary benevolent monarch. Hence the fact that basic equality is already up and running *matters*, for this in itself gives it a claim on our ongoing allegiance, and counts in its favour over speculative alternatives. Attempting to replace commitment to basic equality with something else would be a big risk, because even if basic equality isn't perfect in terms of eliminating cruelty and injustice, the historical evidence at this point indicates that it is a very strong bet for *reducing* their prevalence. Attempting to replace commitment to basic equality with something else would carry a severe risk of making things much worse, albeit under the guise of trying to make them better—and hence of our ending up being sorry for what we had wished for.

6. However, insofar as basic equality is a contingent and highly localised phenomenon (at least in global-historical terms), that genealogy will be unlikely to take the form of a "state of nature" story, as the recent pragmatic genealogies that Queloz (2021b) surveys have tended to do (for example Edward Craig's [1999] analysis of knowledge, or Bernard Williams's [2002] account of truth and truthfulness). This is because basic equality is not a concept that we can posit all human groups will need to hit upon some version of if they are to instantiate successful cooperation, and thus fulfil various shared needs (as evidenced by the fact that most human societies in most of history have gotten along without it). The needs that basic equality serves are much more localised and specific to our history and culture, and thus it is unlikely that they will be most effectively modelled via a state of nature story which strips things back to various universal human needs. This does not mean that a fully fleshed out pragmatic genealogy is not possible for basic equality, but that it would have to be one that looks a lot more like real history. Due to the level of historical detail required for such a pragmatic genealogy of basic equality to be adequate, I have omitted attempting to provide such an account here. However, I invite others to do so.

7. Furthermore, we can also point to the fact that the bigot's worldview will have to rest on lies and falsehoods about what sets some groups of humans apart from others. Yet we now know, beyond doubt, that all the putative legitimations as to why

one subset of humans is allegedly superior to the rest turn out to be bogus. A commitment to basic equality relies on the use of fictions, but it is not itself *untruthful*, in the way that racism, sexism, and other forms of bigotry will have to be if they attempt to legitimate hierarchies within the human set based on some (bogus, and ultimately self-servingly ideological) account of why one group of humans is allegedly superior to the rest. Whilst the bigot's worldview must ultimately rest on lies and falsehoods, the partisan of basic equality does without lies and falsehoods because fictions are a different class of thing. Insofar as we value being truthful about what we are up to, that is an advantage we have over the bigot: we can give honest reasons for why and how the practice does what it does in the specific ways that it does them. The bigot cannot do that, for the bigot must appeal to lies and falsehoods about what sets different groups of humans not just apart, but into relations of hierarchy. This is an advantage it is worth reminding ourselves that we have, even if the bigot might not be willing to listen to us when we point it out. More on this below.

8. Something like a grounding account is suggested, though the details are far from straightforward (not least because trying to avoid the pitfalls of foundationalism), in Sangiovanni 2017, chap. 2.

9. Although I have foregrounded an aversion to cruelty and injustice, and believe that these are the most important features to draw attention to, and which secure the required vindication, it is of course the case that *other* desirable normative values are also realised in part by the commitment to basic equality. Civility, the better functioning of peaceful political processes, and a meaningful commitment to mutual dignity, are obvious cases in point. Although I do not address these further values here, it is not part of my argument to claim that *only* cruelty and injustice are of pertinent concern—although I do take them to be the primary and most important features to recognise.

10. In the technical nomenclature, it is the distinction between "fictionalism" and "quasi-realism" when it comes to metaethics, and the associated analysis of moral attitudes and semantics. The position I adopt here is, following Simon Blackburn (e.g., 1984, chap. 6; 1988) quasi-realist. On the distinction between fictionalism and quasi-realism, see Lewis 2005; Blackburn 2005; and Jenkins 2006.

11. For relevant discussion on this matter, see Dennett 1986, chap. 1, pp. 6ff. There is a further wrinkle here, in terms of whether this quasi-realist position is intended to be *descriptive* of what people at present are *actually doing* when they think of each other as basic equals, or if it is *revisionary*, i.e., in terms of how we *ought* to think about what we are doing, once we get clear on what the issues are in terms of a coherent second-order account. My hunch is that the latter is more plausible. However, working through such matters would require a chapter in itself, and this is not the time for that.

12. To this extent, my deflationary use of the language of truth here shares much in common with the outlook of Richard Rorty (e.g., 1989), though again for the

reasons well marked by Williams (2006b), Rorty's wider "ironist" story cannot be finally right, or give us what we need.

13. This is another point at which the quasi-realist position taken here is at an advantage over metaphysical fictionalism. For the metaphysical fictionalist would have to say that it would be *really true* that we are all basic equals even if, counterfactually, the relevant practices had never been developed, or disappeared tomorrow, which is akin to saying that it would be *really true* that Sherlock Holmes lives at 221B Baker Street even if Arthur Conan Doyle had never written the relevant novels, which is manifestly incoherent. The quasi-realist approach simply avoids getting into such tangles.

14. This is not to deny that philosophical ideas, when they get out into the real world, can sometimes take on a life of their own, and in turn generate potentially undesirable consequences. Take, for example, Rousseau's notion of the general will, and the sometimes disastrous influence of that idea upon, e.g., France's and Geneva's subsequent political trajectories (Whatmore 2012, chap. 3). There is perhaps not much that can be done in advance about what misuses one's ideas might be put to by others, beyond hoping for the best. For further discussion, see Jubb and Kurtulmus 2012.

15. Queloz 2018; 2021a; 2021b, 54–59, 178–87.

16. Queloz 2021b, 55–56.

17. Queloz 2021b, 56.

Chapter 7. Speciesism

1. I here draw on the influential account put forward in Singer 1975, which popularised the term "speciesism" as earlier used in Ryder [1971] 1976. But see also Cochrane 2018, chap. 2, for an explicit argument that basic equality should be extended to animals and claiming that failure to do so falls afoul of speciesism. Tellingly, Cochrane draws his conclusions directly from the failure to provide a convincing foundationalist account of basic equality of the sorts surveyed in chapter 2, instead following Singer in the prioritising of interests (albeit as related to sentience) regardless of where they are located.

2. Cochrane 2018, chap. 2.

3. Diamond 1978; Williams 2006c. See also Anderson 2005; Crary 2010; Phillips 2021, 57–62. I make no great claim to originality in this part of the book; my aim is simply to show how the arguments already made by Diamond and Williams can be adapted for the defence of basic equality as applying only to humans. Diamond's argument has been responded to in Singer 1980; McMahan 2005; and Dombrowski 2006; and Williams has been responded to in Singer 2009; McMahan 2005; and Cochrane 2018, 25. My view is that none of these come close to touching the Diamond-Williams approach, for the reasons recently set out by Diamond herself

(2018), as well as in Gleeson 2008. See also Diamond 1991 for further pertinent considerations as to what is morally at stake, and how to think adequately about it.

4. A slightly different worry here is that encouraging people to regard humans as basic equals will encourage them to regard nonhuman animals as outside of the scope of moral consideration: that the *psychological tendency* of elevating humans to the status of basic equals will be to license greater indifference to the interests of animals. Whether this is really so is ultimately an empirical question and can only be answered accordingly—but I am doubtful that it will turn out to be so, and if anything, I suspect the connection more likely goes the other way around: that the better we treat each other, the better we tend to treat the animals, too.

5. Diamond 1978, 468.

6. After all, some gorillas might have an important interest in experiencing sexual interactions with humans—though I wouldn't want to be the one tasked with finding out.

7. Though even here our responses are not always uniform: witness those who prefer to use "humane" mouse traps to deal with an infestation, rather than using poison or other more fatal devices.

8. Or, as Arenson (1999, 104) has noted, on the Singer view the toothache of a rat, were it as intense as that of a human, ought to count the same in a social policy calculation.

9. See also Chappell 2011, 17.

10. Williams 2006c, 146; Anderson 2005, 284–85. The point here is very specific, about the philosophical pitfalls of thinking that only interests matter. It is an importantly different issue to note, as Martha Nussbaum (2022, chap. 10) has recently done, that "the wild" is both an invention of recent human imagination (probably starting with nineteenth-century romanticism) and belies the fact that very little of the natural world as it now exists is not thoroughly conditioned and distorted by the ubiquitous presence of human activity. Insofar as a lot of animal suffering takes place in the context of that ubiquitous human activity, there is a legitimate charge that insofar as we are responsible for the suffering of "wild" animals, we ought to take responsibility for it (and stop doing it). That is certainly true—but the reasons need not devolve into an appeal merely to the interests of animals. To say that "wild" animals matter and should be better cared for by us is not the preserve of those who appeal only to interests, any more than vegetarianism is the preserve only of those who sign up to the obtuse Singer-style arguments exposed by Diamond (herself a vegetarian). The philosophical point I am making about absurdity is, however, a different and specific one: that if we do indeed think that only interests matter, then the fact of whether animal interests are harmed *by human activity* is ultimately arbitrary, and thus normatively irrelevant. That the gazelle is killed by the lion or by the marksman is neither here nor there on this outlook—and if we think gazelle interests matter, then ceteris paribus we have reason to prevent the killing in both cases, which are morally on all

fours with each other (e.g., Cochrane 2018, 89). But this, I suggest, reduces the interest view to absurdity—and an absurdity, I will argue below, that is *not* properly dispelled by a suitably hard-headed philosophical revisionism. Nussbaum herself falls into this absurdity (e.g., 2022, 247–52), which is in fact unsurprising because despite ostensibly departing from a Singer-style emphasis on interests and replacing this with "capabilities," her approach is structurally the same: see note 21 below. McMahan (2010) does likewise, again unsurprisingly given his reductive philosophical presuppositions (e.g., McMahan 2001, 2005). Cochrane (2018) suggests that on balance we should tend not to interfere with wild animals—but only because of how the consequences will likely fall out if we try, not because it is *in and of itself* wrong-headed to even think like this (as I suggest is the case; more on this below).

11. If some person reasons "animals are not our basic equals, *therefore* I may treat them cruelly in ways that cause them suffering," the problem here isn't with basic equality, but with the individual in question—more on this below.

12. As seriously considered by, e.g., Donaldson and Kymlicka 2011, 180–83; Cochrane 2018, 89–99; Everett 2001; McMahan 2016; Simmons 2009; Cowen 2003; Tomasik 2015.

13. Or in the case of, e.g., Cochrane 2018, chap. 5, what an impartial conception of justice allegedly requires of us once we recognise the fundamental importance of interests.

14. Diamond 1978, 472–79; Williams 2006c, 144–47.

15. Cochrane writes, "Crucially, the interests that sentient individuals possess are not of importance because they contribute to the total amount of welfare in the universe. Rather, they are of importance because they contribute to the welfare of those with ultimate moral value: sentient individuals" (2018, 27). This might seem to leave his sophisticated synthesis of a Singer-style emphasis on interests with a prioritising of moral rights (that is, a rejection of Singer's welfarist utilitarianism) untouched. But really it just begs the question: for what is this "ultimate moral value" that sentient creatures are somehow supposed to possess simply as such? There is, in fact, only the value that humans bring to bear on any such matters.

16. Williams 2006c, 141, 148; 1985, 118–19.

17. Supposing, that is, that the very worst levels of indoctrination and false consciousness have not been reached.

18. On this see also Gleeson 2008, 169–71.

19. Williams 2006c, 148.

20. It might be objected here that when it comes to, e.g., severely disabled humans, it is likewise always a case of how "we" (the normal capacity humans) are to treat "them" (the severely disabled humans)—so why do they get accorded the status of basic equality, but animals do not? The answer here is that when it comes to the severely disabled humans, we recognise that *this being is one of us*, and that the category "one of us" rightly has weighty normative import. To be sure, it has

not always been this way, in all times and places. But for us, now and around here, it is indeed so, and it is so in part precisely because the practice of basic equality is now up and running. To ignore this crucial normative context and complexity, and instead to try and draw a straight-line comparison between (say) severely disabled human beings and higher mentally functioning animals such as chimpanzees, is to entirely misunderstand how our values operate and make sense in this area, both with how we relate to other humans (even those suffering severe impairment) *and* with how we relate to (different kinds of) animals. On this see Anderson 2005, a helpful refutation of the so-called Argument from Marginal Cases, of which the above example is an instance. See also Diamond 1991, 2018; Chappell 2011.

21. For two recent sophisticated philosophical accounts of animal rights, see Korsgaard 2018 and Nussbaum 2022. Korsgaard's avowedly Kantian approach accepts a relatively sharp demarcation between humans and animals in some regards, and to that extent is not unfriendly to what I have said in this chapter. However, that same Kantianism pulls in the opposite direction from the humanistic approach championed by Diamond and Williams that I follow here. Nussbaum presents her own project as (like Korsgaard's) a synthesis of Aristotelian and Kantian perspectives (e.g., 2022, chaps. 4–5). But this is in an important sense misleading. As she notes, she is highly sympathetic to the Singer-style accusation of speciesism, but rejects its utilitarian underpinning that focuses on interests alone (2022, chap. 3). Instead, she seeks to replace an emphasis on interests with an emphasis on "capabilities"— arguing that we should respect and defend these (in particular, via law) wherever they are found, irrespective of species. By noting that such capabilities are found across many species other than humans, she mounts an argument for granting not just moral, but political, rights to animals (with any refusal to do so emerging as a form of speciesism). This is therefore structurally the same move as the Singer approach, and fails for the same reasons. Nussbaum posits that animal lives matter simply in themselves, and hence all creatures who possess capabilities ought to be weighed equally in the balance regardless of species, sub specie aeternitatis (e.g., 66–67, 191). But as per the above considerations drawn from Williams and Diamond, I do not see how that could coherently make sense: animal capabilities matter *to us*, not to the point of view of the universe (which doesn't exist), and it is a profound mistake to fail to recognise that *being human* is a crucially important component in our moral understandings (on which see especially Diamond 1991). Nussbaum's putatively Aristotelian-Kantian approach is therefore in fact a repeat of the mistakes about speciesism examined above. For other recent accounts which advance the view (like Nussbaum) that animals should have political, and not merely moral, rights, see Donaldson and Kymlicka 2011; Cochrane 2018.

22. Albeit not in the way that, e.g., Nussbaum (2022) supposes: see previous note.

23. Anderson 2005, 283–90.

24. Francione 2005.

Chapter 8. Conclusion

1. Waldron 2008, 1.

2. Waldron 2012, 37–40; Phillips 2021, 49, 63–65.

3. Waldron 2012, 37–38.

4. Waldron 2012, 38, emphasis in original.

5. Piketty 2014.

6. For relevant discussion, though focused on human rights rather than basic equality, see Moyn 2019.

7. As indicated in chapter 5, there is an important connection here between basic equality and the rise of liberalism as the organising mode of modern Western states. Kant was a perceptive—and prophetic—observer when he remarked of the new emerging liberal state form that within it "[t]his uniform equality of human beings as subjects of a state is, however, perfectly consistent with the utmost inequality of the mass in the degree of its possessions, whether these take the form of physical or mental superiority over others, or of fortuitous external property and of particular rights (of which there may be many) with respect to others. . . . Nevertheless, they are all equal as subjects *before the law*" (Kant 1970, 75). See also Sagar 2018c, on the constituting connections between liberalism and economic inequality.

8. To a certain variety of Nietzschean, or the overconfident bigot, who thinks they would like to gamble on something other than basic equality, presumably because they think they would come out on top in a new social order, we simply ask: are you sure? Commitment to basic equality is in part a modus vivendi—and those who think they would do better if this arrangement were shattered should be aware that there is no guarantee that they will be wearing the boots if there is to be kicking further down the line. By contrast, those of us who aren't interested in doing any kicking can simply be happy about a world in which the amount of kicking has been significantly reduced (regardless of whether it is us, personally, who are on the receiving end of it), whilst striving to reduce it yet further.

REFERENCES

Ahmed, Arif (2006)—"Review: John McDowell," *Mind* (115:458): 403–9.

Anderson, Elizabeth (2005)—"Animal Rights and the Values of Nonhuman Life," in *Animal Rights: Current Debates and New Directions*, ed. Cass R. Sunstein and Martha C. Nussbaum. Oxford: Oxford University Press, 277–96.

Arneson, Richard J. (1999)—"What, If Anything, Renders All Humans Morally Equal?," in *Peter Singer and His Critics*, ed. Dale Jamieson. Oxford: Blackwell, 103–28.

Arneson, Richard J. (2015)—"Basic Equality: Neither Acceptable nor Rejectable," in *Do All Persons Have Equal Moral Worth?*, ed. Uwe Steinhoff. Oxford: Oxford University Press, 30–52.

Atran, Scott (1998)—"Folk Biology and the Anthropology of Science: Cognitive Universals and Cultural Particulars," *Behavioral and Brain Sciences* (21:4): 547–609.

Augustine, Saint (of Hippo) (2009)—*The City of God*, trans. Marcus Dods. Peabody, MA: Hendrickson Publishers Inc.

Beillard, Julien (2013)—"Equality and Transparency," *American Philosophical Quarterly* (50:1): 51–62.

Bejan, Teresa (2022)—"What Was the Point of Equality?," *American Journal of Political Science* (66:3): 604–16.

Blackburn, Simon (1984)—*Spreading the Word: Groundings in the Philosophy of Language*. Oxford: Oxford University Press.

Blackburn, Simon (1988)—"Attitudes and Contents," *Ethics* (98:3): 501–17.

Blackburn, Simon (2005)—"Quasi-Realism No Fictionalism," in *Fictionalism in Metaphysics*, ed. Mark Eli Kalderon. Oxford: Oxford University Press, 314–21.

Bloom, Paul (2011)—*How Pleasure Works: Why We Like What We Like*. London: Vintage.

Britannica, The Editors of the Encyclopedia (2018)—"Legal Fiction," 12 April, https://www.britannica.com/topic/legal-fiction. Accessed 18 January 2022.

Carter, Ian (2011)—"Respect and the Basis of Equality," *Ethics* (121:3): 538–71.

Chappell, Timothy (2011)—"On the Very Idea of a Criteria for Personhood," *Southern Journal of Philosophy* (49:1): 1–27.

Charvet, John (2013)—*The Nature and Limits of Human Equality*. Basingstoke: Palgrave Macmillan.

Christiano, Thomas (2015)—"Rationality, Equal Status, and Egalitarianism," in *Do All Persons Have Equal Moral Worth?*, ed. Uwe Steinhoff. Oxford: Oxford University Press, 53–75.

Cochrane, Alasdair (2018)—*Sentientist Politics*. Oxford: Oxford University Press.

Cowen, Tyler (2003)—"Policing Nature," *Environmental Ethics* (25:2): 169–82.

Craig, Edward (1999)—*Knowledge and the State of Nature: An Essay in Conceptual Synthesis*. Oxford: Oxford University Press.

Crary, Alice (2010)—"Minding What Really Matters: A Critique of Moral Individualism," *Philosophical Topics* (38:1): 17–49.

Cupit, Geoffrey (2000)—"The Basis of Equality," *Philosophy* (75:1): 105–25.

Curtice, J., E. Clery, J. Perry, M. Phillips, and N. Rahim (eds.) (2019)—*British Social Attitudes: The 36th Report*. London: The National Centre for Social Research.

Dennett, Daniel (1986)—*Content and Consciousness*. London and New York: Routledge.

Diamond, Cora (1978)—"Eating Meat and Eating People," *Philosophy* (53:206): 465–79.

Diamond, Cora (1991)—"The Importance of Being Human," *Royal Institute of Philosophy Supplement* (29): 35–62.

Diamond, Cora (2018)—"Bernard Williams on the Human Prejudice," *Philosophical Investigations* (41:4): 377–481.

Dombrowski, Daniel A. (2006)—"Is the Argument from Marginal Cases Obtuse?," *Journal of Applied Philosophy* (23:2): 223–32.

Donaldson, Sue, and Will Kymlicka (2011)—*Zoopolis: A Political Theory of Animal Rights*. Oxford: Oxford University Press.

Dworkin, Ronald (1983)—"Comment on Narveson: In Defense of Equality," *Social Philosophy and Policy* (1:1): 24–40.

Dworkin, Ronald (2000)—*Sovereign Virtue: The Theory and Practice of Equality*. Cambridge, MA: Harvard University Press.

Everett, Jennifer (2001)—"Environmental Ethics, Animal Welfarism, and the Problem of Predation," *Ethics and the Environment* (6:1): 42–67.

Fawcett, Edmund (2018)—*Liberalism: The Life of an Idea*, 2nd ed. Princeton, NJ: Princeton University Press.

Fleming, Sean (2020)—*Leviathan on a Leash: A Theory of State Responsibility*. Princeton, NJ: Princeton University Press.

Floris, Giacomo (2019)—"On the Basis of Moral Equality: A Rejection of the Relation-First Approach," *Ethical Theory and Moral Practice* (22): 237–50.

Floris, Giacomo (2020)—"Two Concerns about the Rejection of Social Cruelty as the Basis of Moral Equality," *European Journal of Political Theory* (19:3): 408–16.

Fodor, Jerry (1998)—*Concepts: Where Cognitive Science Went Wrong*. Oxford: Oxford University Press.

Francione, Gary L. (2005)—"Animals—Property or Persons?," in *Animal Rights: Current Debates and New Directions*, ed. Cass R. Sunstein and Martha C. Nussbaum. Oxford: Oxford University Press, 108–34.

Frankfurt, Harry (1997)—"Equality and Respect," *Social Research* (64:1): 3–15.

Fricker, Miranda (2007)—*Epistemic Injustice: Power and the Ethics of Knowing*. Oxford: Oxford University Press.

Friday, Jonathan (2004)—"Moral Equality and the Foundations of Liberal Moral Theory," *Journal of Value Inquiry* (38:1): 61–74.

Gelman, Susan A. (2003)—*The Essential Child: Origins of Essentialism in Everyday Thought*. Oxford: Oxford University Press.

Gelman, Susan A., and Henry M. Wellman (1991)—"Insides and Essences: Early Understandings of the Non-Obvious," *Cognition* (38:3): 213–44.

Gillespie, Michael Allen (2008)—*The Theological Origins of Modernity*. Chicago: University of Chicago Press.

Gil-White, Francisco J. (2001)—"Are Ethnic Groups Biological 'Species' to the Human Brain? Essentialism in Our Cognition of Some Social Categories," *Current Anthropology* (42:4): 515–53.

Gleeson, Andrew (2008)—"Eating Meat and Reading Diamond," *Philosophical Papers* (37:1): 157–75.

Godwin, Morgan (1708)—"A Brief Account of Religion, in the Plantations, with the Causes of the Neglect and Decay Thereof in Those Parts." Preface to Fracis Brokesby, *Some Proposals Towards Promoting the Propagation of the Gospel in Our American Plantations*. London: Three Golden Fleur de Luces, 1–3.

Gray, Kevin (1991)—"Property in Thin Air," *Cambridge Law Journal* (5:2): 252–307.

Griffiths, Paul E. (2002)—"What Is Innateness?," *The Monist* (85:1): 70–85.

Grossman, Dave (1995)—*On Killing: The Psychological Cost of Learning to Kill in War and Society*. London: Little Brown.

Hampton, James A., Zachary Estes, and Sabrina Simmons (2007)—"Metamorphosis: Essence, Appearance and Behavior in the Categorization of Natural Kinds," *Memory and Cognition* (35:7): 1785–800.

Haslam, Nick (2006)—"Dehumanization: An Integrative Review," *Personality and Social Psychology Review* (10:3): 252–64.

Haslam, Nick, and Steve Loughnan (2014)—"Dehumanization and Infrahumanization," *Annual Review of Psychology* (65): 399–423.

Hirschfeld, Lawrence (1996)—*Race in the Making: Cognition, Culture, and the Child's Construction of Human Kinds*. Cambridge, MA: MIT Press.

Heath, Joseph (2020)—*The Machinery of Government: Public Administration and the Liberal State*. Oxford: Oxford University Press.

Hobbes, Thomas (2017)—*Leviathan*, ed. Christoper Brooke. London: Penguin.

Hoekstra, Kinch (2012)—"Hobbesian Equality," in *Hobbes Today*, ed. S. A. Lloyd. Cambridge: Cambridge University Press, 76–112.

Holland, Tom (2019)—*Dominion: The Making of the Western Mind*. London: Abacus.

Hont, Istvan (2005)—"Introduction," in *Jealousy of Trade: International Competition and the Nation-State in Historical Perspective*, 1–36. Cambridge, MA: Harvard University Press.

Hull, David L. (1986)—"On Human Nature," *Proceedings of the Biennial Meeting of the Philosophy of Science Association* (2): 3–13.

Hume, David (2007)—*A Treatise of Human Nature*, ed. David Fate Norton and Mary J. Norton. Oxford: Oxford University Press.

Husi, Stan (2017)—"Why We (Almost Certainly) Are Not Moral Equals," *Journal of Ethics* (21:4): 375–401.

Jenkins, C. S. (2006)—"Lewis and Blackburn on Quasi-realism and Fictionalism," *Analysis* (66:4): 315–19.

Johnson, Boris (2013)—"The Margaret Thatcher Lecture," delivered to the Centre for Policy Studies, 27 November 2013, available at https://www.cps.org.uk/events/q/date/2013/11/27/the-2013-margaret-thatcher-lecture-boris-johnson/.

Jubb, Robert, and A. Faik Kurtulmus (2012)—"No Country for Honest Men: Political Philosophers and Real Politics," *Political Studies* (60:3): 539–56.

Kampa, Samuel (2018)—"Imaginative Transportation," *Australasian Journal of Philosophy* (96:4): 683–96.

Kant, Immanuel (1970). *Political Writings*, ed. H. S. Reiss. Cambridge: Cambridge University Press.

Kant, Immanuel (1996)—*The Metaphysics of Morals*, ed. Mary J. Gregor. Cambridge: Cambridge University Press.

Kant, Immanuel (1997)—*Groundwork of the Metaphysics of Morals*, ed. Mary J. Gregor. Cambridge: Cambridge University Press.

Kant, Immanuel (2007)—*Anthropology, History, and Education*, ed. Günter Zöller and Robert B. Louden. Cambridge: Cambridge University Press.

Keil, Frank C. (1989)—*Concepts, Kinds, and Cognitive Development*. Cambridge, MA: MIT Press.

Kelley, Nancy, Omar Khan, and Sarah Sharrock (2017)—"Racial Prejudice in Britain Today." London, NatCen. https://assets.website-files.com/61488f992b58e687f1108c7c/61c209424ce8cec640976cfb_racial-prejudice-report_v4.pdf.

Kelly, Paul (2010)—"Why Equality? On Justifying Liberal Egalitarianism," *Critical Review of International Social and Political Philosophy* (13:1): 55–70.

Kirby, Nikolas (2018)—"Two Concepts of Basic Equality," *Res Publica* (24:3): 297–318.

Korsgaard, Christine (2018)—*Fellow Creatures: Our Obligations to the Other Animals*. Oxford: Oxford University Press.

Kripke, Saul (1980)—*Naming and Necessity*. Cambridge: Cambridge University Press.

Laconi, Stéphanie, Sophie Pirès, and Henri Chabrol (2017)—"Internet Gaming Disorder, Motives, Game Genres and Psycopathology," *Computers in Human Behaviour* (75): 652–59.

Leiter, Brian (2019)—"The Death of God and the Death of Morality," *The Monist* (102:3): 386–402.

Leslie, Sarah-Jane (2013)—"Essence and Natural Kinds: When Science Meets Pre-schooler Intuition," in *Oxford Studies in Epistemology*, vol. 4, ed. Tamar Szabó Gendler and John Hawthorne. Oxford: Oxford University Press, 108–65.

Levi, Primo (1959). *If This Is a Man*, trans. Stuart Woolf. New York: Orion Press.

Lewis, David (2005)—"Quasi-realism Is Fictionalism," in *Fictionalism in Metaphysics*, ed. Mark Eli Kalderon. Oxford: Oxford University Press, 322–28.

Leyens, Jacques-Philippe, Armando Rodriguez-Perez, Ramon Rodriguez-Torres, Ruth Gaunt, Maria-Paola Paladino, Jeroen Vaes, and Stéphanie Demoulin (2001)—"Psychological Essentialism and the Differential Attribution of Uniquely Human Emotions to Ingroups and Outgroups," *European Journal of Social Psychology* (31:4): 395–411.

Locke, John (1960)—*Two Treatises of Government*, ed. Peter Laslett. Cambridge: Cambridge University Press.

Locke, John (1975)—*An Essay Concerning Human Understanding*, ed. Peter Nidditch. Oxford: Oxford University Press.

MacDonald, Margaret (1947)—"Natural Rights," *Proceedings of the Aristotelian Society* (47): 225–50.

Machery, Edouard (2008)—"A Plea for Human Nature," *Philosophical Psychology* (21:3): 321–29.

Malt, B. C. (1989)—"An On-line Investigation of Prototype and Exemplary Strategies in Classification," *Journal of Experimental Psychology: Learning, Memory and Cognition* (15:4): 539–55.

McDowell, John (1998)—*Mind, Value, and Reality*. Cambridge, MA: Harvard University Press.

McMahan, Jeff (2001)—*The Ethics of Killing: Problems at the Margins of Life*. Oxford: Oxford University Press.

McMahan, Jeff (2005)—"Our Fellow Creatures," *Journal of Ethics* (9:3–4): 353–80.

McMahan, Jeff (2010)—"The Meat Eaters," *New York Times*, 19 September, https://archive.nytimes.com/opinionator.blogs.nytimes.com/2010/09/19/the-meat-eaters/.

McMahan, Jeff (2013)—"Bernard Williams: A Reminiscence," in *The Moral Philosophy of Bernard Williams*, ed. C. D. Herrera and Alexandra Perry. Newcastle: Cambridge Scholars, 18–25.

McMahan, Jeff (2016)—"The Moral Problem of Predation," in *Philosophy Comes to Dinner: Arguments about the Ethics of Eating*, ed. Andrew Chignell, Terence Cuneo, and Matthew C. Halteman. Abingdon: Routledge, 268–94.

Medin, Douglas (1989)—"Concepts and Conceptual Structure," *American Psychologist* (44:12): 1469–81.

Medin, Douglas, and Andrew Ortony (1989)—"Comments on Part 1: Psychological Essentialism," in *Similarity and Analogical Reasoning*, ed. Stella Vosniadou and Andrew Ortony. Cambridge: Cambridge University Press, 179–96.

Miller, Sidney T. (1910)—"The Reasons for Some Legal Fictions," *Michigan Law Review* (8:8): 623–36.

Mill, J. S. (1989)—*On Liberty and Other Political Writings*, ed. Stefan Collini. Cambridge: Cambridge University Press.

Mill, J. S. (1998)—*On Liberty, Utilitarianism, and Other Essays*, ed. Mark Philp and Frederick Rosen. Oxford: Oxford University Press.

Mills, Charles W. (1998)—"'But What Are You *Really*?' The Metaphysics of Race," in *Blackness Visible: Essays on Philosophy and Race*. Ithaca, NY: Cornell University Press, 41–66.

Misak, Cheryl (2020)—*Frank Ramsey: A Sheer Excess of Powers*. Oxford: Oxford University Press.

Moyn, Samuel (2012)—*The Last Utopia: Human Rights in History*. Cambridge, MA: Harvard University Press.

Moyn, Samuel (2019)—*Not Enough: Human Rights in an Unequal World*. Cambridge, MA: Harvard University Press.

Nathan, Christopher (2011)—"Need There Be a Defence of Equality?" *Res Publica* (17:3): 211–25.

Nathan, Christopher (2015)—"What Is Basic Equality?," in *Do All Persons Have Equal Moral Worth?*, ed. Uwe Steinhoff. Oxford: Oxford University Press, 1–16.

Nilsson, Niels Christian, Rolf Nordahl, and Stefania Serafin (2016)—"Immersion Revisited: A Review of Existing Definitions of Immersion and Their Relation to Different Theories of Presence," *Human Technology* (12:2): 108–34.

Nozick, Robert (1974)—*Anarchy, State and Utopia*. Oxford: Blackwell.

Nussbaum, Martha (2022)—*Justice for Animals: Our Collective Responsibility*. New York: Simon and Schuster.

O'Neill, Martin (2008)—"What Should Egalitarians Believe?," *Philosophy and Public Affairs* (36:2): 119–56.

Parfit, Derek (1997)—"Equality or Priority?," *Ratio* (10:3): 202–21.

Parr, Tom, and Adam Slavny (2019)—"Rescuing Basic Equality," *Pacific Philosophical Quarterly* (100:3): 837–57.

Pettit, Philip (1997)—*Republicanism: A Theory of Freedom and Government*. Oxford: Oxford University Press.

Phillips, Anne (2021)—*Unconditional Equals*. Princeton, NJ: Princeton University Press.

Piketty, Thomas (2014)—*Capital in the Twenty-First Century*. Cambridge, MA: Harvard University Press.

Pojman, Louis P. (1992)—"Are Human Rights Based on Equal Human Worth?," *Philosophy and Phenomenological Research* (52:3): 605–22.

Pritchard, Duncan (2011)—"Wittgenstein on Scepticism," in *The Oxford Handbook of Wittgenstein*, ed. Oskari Kuusela and Marie McGinn. Oxford: Oxford University Press, 523–49.

Przybylski, Andrew K., Netta Weinstein, Kou Murayama, Martin F. Lynch, and Richard M. Ryan (2012)—"The Ideal Self at Play: The Appeal of Video Games That Let You Be All You Can Be," *Psychological Science* (23:1): 69–76.

Putnam, Hilary (1975)—"The Meaning of 'Meaning,'" in *Mind, Language, and Reality*. Cambridge: Cambridge University Press, 215–71.

Queloz, Matthieu (2018)—"Williams's Pragmatic Genealogy and Self-Effacing Functionality," *Philosopher's Imprint* (18:17): 1–20.

Queloz, Matthieu (2021a)—"The Self-Effacing Functionality of Blame," *Philosophical Studies* (178:4): 1361–79.

Queloz, Matthieu (2021b)—*The Practical Origins of Ideas: Genealogy as Conceptual Reverse Engineering*. Oxford: Oxford University Press.

Queloz, Matthieu, and Damian Cueni (2021)—"Left Wittgensteinianism," *European Journal of Philosophy* (29:4): 758–77.

Rashdall, Hastings (1924)—*The Theory of Good and Evil: A Treatise on Moral Philosophy*, 2nd ed. Oxford: Oxford University Press.

Rawls, John (1971)—*A Theory of Justice*. Cambridge, MA: Harvard University Press.

Raz, Joseph (1986)—*The Morality of Freedom*. Oxford: Oxford University Press.

Rips, L. J. (2001)—"Necessity and Natural Categories," *Psychological Bulletin* (127:6): 827–52.

Rorty, Richard (1989)—"Solidarity or Objectivity," in *Relativism: Interpretation and Confrontation*, ed. Michael Krausz. Notre Dame: University of Notre Dame Press, 35–50.

Rorty, Richard (1998)—"Human Rights, Rationality and Sentimentality," in *Truth and Progress: Philosophical Papers*. Cambridge: Cambridge University Press, 167–85.

Rosenblatt, Helena (2018)—*The Lost History of Liberalism: From Ancient Rome to the Twenty-First Century*. Princeton, NJ: Princeton University Press.

Rozeboom, Grant J. (2018)—"The Anti-Inflammatory Basis of Equality," *Oxford Studies in Normative Ethics* (8): 149–69.

Runciman, David (2000)—"What Kind of Person Is Hobbes's State? A Reply to Skinner," *Journal of Political Philosophy* (8:2): 268–78.

Ryder, Richard (1976)—"Experiments on Animals," in *Animal Rights and Human Obligations*, ed. Tom Regan and Peter Singer. Englewood Cliffs, NJ: Prentice-Hall, 33–47.

Sagar, Paul (2018a)—*The Opinion of Mankind: Sociability and the Theory of the State from Hobbes to Smith*. Princeton, NJ: Princeton University Press.

Sagar, Paul (2018b)—"Smith and Rousseau, after Hume and Mandeville," *Political Theory* (46:1): 29–58.

Sagar, Paul (2018c)—"Istvan Hont and Political Theory," *European Journal of Political Theory* (17:4): 476–500.

Sagar, Paul (2018d)—"What Is the Leviathan?," *Hobbes Studies* (31:1): 75–92.

Sagar, Paul (2022)—"Why Are We Equals? Just Because?," *Political Quarterly* (93:2): 357–58.

Sangiovanni, Andrea (2017)—*Humanity without Dignity: Moral Equality, Respect, and Human Rights*. Cambridge, MA: Harvard University Press.

Schellenberg, Susanna (2013)—"Belief and Desire in Imagination and Immersion," *Journal of Philosophy* (110:9): 497–517.

Schuppert, Fabian (2016)—"Review of John Charvet, *The Nature and Limits of Human Equality*," *Res Publica* (22:2): 243–47.

Sen, Amartya (1992)—*Inequality Reexamined*. Cambridge, MA: Harvard University Press.

Shelby, Tommie (2012)—"Race," in *The Oxford Handbook of Political Philosophy*, ed. David Estlund. Oxford: Oxford University Press, 336–53.

Sher, George (2014)—*Equality for Inegalitarians*. Cambridge: Cambridge University Press.

Shklar, Judith (1984)—*Ordinary Vices*. Cambridge, MA: Harvard University Press.

Shklar, Judith (1989)—"The Liberalism of Fear," in *Political Thought and Political Thinkers*, ed. Stanley Hoffman. Chicago: University of Chicago Press, 3–20.

Shklar, Judith (1990)—*The Faces of Injustice*. New Haven, CT: Yale University Press.

Siedentop, Larry (2014)—*Inventing the Individual: The Origins of Western Liberalism*. London: Penguin.

Simmons, Aaron (2009)—"Animals, Predators, and the Right to Life and the Duty to Save Lives," *Ethics and the Environment* (14:1): 15–27.

Singer, Peter (1975)—*Animal Liberation*. New York: Avon Books.

Singer, Peter (1980)—"Utilitarianism and Vegetarianism," *Philosophy and Public Affairs* (9:4): 325–37.

Singer, Peter (2009)—"Reply to Bernard Williams," in *Peter Singer Under Fire: The Moral Iconoclast Faces His Critics*, ed. Jeffrey A. Schaler. Chicago and La Salle, IL: Open Court, 97–101.

Sioni, Sasha, Mary H. Burleson, and Debra A. Bekerian (2017)—"Internet Gaming Disorder: Social Phobia and Identifying with Your Virtual Self," *Computers in Human Behaviour* (71): 11–15.

Skinner, Quentin (2009)—"A Genealogy of the Modern State," *Proceedings of the British Academy* (162): 325–70.

Smith, David Livingstone (2011)—*Less Than Human: Why We Demean, Enslave and Exterminate Others*. New York: St Martin's Press.

Smith, David Livingstone (2014)—"Dehumanization, Essentialism, and Moral Psychology," *Philosophy Compass* (9:11): 814–24.

Smith, David Livingstone (2016)—"Paradoxes of Dehumanization," *Social Theory and Practice* (42:2): 416–43.

Smith, David Livingstone (2020)—*On Inhumanity: Dehumanization and How to Resist It*. Oxford: Oxford University Press.

Smith, David Livingstone (2021)—*Making Monsters: The Uncanny Power of Dehumanization*. Cambridge, MA: Harvard University Press.

Solomon, Gregg E. A., and Susan C. Johnson (2000)—"Conceptual Change in the Classroom: Teaching Young Children to Understand Biological Inheritance," *British Journal of Developmental Psychology* (18:1): 81–96.

Springer, Ken, and Frank C. Keil (1989)—"On the Development of Biologically Specific Beliefs: The Case of Inheritance." *Child Development* (60:3): 637–48.

Stavy, Ruth, and Dina Stachel (1985)—"Children's Ideas about 'Solid' and 'Liquid,'" *European Journal of Science Education* (7:4): 407–21.

Stephens-Dougan, LaFleur (2021)—"The Persistence of Racial Cues and Appeals in American Elections," *Annual Review of Political Science* (24): 301–20.

Stock, Kathleen (2021)—*Material Girls: Why Reality Matters for Feminism*. London: Fleet.

Temkin, Larry S. (1986)—"Inequality," *Philosophy and Public Affairs* (15:2): 99–121.

Tomasik, Brian (2015)—"The Importance of Wild Animal Suffering," *Relations: Beyond Anthropocentrism* (3:2): 133–52.

Waldron, Jeremy (2003)—*God, Locke, and Equality*. Cambridge: Cambridge University Press.

Waldron, Jeremy (2005)—"Response to Critics," *Review of Politics* (67:3): 495–513.

Waldron, Jeremy (2008)—"Basic Equality," *NYU School of Law, Public Law and Legal Theory Research Paper Series Working Paper 8* (61): https://papers.ssrn.com/sol3/papers.cfm?abstract_id=1311816.

Waldron, Jeremy (2012)—*Dignity, Rank, and Rights*. Oxford: Oxford University Press.

Waldron, Jeremy (2017)—*One Another's Equals: The Basis of Human Equality*. Cambridge, MA: Harvard University Press.

Westen, Peter (1982)—"The Empty Idea of Equality," *Harvard Law Review* (95:3): 537–96.

Whatmore, Richard (2012)—*Against War and Empire: Geneva, Britain, and France in the Eighteenth Century*. New Haven, CT: Yale University Press.

Williams, Bernard (1973)—"The Idea of Equality," in *Problems of the Self*. Cambridge: Cambridge University Press, 230–49.

Williams, Bernard (1985)—*Ethics and the Limits of Philosophy*. London: Fontana Press.

Williams, Bernard (2002)—*Truth and Truthfulness: An Essay in Genealogy*. Princeton, NJ: Princeton University Press.

Williams, Bernard (2005a)—"Realism and Moralism in Political Theory," in *In the Beginning Was the Deed: Realism and Moralism in Political Argument*, ed. Geoffrey Hawthorn. Princeton, NJ: Princeton University Press, 1–17.

Williams, Bernard (2005b)—"Human Rights and Relativism," in *In the Beginning Was the Deed: Realism and Moralism in Political Argument*, ed. Geoffrey Hawthorn. Princeton, NJ: Princeton University Press, 62–74.

Williams, Bernard (2006a)—"Political Philosophy and the Analytic Tradition," in *Philosophy as a Humanistic Discipline*, ed. A. W. Moore. Princeton, NJ: Princeton University Press, 155–68.

Williams, Bernard (2006b)—"Philosophy as a Humanistic Discipline," in *Philosophy as a Humanistic Discipline*, ed. A. W. Moore. Princeton, NJ: Princeton University Press, 180–99.

Williams, Bernard (2006c)—"The Human Prejudice," in *Philosophy as a Humanistic Discipline*, ed. A. W. Moore. Princeton, NJ: Princeton University Press, 135–52.

Williams, Bernard (2014)—"Why Philosophy Needs History," in *Essays and Reviews 1959–2002*. Princeton, NJ: Princeton University Press, 405–12.

Wittgenstein, Ludwig (1969)—*On Certainty*, ed. E. Anscombe, Denis Paul, and G. H. von Wright. Oxford: Blackwell.

Wolf, Werner (2004)—"Aesthetic Illusion as an Effect of Fiction," *Style* (38:3): 325–50.

INDEX

caste, viii, 9, 172
causality: alternatives and, 50, 60; complexities and, 11–13, 183n21; explanation and, 11, 50, 60, 191n1; personhood and, 29; secularism and, 191nn1–2
Chain of Being, 182n8
Charvet, John, 40–41, 44–45
Chinese, 9–11
Christianity: asserted faith and, 191n6; Augustine and, 82–83, 85; essences and, 82–83, 191n52; fundamentalist, 120; Great Chain of Being and, 182n8; Locke and, 10; Nietzsche and, 191n1; secularism and, 83–85, 91; theism and, 182n14
Citizens United ruling, 94–95, 100
civil rights, 76, 89, 106, 183n19
"claim and commitment", 113, 183n24, 184n26
Cochrane, Alasdair, 197nn1–3, 198n10, 199n15
Cohen, G. A., 171
competition: complexities and, 8, 10, 15; essences and, 64; fictions and, 110, 121, 143; historical perspective and, 171; Johnson on, 8; rational agency and, 23; Rozeboom and, 44; secularism and, 87
complexities: belief and, 11–14; bigotry and, 7–8; Black people and, 7–9; causality and, 11–13, 183n21; competition and, 8, 10, 15; context and, 15; Dworkin and, 12, 14; of egalitarianism, 13–14; explanation and, 11–14; of ideology, 9; intelligence and, 10, 12; intuition and 6; justification and, 8, 11, 13, 183nn22–23; liberalism and, 8; moral issues and, 6, 10; normative approach and, 13; philosophy and, 6–7, 10–15; reflection and, 11; relativism and, 11; truth and, 7, 9, 12–13; women and, 8–10
Conan Doyle, Arthur, 132, 197n13

conservatives, 1
Craig, Edward, 195n6
Crick, Francis, 61
criminality, 9, 176
cruelty: fictions and, 106, 112, 114; injustice and, 123–31, 177; outlawing, 194n5; proper order of things and, 124; respect and, 34; Sangiovanni and, 40–42; speciesism and, 150, 166–67, 199n11; vindication and, 123–33, 136, 140–45, 194n5, 196n9
C-subjectivity, 38–39

decision-making, 17, 43, 100, 137, 183n24
dehumanisation: essences and, 63, 78–82; secularism and, 90; slavery and, 81; vindication and, 120; women and, 176
delusion, 12, 103–4
democracy, 32, 87–88, 90
De Niro, Robert, 102
destabilisation, 43–44, 56, 104, 115, 138–39
Diamond, Cora: interests and, 151–53, 155; on speciesism, 151–53, 155, 162, 197n3, 198n10, 200n21
disabilities, 184n1; mental, 2, 24, 27, 39; rational agency and, 22, 24; secularism and, 87; speciesism and, 199n20
DNA: double-helix structure of, 48, 52–55, 61; genetics and, 48–49, 52–55, 61, 67–69
domains, 108–12
Dostoyevsky, Fyodor, 55
double-helix, 48, 52–55, 61
Dworkin, Ronald: complexities and, 12, 14; egalitarianism and, 1, 12, 14, 33–34, 86, 121, 171; historical perspective and, 86, 171–72; race and, 1; respect and, 33–34; secularism and, 86; vindication and, 121; Waldron on, 12

fictions: alternatives and, 50, 58; artifici-
ality and, 95–96; authorised representation and, 95; authority and, 96,
110; axiomatic approach and, 113,
192n17; belief and, 93, 101–4; bigotry
and, 193n28; Carter and, 108–9;
checking and, 108–12; competition
and, 110, 121, 143; context and, 93–96,
106–14; cruelty and, 106, 112, 114;
delusion and, 12, 103–4; domains
and, 108–12; double, 98–99, 103, 113,
116–22, 126, 130–31, 135, 139, 143, 149,
174; Doyle and, 132; essences and, 84,
97–99, 103–4, 109, 113; essentialism
and, 98, 106, 113; explanation and, 117;
gender and, 113; historical perspective and, 174–77; Hobbes and, 95–97,
192n12; immersion and, 100–113,
116–23, 126, 130–32, 135–36, 139, 174–75,
193n19, 193n30, 193n34; increasing
success over time, 122; injustice
and, 99, 112, 114; intelligence and,
97–98, 109; Internet gaming disorder and, 103; intuition and, 97, 103;
judgement and, 94; justification and,
99, 113–14; legal, 93–95, 100; liberalism and, 113; moral issues and, 84,
98, 104–8, 112–14, 130, 135, 196n10;
natural kinds and, 98; normative
approach and, 98–100, 104, 110–14,
192n17, 193n31, 193n34; Phillips and,
113–14, 119–20, 193n31, 193n34;
philosophy and, 93, 113; prejudice
and, 107; psychology and, 98, 103–6,
117; purity and, 99; race and, 105,
107, 110–11; reflection and, 100, 114;
relativism and, 98–99, 106–7, 113;
secularism and, 85; self-effacement
and, 128, 193n27; speciesism and, 149;
status and, 100, 103–4, 109–11; suffering and, 103; suspending disbelief
and, 93; truth and, 93–114, 192n12,
193n27, 193n31; usefulness and, 96–97,
103, 193n34; value and, 109–13;

vindication and, 116–23, 126, 130–36,
139, 143–44, 195n7, 196n10, 197n13;
Waldron and, 108–9; Williams and, 114
First Amendment, 95
Fodor, Jerry, 188n12
4chan, 121
French Declaration of the Rights of
Man and Citizen, 88
Front National Party, 9
fundamentalists, 120
fundamental value, 109–11

gender, viii; Aristotle and, 192n17;
axiomatic approach and, 16–18,
192n17; fictions and, 113; prejudice
and, 37; status and, 4, 125; women, 4
(*see also* women)
genetics: alternatives and, 50, 59–61,
183n23, 186n22; DNA, 48–49, 52–55,
61, 67–69; essences and, 67–69;
fallacy and, 50, 59–61, 183n23, 186n22
Genghis Khan. *See* Khan, Genghis
genocide, 9, 78, 80
Gil-White, Francisco J., 71
God: Augustine and, 82–83, 85; essences
and, 82–83, 90; Great Chain of
Being and, 182n8; humans in image
of, 82–83, 85; Locke and, 5–6, 10, 82;
love of, 82–83, 85, 191n6; as Maker,
6; Nietzsche and, 182n14, 191n1;
religious representation of, 10;
secularism and, 6, 83–85, 90–91;
theism and, 191n6; vindication and,
132–33; Waldron and, 6
Godfather Part II, The (Coppola), 102
Godwyn, Morgan, 183n19
Great Chain of Being, 182n8

Hamlet (Shakespeare), 102–3
historical perspective: Aristotle and, 91;
belief and, 86, 89–90, 93, 174, 178–79,
183n21; bigotry and, 92; competition
and, 171; context and, 175–78; Dworkin
and, 86, 171–72; egalitarianism and,

people and, 33; Carter and, 31–36, 41–42; cruelty and, 34; Dworkin and, 33–34; egalitarianism and, 33–35; ideology and, 33; judgement and, 35; Kant and, 32–33; liberalism and, 32–36; metaphysics and, 33; moral issues and, 32–36; normative approach and, 32–34; opaque, 31–36, 41–42; philosophy and, 32; racism and, 33; range property and, 31; suffering and, 34; truth and, 33; women and, 33

right vs. wrong, 48–49, 52
Rorty, Richard, 194n4, 196n12
Rousseau, Jean-Jacques, 5, 43, 192n12, 197n14
Rozeboom, Grant J., 40, 43–45, 192n12
Rwanda, 80

Sangiovanni, Andrea, 40–42, 45
Saudi Arabia, 125
secularism: Black people and, 91, 146, 149, 162, 164; causality and, 191nn1–2; Christianity and, 83–84; competition and, 87; context and, 86–92, 191n3; dehumanisation and, 90; Dworkin and, 86; essences and, 83–86, 90–93, 191n52; explanation and, 191n1; fictions and, 85; God and, 90; historical perspective and, 85–93, 191n1; human rights and, 88; identity and, 87–88; ideology and, 87; intuition and, 191n5; justification and, 91; liberalism and, 87–90; Locke and, 6; metaphysics and, 191n1; normative approach and, 90–93; purity and, 90–92; racism and, 86–87, 89, 91; reflection and, 92–93; slavery and, 9, 91, 124; status and, 88–91; vindication and, 120

self-effacement, 128, 141–43, 193n27
senility, 2, 22, 24, 27, 184n2

sexism: bigotry and, 33, 147, 149, 165, 195n7; Locke and, 5; speciesism and, 147–53, 159–62, 165
sexuality, viii, 9, 87, 89, 97, 121, 125, 174
Sheffield Northern General Hospital, viii
Sher, George, 36–39
Shklar, Judith, 34, 182n15, 194n4
slavery, 48; Atlantic trade in, 9, 81, 124; dehumanisation and, 81; essences and, 81; Godwyn and, 183n19; "natural", 4, 51; secularism and, 9, 91, 124; vindication and, 124
Smith, David Livingstone, 78–79, 182n8
socialists, 1, 171
social media, 39, 108, 120–21
speciesism: animal rights and, 165–69, 182n9, 200n21; Aristotle and, 200n21; belief and, 156, 160, 198n10; bigotry and, 147, 159, 164–67; context and, 198n10, 199n20; cruelty and, 150, 166–67, 199n11; dehumanisation and, 78–82; essences and, 149–51; ethics and, 153–65, 168; fictions and, 149; game animals, 157; Great Chain of Being, 182n8; hard-liners and, 161–65; *Homo sapiens*, 72–73, 82–83; human set and, 4, 146–48, 151–53, 158–61, 164–68, 182n9; identity and, 74, 146–69; ideology and, 150, 152, 175; injustice and, 148, 150; intelligence and, 149; interests and, 146–69, 182n9, 197n1, 198n4, 198n10, 199n13, 199n15, 200n21; intuition and, 157–58; justification and, 148–51, 161, 163, 167; Kant and, 200n21; living creatures and, 66–72; moral issues and, 147–52, 163, 165, 168, 197n3, 198n4, 199n15, 200n1; normative approach and, 151–54, 160–69, 198n10, 199n20; pests, 80, 156–57, 161; philosophy and, 161–62, 198n10, 200n21; prejudice and, 148, 151–53, 159–65; psychology and, 166–67, 198n4; racism and, 78–82, 147–53, 159–65, 190n29;

A NOTE ON THE TYPE

This book has been composed in Arno, an Old-style serif typeface in the classic Venetian tradition, designed by Robert Slimbach at Adobe.